Snake Eyes

Murder in a Southern Town

Bitty Martin

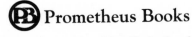 Prometheus Books

Lanham · Boulder · New York · London

Prometheus Books

An imprint of Globe Pequot, the trade division of
The Rowman & Littlefield Publishing Group, Inc.
4501 Forbes Boulevard, Suite 200, Lanham, Maryland 20706
www.rowman.com

Distributed by NATIONAL BOOK NETWORK

British Library Cataloguing in Publication Information Available

Library of Congress Cataloging-in-Publication Data

Names: Martin, Bitty, 1951– author.
Title: Snake eyes : murder in a southern town / Bitty Martin.
Description: Lanham, MD : Prometheus, [2022] | Summary: "By 1966, Hot
   Springs, Arkansas, wasn't your typical sleepy little Southern town. Once
   a favorite destination for mobsters like Al Capone and Lucky Luciano,
   illegal activities continued to lure out-of-state gamblers, flim-flam
   men, and high rollers to its racetracks, clubs, and bordellos. Still,
   the town was shaken to its core after a girl was found dead on a nearby
   ranch. The ranch owner claimed it was an accident. Then the rancher was
   found to be the killer of another woman—his fourth wife"— Provided by
   publisher.
Identifiers: LCCN 2021026086 (print) | LCCN 2021026087 (ebook) | ISBN
   9781633887763 (cloth) | ISBN 9781633887770 (epub)
Subjects: LCSH: Davis, Frank, died 1984. | Ward, Cathie, 1953–1966. |
   Davis, Sharron Knight, died 1967. | Murderers—Arkansas—Hot
   Springs—Biography. | Murder victims—Arkansas—Hot Springs—Biography.
   | Murder—Arkansas—Hot Springs—History—20th century. | Hot Springs
   (Ark.)—History.
Classification: LCC HV6534.H7 A2 2022 (print) | LCC HV6534.H7 (ebook) |
   DDC 364.152/30976741—dc23
LC record available at https://lccn.loc.gov/2021026086
LC ebook record available at https://lccn.loc.gov/2021026087

♾™ The paper used in this publication meets the minimum requirements of American
National Standard for Information Sciences—Permanence of Paper for Printed Library
Materials, ANSI/NISO Z39.48-1992.

Contents

Part III: Cowboy Convict

Author's Note

This true story was told with the help of microfilm/newspaper articles; cemetery records, historical papers, and maps from the Garland County Historical Society; my and others' personal memorabilia; documents from the Garland County Circuit Court/Clerk's office; internet searches; e-mailed documents; copyrighted crime scene photographs by Bill Dever; prison files from the Arkansas Department of Corrections; historical Blacksnake Ranch real estate documents from the current owner; Frank Davis's personal prison files; and interviews with more than sixty persons. The names were changed for nine people to protect their anonymity or memory; however, the rest are as they appeared in public accounts or were allowed by personal permission.

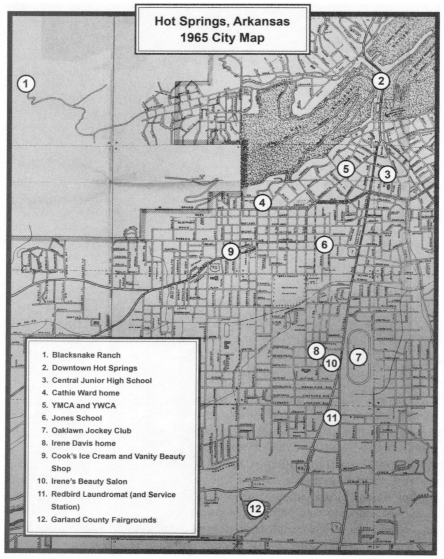

Hot Springs, Arkansas 1965 City Map

1. Blacksnake Ranch
2. Downtown Hot Springs
3. Central Junior High School
4. Cathie Ward home
5. YMCA and YWCA
6. Jones School
7. Oaklawn Jockey Club
8. Irene Davis home
9. Cook's Ice Cream and Vanity Beauty Shop
10. Irene's Beauty Salon
11. Redbird Laundromat (and Service Station)
12. Garland County Fairgrounds

Note: The concentration of story locations does not allow the entirety of the Hot Springs geographical area to be displayed.

I

BLACKSNAKE

• *1* •

The Teenage Girl and the Ranch Owner

*C*athie Ward had been a teenager for only sixty-five days when she woke up on June 24, 1966. Already the Hot Springs, Arkansas, morning was turning hot and sticky, and even with her bedroom window open, Cathie could tell the day would be stifling. She didn't care, though. Today, she was going to Blacksnake Ranch with her junior high school girlfriends Madelyn and Peg.

Cathie dressed in a hurry, pulling on red riding pants and brown leather jodhpur boots. Then she looked into a mirror and put on the necklace Mike had given her as a surprise gift days earlier, fixed a stretchy red headband behind her bangs, and fluffed her shoulder-length flip.

For months she'd badgered her mother, Sarah, for permission to ride horses at Blacksnake Ranch on the outskirts of town, but each time, Sarah'd been hell-bent on refusing her. However, when school was out for summer break, Sarah not only changed her mind but also, on a whim, took Cathie shopping for the occasion. She was a doctor's daughter, after all, and even though Sarah and Cathie's father were divorced, she wanted her daughter to ride in style.

Now, fully dressed and unable to contain her excitement, she ran downstairs, out of her house, through the side yard gate, and into the home of her next-door neighbor Gail Rader.

The two families had developed a deep friendship, although when Gail, her brothers, and her parents moved into the house, Gail wondered how Sarah, an unemployed single mother of three, could afford the pricey Prospect Avenue home. Soon she learned about the divorce and the wealthy ex-husband.

Gail, who had just finished her junior year, was up early for cheerleading practice at Hot Springs High School and was also packing for a weekend trip to the University of Arkansas in Fayetteville. She was buckling her suitcase when Cathie burst into her room.

"I'm going horseback riding!" she sang out to her startled neighbor.

There was no mistaking the excitement in Cathie's voice. Then Gail looked at her outfit.

"Isn't it a little bit early to be dressed like that?" she asked.

"Uh, no." Cathie smiled and stuck a hand into the pocket of her red riding breeches.

"Have you ever ridden a horse?"

"No," she admitted.

"Well, your outfit looks brand new and really expensive!"

Although she'd ridden horses before, Gail never owned any fancy riding attire. *Never ridden a horse*, she thought, *but wearing fancy riding pants and boots?*

The neighbor kids didn't go without anything, and Gail suspected Sarah had taken Cathie to the upscale Oaklawn Sportswear to purchase the clothes.

Gail straightened her white cotton short-sleeve shirt and tugged at her black shorts. Then she turned to Cathie. "You say you've never ridden a horse, right?"

Cathie shook her head, "No."

"Well, be careful because they can get spooked!" She grabbed her practice bag with the pom-poms and said, "Come on. I gotta go."

Then she walked out of her house with Cathie, unaware that she'd never see her little friend again.

THE DYSFUNCTIONAL FAMILY

Sarah Ward sat in the den that overlooked the tall pine trees in the backyard, waiting for the phone to ring. Earlier, the mother who'd taken the girls to the ranch had called to tell her Cathie was lost somewhere on the trails but said they knew she'd be all right when they found her. Despite their concern and encouragement, Sarah jumped up from her chair in the den and began pacing the three-story house. Visions of Cathie flashed in her mind as she thought of her efforts to re-create their previous life of living in a household headed by a physician.

During the mid-1950s, everything seemed idyllic when they lived in the small town of Murfreesboro, Arkansas, where a doctor's family was the closest thing to royalty. Sarah's husband, Dr. Hiram Ward, a tall man resembling Gregory Peck, was dedicated to his profession. However, he spent more time at his clinic and the hospital than at home, so Sarah turned to the most comforting replacement: a bottle.

In 1960, unable to tolerate her marriage even with the cushion of liquor, Sarah whisked Cathie and her two siblings, Dick and Lilly, away to Hot Springs. Unlike any other town in the southern state, Hot Springs attracted a variety of sophisticated visitors along with well-dressed men who came to patronize illegal gambling casinos and wager bets on thoroughbred horses at Oaklawn Jockey Club's spring meet. More than thirty years earlier, Al Capone frequented the racetrack, clubs, and bordellos.[1] The notorious Italian mobster Lucky Luciano had been spotted in Hot Springs during a nationwide manhunt by New York special prosecutor Thomas E. Dewey, who proclaimed him "Public Enemy Number One" for running a $12 million prostitution syndicate.[2]

By 1966, Hot Springs still wasn't your typical sleepy little southern town. Illegal activities continued to lure out-of-state gamblers, flimflam men, and high rollers. Nonetheless, residents turned their heads the other way because the vice trickled down into their bank accounts and afforded them a comfortable existence.

Perhaps that colorful lifestyle enticed Sarah to leave Murfreesboro for Hot Springs. Or maybe she wanted anonymity and felt the cosmopolitan atmosphere of Hot Springs would be more accepting of a single parent, something out of the ordinary in the polite society of the 1960s.

Although Sarah was assured that Cathie was at the ranch, she was still upset and wondered why she had given her permission this time. She'd dodged every plea during the school year but for some reason relented this week during Cathie's quest to ride horses with her friends. Sarah had also given in four years earlier when her husband said, "This has been long enough. We don't intend to get back together. Either you get a divorce, or I will."

She accepted his demands but suggested splitting the children's time through a part-time living arrangement.

"That's not going to happen," Hiram replied. "You take them or I'll take them, but they're not going to be going back and forth like that."

They compromised. The children would live full-time with her, and he could visit. During the summer, Cathie and her little sister Lilly would go separately to their father's Murfreesboro home for weeklong visits while their older brother, Dick, would stay the entire three months.

Hiram Ward was vigilant during the school year, driving to Hot Springs once a week to visit his three children. He normally picked them up and took them to dinner at McClard's Barbecue and then returned them home to their mother. Dick, who at age sixteen was three years older than Cathie, admired his father and thought he was a brilliant man. He recalled Hiram telling him that he had a photographic memory and could turn the pages of a book and then later recite contents verbatim.

A year after the divorce was final, Sarah bought the Prospect home and accepted Hiram's monthly stipend and child support. Despite her lovely new home and financial stability, she appeared dissatisfied.

"She was unhappy and drank a lot," Dick said. "There was wide-open gambling, and she spent time in those places." He remembered his mother going to the clubs and casinos, leaving him, Cathie, and their little sister at home, sometimes under the watch of her close friend, Martha Wayman, who worked at the local radio station, KBHS.

Tall and attractive, Sarah stood out in the nighttime pack the same as her appearance in a May 1964 newspaper photo of arts supporters.[3] More affluent than avant-garde, the other women in the photograph couldn't match Sarah's dark beauty.

Although Sarah was trying to make positive changes in her life, she was far from happy. One of her Fine Arts (Center) friends said, "It was becoming harder for her to be a parent, especially since it wasn't planned that she'd be a single parent. She had never imagined the sacrifices she'd make, getting her husband through medical school, and then, when it was time to be the doctor's wife, she would be put aside."

Cathie and her little sister befriended the daughters of another physician who lived nearby in their Prospect neighborhood. The oldest daughter, Kathy, and her little sisters would spend the night with the Ward sisters and felt odd because "they'd never been around anybody divorced." Kathy could tell Cathie Ward's mother was very bitter. "We couldn't even mention her daddy's name or ask, 'Where's your dad?'" she said.

THE BOYFRIEND

Cathie Ward and her new boyfriend, Mike Langley, had sat on the living room couch on Wednesday, June 22, 1966. Both were seventh graders but attended rival junior high schools. He was the tall, handsome quarterback at Southwest who led his junior varsity team to a winning season, and she was the pretty flutist at Central with all the band boys swooning over her. They met at a "Y-Teen" dance in the spring of 1966 and exchanged phone numbers after spending the whole night dancing together. Their budding romance was revolutionary at the time with their dating across school lines.

"I really had a crush on her," Mike recalled. "I thought she was a really nice girl and really pretty, and I liked her a lot."

He still remembers the last time they were together.

"We were at her house a day or so before she was going to go horseback riding, and I remember how excited she was. I remember hoping she wasn't going to go because I wanted us to do something together that day."

THE RANCH OWNER

At 3:48 p.m. on Friday, June 24, 1966, Frank Davis, the forty-two-year-old Blacksnake Ranch owner, called the sheriff's department to report an "accident."[4] Cathie hadn't shown up at the stables when she and the other two girls were to leave for home, so Frank insisted that one of them accompany him to search. When the friend finally spotted her, sprawled in one of the fields far back on the north side of the property, Cathie was dead.

However, Frank told the sheriff's deputies another story—that he had witnessed the young girl's death and that it was an unavoidable accident, something that even he, a skilled horseman, couldn't prevent.[5] "She was dragged to death by the horse when her foot caught in the stirrup," he said. "I couldn't catch it before she was killed," he explained.

Frank knew he was convincing when he spoke, whether in a gentle, humble manner or by threats. But he dazzled women, especially his fourth wife, Sharron, who was nineteen years old when they married two years earlier on the same day the divorce from his twenty-seven-year-old third wife was final.

Frank always got what he wanted, thanks to his mother's checkbook, which bankrolled his marriages and business ventures. His most recent was the 126-acre ranch that sat next to the Bull Bayou Creek on Blacksnake Road about six miles outside Hot Springs, where the majority of men wore patent leather shoes instead of cowhide leather boots. Frank Davis signed the papers on June 1, 1965, eleven months after the birth of his son, with plans to support his new family by selling angus cattle and trading horses while also offering "A Day on the Ranch"—trail rides, swimming, fishing, barbecues, hayrides, and saddled horse rentals.[6] He also expected to make money, lots of it, like his parents had done with their grit and hard work.

Ray and Irene Davis had hip-hopped across the Texas Panhandle and then in 1947 moved to Bismarck, a rural community eighteen miles south of the Hot Springs city limits. They were attracted to the resort town, famous for its thermal-water bathhouses, along with the bawdy side of illegal gambling, wild nightlife, and unbridled fun that attracted visitors from across America. The frenetic atmosphere was similar to Frank's childhood home in McCamey, Texas, sixty-seven miles east of the Pecos River, where a wildcatter hit a gushing oil well.[7] Overnight, the town named after him exploded with others seeking their fortunes, including bootleggers and gamblers.

Ray spent long hours as a barber in the rambunctious oil town while Irene remained at their $10-a-month apartment in a boardinghouse occupied by refinery workers, truck drivers, carpenters, nurses, bakers, bookkeepers, and private home cooks.[8] By the time Frank was six, he was headstrong and wanted no one to advise him or tell him what to do. His father was a strict disciplinarian and believed he could straighten out his son's stubbornness with daily spankings. Frank felt otherwise, thinking they had an opposite effect, making him meaner.

A year later, the seven-year-old was jumping on horses and enduring many falls that resulted in trauma, his badges of courage. One day, he proved another version of bravery by setting a jailhouse on fire to bust out some Mexican men. The sheriff was confused when he discovered the blaze had been started by a kid and then startled when Frank said, "My friend's in there, and he's a helluva good cowboy!" Ray Davis's punishment for his only child was *an ass whipping that wouldn't hold shot*—a scene Frank would remember and describe by those exact words not eight months after June 24, 1966, when Cathie Ward died at his ranch.

THE SHOCK

After Sarah Ward received the harrowing news of her daughter's tragic death, she ran out the front door screaming, "She's gone! Cathie's dead!" Her next-door neighbor Faye Vaught heard the commotion and went outside to check. There stood Sarah, doubled over in the middle of the street, crying. Faye ran, grabbed her, and then slowly walked her back inside. Before Sarah could explain how Cathie had died, Faye called her husband, L. A. Vaught, who managed the Hale Bath House.

"Come home," she told him. "Something terrible's happened to Cathie."

Faye and Sarah became very close when Faye married L. A., and they bought the house next to the Wards. Sarah was a stay-at-home mom, and Faye worked at the telephone company. Between the two families, there were six children, including Faye's twins, Gail and Gary. Before long, the next-door neighbors were walking through the side yard gate for visits in each other's homes. Sarah even offered her huge backyard as a place for Gail and her Hot Springs High School cheerleaders to hold practices, especially after Gail had been chosen alternate captain for her senior year.

Gail was in her bedroom when she heard Sarah crying in the kitchen. Walking over there, she asked, "What's the matter?"

"It's Cathie." Faye went to her daughter and placed her arms on her shoulders. "She was killed today. At that ranch. A horse dragged her to death."

"Huh? No, I don't believe that!" Gail jerked away from her mother and rushed to her bedroom in tears. All she could think about was the last time she'd seen Cathie—that morning.

Now, eight hours later, Gail sat in her room thinking how happy Cathie had been. Gail felt bad, remembering how she felt when she saw Cathie in the fancy outfit and compared it to her own riding clothes, old blue jeans, and scruffy cowboy boots.

But she felt worse, recalling an incident a few months earlier when Cathie had broken her arm skateboarding, and she'd made fun of her, calling her "klutz." Gail sobbed, thinking how mean she'd been to Cathie, and now she could never take it back.

THE TEACHER

The ambulance took Cathie Ward's lifeless body to Gross Mortuary on Central Avenue, one block west of Central Junior High School, where, three weeks earlier, she was given her year-end report card.[9] Her good grades didn't reflect the problems at home that she hid from her seventh-grade classmates.

During grade school, Mary Sue Tracy walked into her classroom and announced she was replacing the regular teacher. "She's taking an extended sick leave. So, to help me get to know you, I'd like you to write something about yourself," she said.

Cathie sat at her desk, laboring over her paper just like the other students, but none moved Mary Sue like hers. "My father is a doctor, but my parents are divorced, and I miss him. I like it here now that I'm making friends, but I don't like being here," she told her new teacher—what she wouldn't tell her friends.

Mary Sue was amazed as she read Cathie's story and wondered how someone that young could write with such feelings. But from the standpoint of a mother's view, she was sad. After class was over, she slipped Cathie's paper into her purse, took it home, and then tucked it away in her bedroom drawer, maybe planning to give it to Cathie's mother so that she could get her daughter some help.

She also decided to introduce Cathie to her daughter, Leslie. The two girls were in different homerooms but were the same age and lived a few blocks apart. They became fast friends and visited at each other's homes despite being extreme opposites. Cathie was tall, dark, a bit clumsy, and unsure of herself, while Leslie was short, blond, and known as the fastest runner in their grade at Jones School.

When Cathie came to Leslie's house, she would first sit and talk with Mary Sue. Leslie knew their unusual bond resulted from their time in the classroom. She was always patient and stayed in her bedroom until Cathie and her mother were finished visiting. Leslie wasn't jealous or threatened by their closeness. In fact, she was glad because she knew they would talk whenever Cathie became sad, which she thought happened every time Cathie started missing her father. Leslie also knew Cathie's mother had a drinking problem that may have contributed to her friend's longing to talk to a mother figure.

THE SIGHTING

That afternoon, Mitsy, my twin, and I were sitting in the backseat of Mrs. Letha Smith's Rambler sedan with our neighbor, Leslie Tracy. We were headed home from summer church camp when I spotted Cathie Ward walking down the West Grand hill not far from her house.

"There's Cathie," I told Mitsy and Leslie.

We all leaned out the window and waved as we yelled, "Hi, Cathie!" But she didn't respond. We figured she was preoccupied and didn't hear us because she looked like she was in a rush to get home.

Mrs. Letha, as we called her, veered left onto Summer Street and drove two blocks. Then she dropped us off at our homes on the corner of Summer and Garland. Later, Leslie was sitting on her bed when her mother walked into her room. Mary Sue hesitated and then said, "I've heard Cathie Ward was killed in a horseback riding accident. I'm not a hundred percent sure, but that's what I've heard."

"But we just saw her walking home," Leslie said.

"It couldn't have been her," Mary Sue snapped. "It happened at a ranch out in Mountain Pine."

"Yes, it was," Leslie insisted.

"I'm sorry. I wish you had seen her, but you didn't. That poor child is dead." She rubbed her eyes and walked away.

Leslie was confused. She called her best friend, Debbie. "I just got back from church camp and heard something happened to Cathie Ward today," she said. "Do you know about it?"

"Yes," Debbie replied. "I heard something but don't know if it's true."

They decided to call Cathie's house and see if she answered, but neither could summon the courage to follow through.

That evening, their friend Mary Claire Atkinson was at the junior high school Y-Teen dance when the news of Cathie's tragic death roared through the YMCA gymnasium. As Mary Claire remembers, "It was so shocking to my brain, that I can close my eyes, [and see it] as if it were a photograph—a dim, bluish-lit gym, and I am standing fairly close to the center of the gym floor. The news didn't come with any details, just that she had been horseback riding, and there was an accident, and she had died."

Jan Johnson, a year older than Mary Claire, was also at the dance but outside on the steps leading into the YMCA building. She was standing with a group of eighth graders who couldn't believe Cathie had actually died, so they decided to validate the story. Somehow, one of them got to a phone, called Cathie's house, and asked for her.

"We never really found out what happened," Jan said. "It was never talked about. Nothing was in the newspaper that I remember, and nobody knew what happened. It was hush-hush, and it was one of those experiences where you dealt with the death of a peer for the first time, and you think, *Can something like this really happen?*"

While the news of Cathie's death was startling to her friends at the YMCA, two others were preparing to leave for her house. Earlier in the week, Cathie had invited Jan Harrison and Candy Brown to a Friday night bunking party. Jan Harrison was at her home waiting for her ride to Cathie's house when the phone rang. As Jan Harrison remembers it, "Candy called about the time she and her mom were to pick me up and told me Cathie was dead, but I thought she was kidding."

Cathie's boyfriend, Mike Langley, hadn't gone to the dance because he couldn't bear to attend without her. Not remembering how he heard the news of her death, he vividly recalls a phone call his parents received regarding Cathie. "When they found her, she was wearing a piece of jewelry I had given her. One of her parents called my parents and wanted to know if I wanted it back, and I said, 'Absolutely not, that was hers.'"

The disturbing account of Cathie's death thrashed through the ranks of the Hot Springs junior high schools. Everyone was stunned and frightened. No one had dealt with death on a personal level and didn't understand how fast and complete it could arrive. The adults, however, knew the finality of Cathie's tragedy. Some, like Frances Gabriel Forsberg, whose daughter was a friend of Cathie's younger sister, recalled the townspeople's suspicions after hearing about the fatal accident.

"They said her foot caught in a stirrup and she was dragged for a long time," Forsberg said. "And most people thought it was a cover-up because that man [Frank Davis] had a bad reputation."

That was 1966. The next year, when a vicious killing by Frank Davis connected him to Cathie's suspicious death, most everyone in Hot Springs was certain we had a multi-murderer in our midst.

Those of us who knew Cathie were touched by her short life like a high-water mark after a flood and have been tethered to her all these years. Perhaps because it was my first connection with senseless violence, I moved into adulthood with jumbled memories. Since then, Cathie's death and the chaos that followed have been running in my mind on a perpetual loop.

Then something happened that stopped the replay—a cell phone conversation with my childhood friend Leslie Tracy Swinford late one night in August 2014. I was driving from New Rochelle, New York, to Yonkers after work and couldn't wait to tell her I'd be home for a short visit. "I'll be there in two weeks and want to look up Cathie on the library's microfilm," I told her.

"I want to go," she said, and then added, "you won't believe what happened."

Leslie began telling me about Cathie's skateboard and how it had wound up in her possession and had been with her all these years. I was surprised to hear this story but more surprised she'd kept this secret from Mitsy and me. We'd grown up across the street from each other and had stayed close throughout adulthood, yet this was the first time she'd ever mentioned Cathie's skateboard.

Leslie said that sometime after the millennium, the skateboard had been lost or stolen and that her handyman then found it up in the attic recently. I asked her when because for some reason that seemed important. Leslie told me she had written him a check and would look up the date and send me a text.

Two weeks later, on August 20, I was home, and we went to the library to start searching for Cathie. Neither of us knew her actual death date, not even the year. It was blurry in our minds, but we knew she'd died sometime during junior high, so I just asked for microfilm during those years. We both went through our separate boxes, looking from beginning to end of each reel, but had no success. So I decided we'd have better luck at the sheriff's office. Wrong. They didn't have files that went back to the 1960s. Gross Mortuary had burned, destroying their files, and, the owner, who'd conducted decades of funerals, couldn't remember anything about Cathie. The coroner said he had nothing from that era. And another official's mind was blank. I felt as if every door was being slammed in my face and couldn't help feeling discouraged. I was stumped but not giving up.

I returned to the library two days later, on Friday, August 22, armed with new information. An internet search of Frank Davis produced a story with Cathie's name and the date 1966. But my results were the same. Nothing. As I returned the reels, I mentioned my dilemma to Greg at the reference desk. He made a suggestion. "Go to the Garland County Historical Society. They have funeral home records and can look it up for you."

Arriving there, Donnie, a volunteer, said, "I'll go see what I can find."

A few minutes later, he walked back into the room, holding up several sheets of paper in his right hand. He placed them on a table in front of me and bent down. "Look right here," he said, pointing at one of them. "Ward, Catherine Ann."

He'd highlighted her name in yellow on a long list, titled "Gross Funeral Home Records." It included the names of the deceased, death and birth dates, spouse, father, and mother.

Donnie said, "She died on June 24, 1966, and her father was Dr. Hiram Ward."

Then Donnie whipped out another sheet from his stack that had a picture of a cemetery headstone. "It says here, she's buried in Murfreesboro."

I thanked Donnie and rushed back to the library, trying to hide my excitement as I stood in front of Greg at the reference desk and asked, "Could I have the June 1966 *Sentinel-Record*?"

I knew Cathie's obituary or story of her accident would show up somewhere between June 25 and 27. I sped through the reel until June 24 appeared, then crawled the tape and was surprised when the June 25 issue was missing. Not only that, but her name never appeared on any pages from June 26 through the end of the month.

My disappointment in not finding her obituary was buoyed by the fact that I'd at least obtained her death date, which was ground zero for my search. Friday night, I called Leslie to tell her the good news.

Then Saturday afternoon, I called her again. "Let's go on a drive out by Blacksnake Ranch." I thought some kind of magic mojo would rub off on me where Cathie had died.

When we reached the Mountain Pine Road and Blacksnake intersection, I saw a big sign on our right. "Look at the name on that sign!" I said to Leslie as I pointed at the large wooden sign.

"Ward's Country Store!" she said.

"What are the odds on that?" I asked.

"Yeah, none of her family live here anymore, and they sure wouldn't own a store."

"That's unbelievable! Her name right here at Blacksnake Road after all these years!" I said.

As unusual and unsettling as it was, we both knew that what we had just seen was not a coincidence.

The next day as I sat drinking coffee and reading the Sunday newspaper, my mind wandered to the sequence of events in my search for Cathie—Leslie's story about the reappearance of her skateboard, the struggle to obtain Cathie's death date, and the freaky "Ward sign." Then I thought, *Leslie's text!*

I remembered she promised to send me the date her handyman found Cathie's skateboard, so I grabbed my cell phone and began scrolling through her text messages. When I found it, Leslie had simply written, "June 24, 2014."

I gasped when I saw the date because I knew Cathie wanted her story told. She died on June 24, 1966, and her skateboard appeared on June 24, 2014—the forty-eighth anniversary of her death.

I took that as my sign to start digging up the true accounts of her tragedy and its connection to the other murder in town by a man so vile that he kept us in an anxious sweat for almost two decades. In my search, I procured documents from all levels of government as well as personal items from many, but the true prize was when one of the killer's family members granted me access to Frank Davis's prison files. Much of the information I gleaned in my research was shocking, and I soon saw a common thread weaving through the victims and their killer. The story wound up in a hairpin curve with an ending none of us who were there at the time saw coming.

As I interviewed almost sixty people connected to Cathie and her killer, I learned that the fear Frank Davis instilled then exists today. Some believe he is still in town, hiding and waiting for his next victim.

I can still picture Cathie the last time I saw her, three of us girls, watching her determined to get home. We had no idea what was to follow. Many times, I've wished I could go back and change the past. What I can do now is share this story so that all these years later, Frank Davis will not get away with murder.

• 2 •

The Father and the Friend

On June 24, 1966, after 8:30 p.m., the phone rang at Dr. Hiram Ward's home in Murfreesboro, Arkansas. The summer solstice had occurred three days earlier, and it was getting dark outside when he heard the familiar sound. Thinking it was a hospital emergency, Hiram answered the call and knew immediately it was much worse.

"Cathie's been killed," his ex-wife blurted through sobs.

"What?" he asked.

"She had an accident. She's dead," Sarah repeated. Then she gave him the details the best she could through hiccups of tears.

He listened to Sarah recount the tragedy and realized she wasn't hysterical. "She was drunk," he recalled. "As long as we were living together, she drank alcohol but wasn't ever drunk. But this wasn't true after she left me."

He ended the heartbreaking call from his ex-wife and walked into the den, where his son and second wife, Pat, were watching television. "Cathie's dead," he told them.

Dick could tell his father was shaken but never expected to hear those words. "It was stressful," Dick said. "I was sad but don't remember crying. I was always pretty emotionally repressed and kept a damper on emotions all the time, so I can't say I felt a lot."

Pat Ward packed her husband's suitcase while Dick grabbed his, then Hiram and his son were off to Hot Springs, sixty miles away. Remembering the drive, Hiram told me, "I felt a sense of loss and was not happy that she was dead, but I knew the fact that it was an accident—nobody could help that."

Hiram and his son arrived at Sarah's home by 10 p.m. and went inside to the living room, where Sarah and a friend were seated. Dick left his parents to

15

talk and then climbed the stairs to his bedroom, located across the hall from his sisters' room—now full of Cathie's memory.

THE FRIEND

Another out-of-town call was made to the home of thirteen-year-old Bettye Jo Tucker on Oak Street in Hot Springs. Her father, James, answered it and began talking with his cousin, Janice, who worked with Dr. Ward in Murfreesboro. She was best friends with his wife Pat, who was also a nurse, and Janice was just as familiar with Ward's children as Pat. Janice knew Cathie's older brother and younger sister were introverts and bookworms. She thought they were above average and had different personalities than Cathie, who was more outgoing and hung out with the popular crowd.

Janice also knew what was happening in the children's lives back home in Hot Springs from conversations with Hiram and Pat. "The kids were young, and they might stay gone all day long," she said. "Their mother didn't work, but she was bad to drink."

❧

Cathie Ward's and Bettye Jo Tucker's biggest desire during their 1966 spring semester at Central Junior High School was to go horseback riding. They had other similarities, such as the same dark, long hair. Although Bettye Jo's skin was much fairer than Cathie's, they could've passed as sisters because on the inside they were both genuinely kind and somewhat innocent.

"Cathie reminded me of myself in her naïveté," Bettye Jo recalls. "She was vulnerable like me and probably not as streetwise as some of our friends."

Bettye Jo would never go inside Cathie's house. She stayed out on the curb in the Tuckers' blue-and-white Dodge station wagon as her father drove her and her friends around Hot Springs. If any of them needed a ride, she and James were off in the car to pick them up and take them to Girl Scouts, Camp Clearfork, or downtown to a movie or a shopping trip. The kids would all pile in the backseat, and he'd drop them off and pick them up later. James didn't mind that, but he was very leery of his daughter going to any of her friends' homes for an overnight stay.

Bettye Jo invited Cathie to join Girl Scouts, which was the major focus of her childhood. She thought her new troopmate, with her olive complexion and dark hair and eyes, was beautiful.

"I remember always being drawn to her, you know, sit by her, talk to her, because she was so sweet," Bettye Jo said.

By the time the two friends reached junior high school, their interests changed. Cathie joined the band and Bettye Jo the pep squad, a prelude to her becoming a cheerleader.

Despite their emerging differences, they were still connected and had acquired a mutual new interest—thanks to their friend Madelyn, who loved horses. The three girls had become good friends in Mrs. Freeman's fifth-grade class at Jones School. And when the class photo came out, they were coincidentally pictured side by side with Bettye Jo in the middle. She seemed to be the glue that held their friendship together.

Madelyn asked them to ride horses at Blacksnake Ranch throughout the spring of 1966 school year. The way she described the rustic place, it seemed a world away from Hot Springs with neon signs that advertised motels, restaurants, bars, and nightclubs. But Cathie's mother wouldn't give her permission, and it never seemed to happen. However, when summer arrived, Madelyn once again extended an invitation for June 24, 1966. All the girls were excited, and one by one they began asking their parents for permission.

Bettye Jo, the only child of hardworking parents who owned the Mary Carter Paint store, approached her father.

"Can I go horseback riding?" she asked.

"When?" James walked into the living room and sat down in his easy chair.

"Friday."

"With who?" he asked, reaching for the newspaper on the coffee table.

"Madelyn and Peg, and I think Cathie and maybe Paula. I'm not sure who else."

"Where are you going?"

"Blacksnake Ranch."

James shot up in the chair. His body became rigid, as if he were bracing for an impact. He looked his daughter straight in the eye and said, "No!"

Bettye Jo was startled. Her father rarely denied her anything. But she couldn't have known his abruptness had nothing to do with her.

James sold paint to many people in Hot Springs and could size up a person during the transactions, especially customers such as Frank Davis, the owner of Blacksnake Ranch. The two men were similar in age but not in behavior. Although James Tucker had to be nice to his customers, he didn't have to like them, and he didn't care one iota for Frank Davis.

"Oh Daddy, please let me go," Bettye Jo begged.

"You will never go any place that involves that man!"

She looked at her father, not understanding his reasoning. "They're my friends. I want to go with them."

"I know him. You will not!" He shook his head in opposition at the idea of his daughter going anywhere near Frank Davis.

Bettye Jo smiled at her father, trying to melt his stern opposition. "Please let me go horseback riding, please, please, please?"

The more she begged, the more stubborn her father became. "Do not ask me again. I know better. I know that man's character, and I don't want to have anything to do with him. You're *not* going!"

"Okay," she said, accepting his final ultimatum while trying to hide her disappointment.

Not wanting her father to see her crying, she walked across the street to Peg's house and then erupted in tears. Peg, who was a year younger than Bettye Jo, had also been invited and had no problem receiving permission. The two girls were as close as sisters and constant companions, which made it that much worse for Bettye Jo. She wanted to do what her friends were doing and didn't want to feel left out because her father didn't like the man who owned Blacksnake Ranch.

⌒

The news of Cathie Ward's tragic death infiltrated Murfreesboro on Friday evening, June 24, 1966, which prompted a phone call to James Tucker in Hot Springs. His cousin Janice, who worked with Cathie's father and stepmother, called to tell him her firsthand news. James listened to her quietly and thanked her for calling, then walked into the living room to tell his wife.

"Now, I need to tell Bettye Jo," he said after finishing the sad story.

He was known to be loving but overprotective. However, nothing could protect his daughter from what he had to tell her.

Knocking on her door, he asked, "Can I come in?"

"Yes sir," Bettye Jo said, masking hurt feelings from his unusual denial to go with her friends to the ranch that day.

James walked into the room, sat down on Bettye Jo's bed, and said in a calm tone, "I hate to have to tell you this, but your friend Cathie is dead."

"Dead?" She screamed, pushed away her cotton top sheet, and sat up in bed.

He looked at her and silently nodded.

"Why?" Bettye Jo asked, not believing what she'd just heard.

James didn't answer.

"How did it happen?"

"We don't know all the details, but I wanted you to know she is dead."

He leaned down, kissed her forehead, and then walked out of the room, slowly shutting the door behind him.

She'd spent the day envying her friends out there horseback riding, but now Bettye Jo was numb after hearing the news of Cathie's death. Thoughts swirled through her head, and then she remembered something. She bent down to look in her nightstand drawer and grabbed the autograph book her friends signed before school let out for summer break.

Bettye Jo began thumbing through the small book and saw Leslie Tracy's funny words: "2 in a car, 2 little kisses, that adds up to Mr. and Mrs."

Leslie also wrote, "U R TO SWEET 4 me." She drew a ladder with each rung containing a word of her verse: "I came all the way down this long, long ladder to sign my name Leslie Tracy. Best Luck, always."

On another page, Leslie showed her serious side: "Bettye Jo, You're a real nice person to know and I like you a lot. Stay as cute and nice as you are now and you will get the best things out of life. Love Leslie Tracy. P.S. You've been a real nice school buddy to me. Good Luck in the future (Bye Now See you Next Year)."

Madelyn's entry said, "Bettye Jo, Bettye Jo, you bad little girl. You poured milk on little Linda Curll. I love you always."

Then Bettye Jo found Cathie's page. Unlike the other girls' humorous inscriptions, the message seemed prophetic, almost like a sweet good-bye. Cathie wrote, "Bettye Jo, This is to a sweet girl I've known for a long time. Good luck in the future. I'll always remember you. How could I forget!? (not really) Cathie Ward." On the lower left side, below her words, she included "7th Grade '65–'66."

After reading Cathie's message, Bettye Jo made three notations. Under the date, she penciled in "1965-1966," and below Cathie's signature she printed, "Wrote May ——, 1966. She died June 24, 1966."

Her seventh-grade autograph book was meant to hold happy memories, but that changed with Cathie's death. That evening, Bettye Jo and her father's cousin, Janice, were unaware how much their lives would be affected in the future by Cathie and Hiram Ward.

· 3 ·

The Funeral and the Skateboard

*H*iram Ward woke up in a Hot Springs motel on Saturday morning, June 25, 1966, wanting to see his daughter. He rushed into the shower then dressed and drove straight to Gross Mortuary, which shared a parking lot with Central Baptist Church. The two buildings sat side by side on Central Avenue, a block below the junior and senior high schools, where Cathie and Dick just twenty-four days earlier had completed the school year.

Hiram entered the mortuary prepared to assess the severe trauma that killed his daughter. He wanted to see it from a medical perspective, but the mortuary denied his request. They were adamant her casket would remain closed, even to her physician father. Standing for a moment to consider his next option, Hiram chose to honor Cathie's memory peacefully and relinquished his quest to view her fatal injuries.

Teacher Mary Sue Tracy and many other Hot Springs residents rushed outside to fetch the Saturday *Hot Springs News Era* with a mixture of anticipation and dread, hoping the newspaper would be void of Cathie Ward's tragic death. If it wasn't in print, that meant the rumor wasn't true.

The newspaper's front page normally covered only national and state news, but this morning there were two local stories, both of deaths: the closing of the Hot Springs Merrill Lynch office *and* Cathie's fatal accident. Hers was on the bottom of the ninth column, the final article on the page. "Girl Killed in Horseback Riding Accident," the headline shouted.[1]

"Catherine Ann Ward, 13, daughter of Mrs. Sarah Ward of 1003 Prospect Ave, was killed Friday in an accident at the Davis Ranch on Blacksnake Road," the newspaper reported. "The girl was apparently dragged to death

21

by a horse she was riding when her foot caught in a stirrup. Allen [*sic*] Frank Davis, owner of the ranch which specializes in horse rentals, pursued the running horse but was unable to catch it before the girl was killed," it explained.

At this point, some readers may have taken pause, especially Frank Davis's friends and customers. They knew he was an expert horseman, fearless in the saddle, and a daredevil who, as tales went, regularly jumped off a cliff atop his horse into a deep swimming hole on his property. Catching a runaway horse would have been an easy feat for him. Knowing his shady reputation, they were already questioning the validity of his explanation and felt he'd duped the deputies. However, they were pleased to read Dr. William Mashburn, the county coroner, promised the cause of death would be filed in an official report when the investigation of her accident was concluded.

Cathie's survivors, which included her maternal and paternal grandparents, were listed, but the sad reality of her death came at the end of the short obituary—the announcement of her funeral service that afternoon, followed by burial out of town at the Murfreesboro Cemetery. Not only had Cathie died tragically, but she was being rushed to the grave less than twenty-four hours after her death. Southern tradition meant family and friends would bring covered dishes of food and share memories of the deceased over a three-day period from death to internment. But there would be no time for Cathie's mourning, just a quick good-bye. The Brenner family, Gross Mortuary owners, pulled her funeral together overnight, which was an amazing feat for a service being held in one town and the burial in another.

Saturday afternoon at the stroke of 1:30 p.m., Katrina Williams began playing the organ as the funeral director escorted the Ward family into St. Luke's Episcopal Church. A hundred years earlier, it was founded by a crowd, holding a full morning service and grand sermon in a local saloon.[2] Now, in a gothic revival building before a high altar, the Wards' sad procession walked down the center aisle to the front pews of the nave.

Earlier, Mary Claire and her mother Dinks Atkinson walked up the steps to enter St. Luke's and sat down in a pew. Mary Claire had never experienced the loss of a relative, much less a close, healthy friend, and she had difficulty comprehending what had happened. The twelve-year-old decided the way she would handle Cathie's death would be to pretend her friend had just moved away, and that's why she would never see her again.

Cathie's closed casket sat in front of the altar rail as a private exhibit of a death too horrific to allow family and friends a face-to-face good-bye. The white pall draped over her casket signified the belief that everyone was equal in the eyes of God. Reverend Wayne L. Buchanan followed the traditional burial service of his Episcopalian faith found in the 1928 version of *The Book of Common Prayer*.

Kathy McConkie sat with her mother "partway back" in the "jam-packed" sanctuary. The youngster, who had once been in Jones School's junior high preparatory band with Cathie, looked around and noticed there weren't any flowers and was sad. For some reason, she thought the church wouldn't allow them. Kathy couldn't help but think how four days earlier she'd received a phone call from Cathie Ward, inviting her to go horseback riding that Friday.

Having just returned home from camp, she said, "I'm tired. I don't want to go horseback riding but thank you anyway."

"It was one of those things that you're going to go horseback riding, you didn't go, Cathie was killed, and the funeral was the next day or two," Kathy McConkie remembers. "It was quick, and especially at that age I hadn't even gotten it processed in my brain."

Sarah had chosen pallbearers from different avenues of her life, such as the Hot Springs Fine Arts Center with John Baran, Charles Beyers, and James Few; her next-door neighbor, L. A. Vaught; and from her married years in Murfreesboro, her friends Buddy Bond and Grady McCarty. Cathie's attachments were represented by the Central Junior High School Spartan Band, who served as honorary pallbearers.

Janette Woodcock sat with her father in the church as the pallbearers carried Cathie's casket past their pew. She and Cathie attended confirmation class together at St. Luke's. They were also fellow seventh graders and Girl Scout troopmates. She and Cathie had recently shared a bunk bed at Girl Scout camp. Janette, the smaller of the two, was happy to take the top bunk until she felt something poking through her mattress. When she realized it was Cathie's big toe, she yelled, "Stop!" But the more she yelled, the more Cathie giggled and kept poking.

Janette walked outside to see the pallbearers load the casket in the hearse parked in front of the church. The mortuary's family car was second in line, and Sarah was just about to climb into the back of the stretch limousine when she turned around and began staring at Janette. Standing on the church steps, the thirteen-year-old could feel Sarah's gaze locked on her. Then Janette smiled and broke her trance.

The memory of Cathie's funeral would be impossible for the family to retain. Fifty years later, her brother Dick would have no recollections, and his eighty-three-year-old father, who Dick said had a mind like a steel trap, could summon only one. "We had a procession from Hot Springs, and they did not turn on their lights at all to avoid traffic."

Cathie's coffin was carried to her grave site more than twelve feet east of the large Ward family headstone in the Murfreesboro cemetery around the corner from the town square. Hiram stood alongside his immediate family while his Murfreesboro friends and patients came to offer their condolences. He didn't know who made the decision to bury Cathie in the Ward family's Murfreesboro plot instead of her mother's hometown of El Dorado, Arkansas.

"It was probably her mother since she was Cathie's legal guardian," he said. Later, Cathie's grave would be marked with a somber granite and bronze headstone that bore no displays of affection, such as flowers or angels to soften the impact of a thirteen-year-old's tragedy. It simply stated, "Catherine Ward, April 21, 1953, June 24, 1966."

THE SKATEBOARD

Hours after the last shovel of dirt covered Cathie's grave, Mary Sue, her former teacher, was knocking on the Wards' front door. "I've brought Leslie and the twins with me to pay our respects," Mary Sue told Sarah's friend, who answered the door.

Standing next to her were the three of us in Sunday dresses, who'd somehow seen Cathie walking home the day before at the same time she apparently was found dead at Blacksnake Ranch. When we entered the house, we didn't tell her mother about seeing her. We were still too confused. We kept our secret from her the same as Mary Sue kept the secret about Cathie's sad grade school paper. Neither were mentioned during the uneasy visit with Cathie's mother.

Both women were thirty-eight years old with birthdays only three months apart and daughters the same age. Despite their sameness, the women were exact opposites. Mary Sue was born in Murfreesboro and then moved as a child to Hot Springs, where her father opened Stell and Adams Hardware Store, while Sarah was married to a Murfreesboro physician and moved to Hot Springs as a single parent. Mary Sue loved nothing more than to play bridge all day, while Sarah Ward preferred being out on the town all night. But now that Cathie was gone, all their similarities and differences didn't matter. After this condolence call, the two mothers wouldn't be in each other's company again.

Leslie fidgeted in her chair, wanting her mother to hurry up so she could leave. She wasn't testy, just anxious to get home to see if Cathie's skateboard was still in the side yard bushes at her house. The past Sunday, she'd invited Cathie over and told her since it was Father's Day, she should come around 3:00 after they'd finished their special meal. Cathie walked the two blocks from her house to Leslie's and, as usual, spent time talking with Mary Sue before she reached Leslie's room.

The two girls went outside and began skateboarding down the steep Garland Street sidewalk beside Leslie's house, taking time to also talk about boys. Cathie mentioned an eighth grader named Gary but said she was madly in love with Mike, the quarterback at the other junior high school.

Cathie left before suppertime, and as Leslie was grabbing her skateboard to go inside, she saw Cathie's. That evening, Leslie called her.

"You left your skateboard," she said. "I'm going to church camp tomorrow with the twins, so I put it out in our fort over in the side yard. You want to come get it while I'm away?"

"Sure, I'll walk down there and get it," Cathie said. "When are you coming back?"

"Friday afternoon."

"Groovy! Let's skateboard Saturday, okay?"

"Yes, I'll call you when we get back," Leslie said and ended their final conversation.

Leslie sat quietly in the Ward home, wanting to see if Cathie had retrieved her skateboard. When her mother got up and said, "Let's go, girls," Leslie was the first one out the door. Arriving home, she went to her bedroom and waited for her mother to go into the living room, where her father was watching television. Then she snuck out the backdoor and ran down the high back-porch steps to the side yard, where she and the twins and their summer friend Karen would spend hours sharing stories in a covey of bushes that formed what they'd dubbed "the fort." She pulled apart some low-lying branches, and there it was—Cathie's skateboard. She grabbed it, rushed back inside, and stashed it under her bed.

That night, both Leslie and her mother went to sleep with heavy hearts, unaware they each had a keepsake of Cathie's hidden away in their bedrooms.

THE BOYS

Thirteen-year-old Don Harper was attending Camp Tula at Lake Greeson, north of Murfreesboro, on June 25, 1966. He was serving as a counselor at the Boy Scout annual encampment and making rounds that Saturday evening when one of the Scoutmasters stopped to ask, "Do you know someone named Cathie Ward?"

"Yes," he said.

"Well, she died, was killed on a horse," said the man, who couldn't have known how hard this news would impact the teenage boy.

Don attended parochial schooling at St. Johns, a few blocks north of Cathie's public school, but never crossed her path until they entered seventh grade at Central Junior High School. They both joined the band and shared the spontaneous connection that came with the cohesive group. He was immediately attracted to Cathie and wanted to be her boyfriend, but he heard she was dating the quarterback at the other junior high school, so he settled for being her good friend.

He'd never experienced the death of anyone his own age, much less someone like Cathie, who had won a piece of his heart. Remembering the tragedy, Don said, "The news of her death was pretty traumatic, and I was inconsolable for days."

He married in 1974 and became a radiologist, but he never forgot Cathie.

"She comes up all the time, and I thought about her frequently for years," he said. "I still think about her from time to time. I met her little sister a few years after it happened, and she didn't talk about it. But I didn't either because it hurt to think about it."

Fifteen-year-old John James was walking up Park Avenue on Monday, June 27, 1966, near the Polar Bar, a popular ice cream stand, when Doyce Smith stopped him and asked, "Did you hear about Cathie?"

"No."

"She was killed, and they had her funeral day before yesterday," said Doyce.

John looked at his friend and then turned and continued walking home in a shocked stupor. He'd just returned from a summer visit with his ninth-grade buddy Tommy Stafford, who had moved to Mobile, Alabama, during the school year. The euphoria of a great vacation with his best friend had been broken by this painful news on his first day back home.

John had also met Cathie in the junior high school band. He was two years older, so the only class they shared was first period in the band hall. During both practices and while marching at football games, they were on different rows. She was up front in the flute section, and he was in the back line on the drums.

"We didn't have a lot of interaction. We just didn't," he said. "It was real casual, and in my mind, it was bigger than it was. In Cathie's life, I would have been a very minor character, just fleeting, but she left a real impression on me. She was really friendly, really pretty, and just a nice person. She was easy to talk to. Some people you just like, and I liked her."

There had to be more than what was in John's mind, considering Cathie's invitation to visit her at her home sometime in the spring of 1966. Not yet sixteen and able to drive, he walked everywhere, which made for a long trek from his home in the Park Avenue neighborhood on the northeastern edge of Hot Springs. John left his house and walked three miles, going down Park

Avenue to Central Avenue, through downtown Hot Springs, and then up Prospect to Cathie's home, where Sarah Ward greeted him at the front door.

"I didn't go in because Cathie was a young girl, and you didn't invite boys into the house," he said. They talked outside in the front yard and hung out the way kids did back then. John said, "I was just glad to be spending the afternoon with a pretty girl."

John and Cathie were together again near the end of the 1966 school year. He met her at a band concert at Jones School.

"She said she'd be there and asked would I be there?" he said. "Well, if she was going to be there, for sure I wanted to be there."

John held hands with Cathie as he sat between her and her friend Kathy Fry, who lived off Blacksnake Road.

"I couldn't even concentrate on the show for holding her hand," he remembered. "She may have been my first girlfriend in my mind, but that's okay. It was an innocent time. It was bigger in my mind than I'm sure it was in hers, but I'd never held hands with such a pretty girl."

John's career with AT&T took him away from Hot Springs but not the teenage memories of Cathie.

"I would think of her when something would come up, or I'd see somebody that might look like her," he said. "If Cathie had lived, I probably wouldn't have thought about it again because it wouldn't have lasted. We weren't in the same circles, but that didn't seem to matter to her much. I always felt lucky to have known her. I always cared a lot about her and always wondered what happened to her."

Not having seen her obituary as a teenager, John didn't know where Cathie was buried. He went to the library to search the microfilm for any news on Cathie and found nothing. Then he went to Gross Mortuary, but they had no records. He kept hitting dead ends.

John married in 1986 and talked to his wife in 2013 about his search for Cathie. "I told her I've never been able to find her, and no one I knew knew where she was."

By this time, Find a Grave had arrived on the internet. He used the website to search for obituaries of his departed high school classmates that he placed in a bound book and took to his class reunions. While looking for his school friends, he'd also search for Cathie but never had any luck. Then sometime after he spoke to his wife, he was back on the site, and there it was.

"Finally," he shouted when Cathie's grave appeared online.

Someone had surveyed the Murfreesboro cemetery, and John found Cathie.

"The ironic part was, I'd been driving past it for nearly thirty years because you have to drive to Murfreesboro to get to Nashville [his wife's hometown in Arkansas], and I had driven within a hundred yards of her all that time," he said. "I just happened to be on my way to Nashville after finding out and went and paid my respects. I couldn't believe it."

John knew Cathie's father was a doctor. He also knew there was a Dr. Hiram Ward in Murfreesboro because he was a patient of his clinic but went to a different physician. Once on an appointment at the clinic, John asked a nurse, "Has Dr. Ward ever lived in Hot Springs?"

"No, he's always lived here," she replied.

"Well, coincidence, I guess it's a different person," John said. It never occurred to him that this Dr. Ward could be Cathie's father because he was divorced from Cathie's mother.

"People back then didn't get divorced," John said. "Then, when I found out about her grave, it all came together. Of course that's who that is, and that's Dr. Hiram Ward. But the person I talked to at the clinic didn't put it together. I had seen Dr. Ward and talked to him, but it never occurred to me that Cathie was his daughter."

John retired in Hot Springs with his wife, but while he was still working from 2000 to 2010, they enjoyed a weekend home in Hot Springs on Chincapin Street. By coincidence, it was around the corner from Prospect Avenue where Cathie had lived, and whenever he would drive by her old house, he'd think of her. "Some things just stay with you," he said.

THE SECRET

Cathie kept a secret until the day she died. It wasn't scandalous or risqué, just one that allowed her to get her way. Multiple times, her mother had denied her permission to ride horses at Blacksnake Ranch. But Cathie got her wish covertly.

Gary Sisney, a hyper eighth grader with curly hair, was crazy about Cathie. He knew his friend John Dean, a tall boy who was gentle like a Great Dane, had a mother who would drive him anywhere in town. So, he talked him into going to Blacksnake Ranch and picking up Cathie on the way.

John's mother drove the young threesome to the ranch on two separate occasions. On their second visit, John's horse was really high-spirited and took off for the barn at a gallop—twice—nearly throwing him off both times.

"It was just a real mean horse, and the guy [Frank Davis] didn't say nothing or do anything about it," said John, who was glad for the riding session to end and his mother to take them back to town.

"Gary and Cathie were beginning to be boyfriend and girlfriend when we went riding," he said. "The next time I saw him, he told me Cathie had been killed on a horse. I was shocked. He was in tears. And after that, he didn't come around much."

Six years later, Gary died in a horrific car crash while commuting to college in Arkadelphia, Arkansas, and John Dean had joined the navy, lived in California where he married, divorced, and later earned a special education teaching degree.

John moved home to Hot Springs in 2010 and ran into Leslie Tracy Swinford in 2018. Cathie Ward came up in conversation, and he told her the story about his trips to Blacksnake with Gary and Cathie. Leslie was shocked. She'd always been under the same belief as Cathie's family and friends that the day she died was the first time she'd ever ridden a horse.

Leslie brought John to my house to share this story, and after he was finished, something was bothering me. I was aware Cathie's mother had given her permission to ride only once—and that was the day she died.

So, I asked John, "Where did you pick up Cathie? At her house? Did you meet her mother?"

"I never met her mother," he said. "And when we'd pick her up, she'd come walking through a big field."

Leslie and I both looked at each other. We knew there wasn't a big field near Cathie's home.

"Could I drive you up by her house, and we'll see if that's where you remember getting her?" Leslie asked.

He agreed, so they left, and Leslie drove him up to Prospect Avenue. As they passed the house where Cathie had lived in 1966, Leslie pointed and said, "Is that it?"

"Nope," he replied.

She continued driving, and when they had gone two blocks farther, John said, "That's it! That's where we picked her up."

The property John showed her was a vacant lot situated between Prospect Avenue and Pecan Street. It was a large lot that once contained a freestanding garage next to a three-story house at 108 Pecan, where I rented an apartment after college in the late 1970s. We'd dubbed it "the sorority house" because several of my friends and I had lived in its two apartments at different times. I had valued the garage back then during the cold winter months because I owned a tiny Triumph Spitfire convertible. I'd park it inside the garage, then place a blanket over the hood to keep the engine warm overnight.

Later that evening, Leslie and I talked about Cathie's remote site. It was obvious she'd used it to sneak away from her home to catch a ride with the boys. John remembered stopping there twice to fetch her for their horseback rides at Blacksnake Ranch.

After hearing this, I thought of Cathie, a thirteen-year-old who so badly wanted to ride horses, and it reminded me of a statement by her father. "I was not living with her [Cathie] at the time, and I only saw her when she was here," he said. "Well, she was all right when she was here. She had her own mind that she wanted to do whatever she wanted to do. She was not defiant. It was not that kind of thing. You just weren't going to make her sit down and do anything. She was going to be into something. She was a party girl. She liked to go and do. Well, she was not going to be controlled. She did whatever she wanted to, whether you liked it or not. But as long as she was here, we got along fine."

The day before, after John revealed this blockbuster, Leslie said, "This means Frank Davis saw Cathie *twice* before the day she died. This was Cathie back then." Leslie put her hands in front of her and waved them in the shape of an hourglass. "And this was the rest of us girls back then." She stuck her hands out and ran them straight up and down, like a flat board. "She was more developed than a lot of us," she added.

Couple Cathie's young beauty with the fact that forty-two-year-old Frank Davis had a penchant for young women, and you have a lethal situation. Only two years earlier, he married his nineteen-year-old fourth wife. Frank Davis was probably quite happy to see Cathie arriving at his ranch on June 24, 1966, with two little girls instead of John and Gary, her two bodyguards.

• 4 •

The Killer

$\mathscr{F}$rank Davis and Harold Tankersley, a local horse trader and bar bouncer, frolicked on the outer fringes of respectability in Hot Springs. Although both men were married, they danced, chased women, and did whatever they wanted at "old joints," like the Circle L, Twin Oaks, and Club 88. They limited their carousing to the weekend, though when they stayed late at the clubs, they were usually invited home by women for a nightcap—but only on weekends.

Frank's trusty transportation for these jaunts, among others, was an old gray mare given to him by Irene, his mother, who shared her Lakeshore Drive home with Frank and his first wife, Naomi. Once, Frank rode the mare to a nearby joint that had a makeshift walkway of two long boards flung over a muddy creek at the entrance. Frank took the mare over the boards into the old tavern and tied her to a wooden post inside. Watching his buddy's unorthodox entrance, Harold laughed and thought, *He breaks all the rules!* During the men's wild days and nights, the mare died. "She was like family to Frank, so he drove her out to my farm on a flatbed truck, and we buried her," said Harold.

Harold was the number one bouncer in Hot Springs and Garland County. He earned the title by being kind to people as they entered his establishment but brusque when they became rowdy. If anyone acted up, Harold showed them the door—everyone, that is, except Frank Davis. Harold knew two drinks would mess up Frank's mind and make him fighting drunk.

As he remembers it, "Frank would go into a rage when he got mad. It made no difference what he was mad at, he'd try to kill it or tear it up. He was very high tempered. Frank was the type of guy that if he didn't like you, he didn't like you. But he was always good to me, and he even let me ride his rodeo horse. His mama, Irene, financed twenty-five to fifty horses stabled all over Garland County."

"She took care of him—always," Harold recalled. "Whatever he wanted, she got him. I don't know where her money came from. Whatever he wanted, he got. She leased him a place on Wildcat Road, and she'd meet him up there and baby him. You didn't hear much out of her. She just stayed quiet and spent a lot of money on that boy. Then she bought that place on Blacksnake for him."

Frank wanted to emulate his parents' strong work ethics through his new venture located on Blacksnake Road near the Bull Bayou Creek, which flowed south into Lake Hamilton, where people headed to go boating, fishing, and water skiing. A canopy of rock-rimmed trees lined the long dirt driveway that led up to a rustic ranch house surrounded by beautiful pasturelands and ponds. A service road shot off to the left of the house past the large pond and then on to the barn and stables behind the house. The main drive continued beyond the front-yard wishing well to the pastures, where a tack shed was the starting point for riders to take the riding paths that ambled toward the backside of the ranch and connected to trails. The western perimeter of Blacksnake was bounded by trees and fencing, while the eastern aspect halted at the creek with large rock outcroppings, forming a balcony and equestrian diving board for the pool of cold water.

Frank began marketing Blacksnake Ranch as a recreational destination with a listing in the *Hot Springs National Park City Directory* and the telephone book. But he found the most effective way of drumming up business was through word of mouth from local motels, where he distributed pamphlets. Frank stopped at the Best Tourist Court on Ouachita Avenue, where he met Catherine "Tiny" Browne. The tall and attractive motel manager returned home in the late 1950s with three children after a divorce. Her father, Dr. N. B. Burch, who owned the Best, Burch, and Fountain tourist courts along with the Willow Beach motel on Lake Hamilton, hired his daughter to manage the Best Motel with twenty-six units, each with an attached garage. Wanting to attract more vacationing families in the 1960s, she added a swimming pool at the front of the property.

Regular stops at the Best helped Frank forge a bond with Tiny that soon included her ten-year-old daughter, Cathy (no relation to Cathie Ward, who was a few years older). To repay her for sending her guests to his riding stable, Frank offered a discount for young Cathy. Tiny drove her several times to ride horses at the ranch until Frank offered to chauffeur the young girl both ways. As Cathy remembers it, "I was tall and skinny with short hair that looked like a boy. I was just one of the kids, and he was just Frank. He never bothered me."

Cathy got a thrill each time she entered the greeting area near a wooden Blacksnake Ranch sign with wagon wheels. She'd get out of Frank's car and walk over to the big oak tree out front and then wait on a ranch hand to bring her a horse. They would saddle up her horse, and off she'd go on her own.

"I rode all kinds of horses, and Frank and his hands just let me have free rein to choose which horse I wanted to ride. They'd already explained each of the horses' quirks," she remembered. "My favorite was Postman, but he was too short for my height, but since I was so skinny, it didn't matter. He could run like the wind with my long legs flapping in the stirrups."

Cathy was at home at Blacksnake and felt Frank and his young ranch hands looked out for her. They'd say, "Don't go over here, don't go in this pasture right now, we're bush hogging it" or "You can go down to the creek if you want." They'd tell her so they would know where she was in case something happened and she didn't come back.

She'd watch Frank and his ranch hands break in horses at the corral by the stables with ten or twelve stalls. Sometimes, he or Sharron would invite her into the house. Cathy would enter through the kitchen that overlooked the stables but never went to the back of the house, where the bedrooms were located. She loved playing with their precocious toddler, Allan Ray, and holding Fredrick Allan, the infant.

Frank had dammed up Bull Bayou's cold, spring-fed water to create a swimming pool below a cliff. He loved riding his horse straight up the side of the mountain to that rocky prominence and jumping off like a stunt rider into the pool. One day, he asked Cathy to go with him up the steep incline.

"Naw," she said, "I'm not going to do it. That's too scary!"

Instead, she rode down to another part of the pool, where the young ranch hands bathed the horses. The ten to fifteen teenage boys were closed mouthed when she asked about their living situation, but they did divulge Frank had fostered them to work and housed them somewhere on the ranch. As Cathy remembers, "Mother thought it was kind of strange that Frank had so many boys at the ranch."

Once, Cathy invited her friend Toni to Blacksnake for a day of horseback riding. They were riding out in the pasture with a group of people while Frank led the tour. He was talking about the area when he rode his horse around Cathy, grabbed her tiny friend, tucked her in front of him in his saddle, and raced off.

The group was shocked at his heroics, but Cathy knew he always talked about being "a cowboy out West" and thought he was just showing off his riding skills. Waiting in a pack for their leader, they watched him from a distance—sandwiched in the saddle with the young girl. Then, they saw him gallop back towards them and return Toni to the saddle on her horse.

Cathy turned around to look at Toni, who rode up next to her. "I want to go home," she screamed. "Now!"

"I'm sure that scared the dickens out of yah!" Cathy replied.

"Yeah," said Toni. "I just want to go home!"

Cathy led her back to the stables. Then she went inside the house and called her mother. On the drive home, she kept asking, "Are you okay?"—because she knew her friend was not okay.

Later, whenever they were together, Cathy would say, "Wow, that was really something, him grabbing you off the horse and all that." But Toni would never respond. Cathy didn't know if Frank had said something intimidating or if it was the scary experience of what he'd done that had frightened her so badly.

THE YOUNGSTER

Frank conducted himself by his own set of rules, learning as a kid to fight for respect. He could whip any boy in his Texas town, which elevated his status and gained friends' participation in his clandestine escapades, such as pilfering farmers' annual crops.

"I never stole anything but watermelons. That's the extent of my thievery in my whole life," Frank told someone years later. "I can't stand a thief or a liar. Boys didn't go to reform schools in those days. The sheriff brought them home, and their daddies took care of them like a mule."

Irene Davis tried a different approach to teach her young son the difference between good and evil. She doted on Frank and gave him extra doses of love, hoping it would counterbalance her husband's stern attitude. Every Sunday, she took Frank to the Presbyterian church, which he joined at the age of twelve, the same year he had his first drink.

Making good grades, Frank graduated from Balmorhea High School in 1939 before he was fifteen years old, and his parents quickly enrolled him in a two-year program at the John Tarleton Academy, an agricultural school in Stephenville, Texas, southwest of Fort Worth. During school, he watched as Nazi Germany escalated its European invasions and America declared war. The seventeen-year-old graduated, volunteered for the air force, completed basic training, was selected for aviation cadet school, became a flight officer in 1942 (a rank used only during World War II),[1] and shipped off to the South Pacific. Soon, he realized it was just as dangerous on the ground as in the air when he was blindsided with a steel pipe in the barracks. After falling to the floor and passing out, he was carried to the infirmary, where he remained unconscious for several days.

His childhood toughness from multiple falls off his horse steeled him in his World War II tropical deployment after a crash while copiloting a plane. Before the rescue team could reach him, he rubbed his hand across his head but didn't feel any bumps. He found no evidence of blood or broken bones and waved away the rescuers, who ignored his noble gesture and took him straight to the infirmary. Later, he became angry as his superiors questioned him about the crash. Years later, he maintained their inquisition was so overwhelming and provoked him so badly that it caused him to black out for three days, and when he awoke, he didn't know where he was or where he had been.

Frank developed bleeding ulcers, sometimes so severe that he would go into shock and require hospitalization. After several repetitions of this scenario with no improvement, the air force gave him an honorable medical discharge in 1945 that included a monthly check of $170. Frank received the government's decision without an argument, not realizing their formal rejection had set into motion a pattern that would become personal and, on several occasions, become too much for him to accept.

THE CONNECTION

The week following Cathie's funeral, fifteen-year-old Lorna Garner overheard her parents talking about "the little girl who'd died." Her mother worked at the local newspaper, where the staff discussed the teenager's fatal accident, while her father was a salesman at an auto parts store frequented by policemen.

Something clicked when Lorna overheard her mother and father talking about the incident. She went to the living room and found a stack of newspapers. She rifled through them, grabbed a few, and rushed to her bedroom. Unlike most kids, Lorna was accustomed to reading the daily paper due to her mother's employment, which she emulated at Southwest Junior High School's newspaper as a staffer. She quickly found Cathie's story and after reading it realized she knew her.

Lorna remembered meeting Cathie while playing with her friend Babette, who lived near Jones School. They were in the bell house, which once had a long rope that was used to ring the bell up top, calling students to school each morning. Now, with an electric bell inside the three-story school building, the rope was gone, and the square stucco building with four inside corner benches had become a fun place for kids to play. Lorna remembered how she and Babette played with Cathie one day in the bell house and thought she was really sweet as they jumped from bench to bench.

After Lorna made the connection with Cathie, she realized another. Her parents' conversation about Frank Davis spurred her memory of a frightening encounter that happened a few weeks earlier. Having just finished ninth grade and out for summer break, she and her cousin Kay were at their grandmother's house near Oaklawn School. They walked over to the playground and went to the backside of the school, next to a busy street. Just as they reached the swings, a man drove by in a red truck and stopped.

"I need your help," he hollered.

The girls went over to see what he wanted.

"I know there's a puppy around here somewhere," he told them.

Hearing the word "puppy," Lorna asked, "Where is it?"

She walked over to the truck and stepped up on its running board, then Kay joined her.

"I've been trying to get this puppy back to these people," he said.

"Well, I don't see it," said Lorna, who was looking around the dark-haired man for the little dog when she felt Kay jerking on her arm. She knew her cousin was trying to warn her not to talk to strangers.

"I took it to my house, and I'm keeping it in my backyard until I can find the people that owned it," the man said as he began to unzip his pants.

Knowing that what he was doing was something they shouldn't witness, the two girls jumped off the truck and slowly backed away. They could see him smiling at them as he jerked his hand back and forth from his mouth to below the window where they couldn't see what he was doing down there.

They stood stiff as boards, watching him, until they heard their grandmother yelling, "Come home, girls!" They turned and ran, and as soon as they were inside their grandmother's house, the questioning began.

Lorna and Kay knew they were in trouble for going up to the truck because they'd been taught never to do that. Lorna's mother and Aunt Dorothy sat the two girls down and had "one of those talks girls aren't supposed to hear when they're little."

While the women conducted their serious lecture, Lorna fidgeted in her seat, wanting them to finish so she could get back outside. But first, she wanted to defend her and her cousin's actions. "I have friends over on Henderson Street, and we've seen the truck over there," she said. "We've seen the guy driving the truck around, but we've never ever talked to him. He's just somebody we've seen around."

"There are people who appear to be all concerned about an animal, a puppy, or a kitten," Aunt Dorothy explained. "And they're just trying to hurt you if you get in the truck or go with them."

Lorna and Kay promised to heed their warnings, then asked permission to go back outside to play. However, the scary experience with the man had shook them up for quite a while.

Snapping back from her thoughts, Lorna placed the newspaper on her bed and then called her cousin Kay. She told her about Cathie Ward's death and what she suspected.

"That man who owned the ranch where Cathie Ward died, I think he's the same creep that got us into trouble," Lorna said. "The guy in the truck."

"Nah," Kay replied. "It may not be the same person at all."

"But we've seen him driving around before. I think he's the same guy that stopped and talked to us," said Lorna, trying to convince her cousin.

"Maybe," Kay relented.

"You know if we'd gone with that man, he might have hurt us or killed us! We've walked all around town and been to the carnival, and nothing's happened to us like what that man did in the truck. I mean, who else drives around and talks to little girls? I just think he's weird, and I think he's the same guy."

"Well, maybe," Kay replied, worried now.

"Do you think he tricked her?" Lorna asked.

Each time the two cousins visited their friend Babette, they would talk about what happened to Cathie, the little girl they'd met in the bell house, and one question always came up—*Do you think he tricked her?*

After Cathie died, Lorna wouldn't discuss her death with anyone but Kay and Babette. She didn't want to mention it to her parents because it would bring up the possibility the man in the truck could've gotten them. However, she didn't have to worry because her parents never again spoke of "the little girl's death" or "the man-in-the-truck incident." They just made sure their daughter was well supervised whenever she left the house, a practice in many homes with teenage girls after the incriminating rumors of Frank Davis began swirling through Hot Springs in the summer of 1966.

The Drowning, the Women,
and the Mother

*A*fter June 24, 1966, the clientele at Blacksnake Ranch fell faster than New York's Times Square ball drop. Frank's bar-hopping buddy Harold Tankersley said, "Frank had lots of kids coming out, paying to ride horses. He'd changed quite a bit, and things finally seemed to be going his way—before the girl died at his ranch."

Tankersley, who lived in Garland County on Amity Road, believed all the gossip about Frank Davis's involvement. Discussions of Cathie Ward's suspicious death were being shared from person to person on the outskirts of Hot Springs when a second incident began making the rounds.

"We heard a little black boy drowned at Blacksnake Ranch," said Margie Hill, Tankersley's niece. "And his drowning may have been because of him seeing what actually happened to that girl, that she was already dead when she was connected to the saddle."

"They found the boy drowned in the same area where the girl was at," Harold Tankersley said. "It was a very sad time for all of us, that he had gone that far," said Tankersley.

"It made us stay away from him and not get involved in anything he was doing," Hill added.

THE WOMEN

Everyone was steering clear of Frank Davis except his young fourth wife, Sharron, and their two sons, a toddler and an infant. He and Sharron were married more than two years earlier—the very day his divorce was final from Carrie, his third wife.

39

Carrie was an attractive brunette and graduate of Hot Springs High School's class of 1954, the same as Frank's second wife.[1] She shared that one commonality with her and another with Frank. The reserved young woman from the stylish Trivista neighborhood, north of Oaklawn Park Jockey Club, was also divorced.

A woman who knew many people in Hot Springs said, "After graduating high school, Carrie married the wild son of a wealthy woman who'd recently remarried a prominent attorney, but her father would have nothing to do with the hasty marriage and had it annulled. It was a shock to me that Carrie and Frank even knew each other. Her parents lived on the corner by Judge Britt's home, and her father was a dentist."

Frank was a dozen years older than Carrie. How they met is unknown. However, Linda Livingston Harris, the daughter of the Garland County treasurer, said, "Frank Davis liked to hang out with younger people . . . like he could get a cult or something, a following. He would come out to Bob's Drive Inn on Central Avenue where I went with a group of my friends. I thought he was a cowboy kind of guy and didn't particularly care for him. I just didn't know him that well, but I just remember him always being around, and he and my friend, Princella Cook, rode horses together. He was just, to me—" Linda paused. "He was like a scary person. I felt really uncomfortable around him."

Somehow, Frank and Carrie's odd marriage was working. In May 1962, they became proud parents of a boy. While she cared for their new infant, Frank was experiencing debilitating spells of chronic stomach pain, the same medical issue that earned him a 1945 pink slip from the air force.

Six years after Uncle Sam released him, Frank graduated from Texas Tech with a bachelor's degree in agriculture. He began teaching adult Conservation Service classes and sidelined as a crop duster while working on his father's ranch. Later, he became a U.S. cattle inspector. Then in 1953, he contracted undulant fever, an infectious disease that is transmitted either through contaminated milk and milk products or by direct contact with infected animals, such as cattle.[2] A doctor prescribed Frank some antibiotics, but he claimed they didn't make him feel any better. Only the pampering from his first wife, Naomi (from Denton, Texas), and his mother seemed to relieve the pain. However, it soon escalated, and he was admitted to St. Joseph's Hospital in Hot Springs.

A year later, in 1954, he went to the Army and Navy Hospital, a V-shaped, ten-story majestic building perched atop a hill behind the world-famous Bathhouse Row in Hot Springs. The medical facility, owned and operated by the U.S. government, cared for retired and active armed forces members from across the nation. The hospital chief placed Frank under a thirty-day psychiatric evaluation and on its completion informed him that his stomach symptoms might be coming from his head.

Frank vehemently disagreed and said, "Anyone would know this was foolishness!"

In 1962, during his third marriage with Carrie, his stomach problems accelerated to the point that he'd pass out on the floor, sleep, and then wake up feeling fine. Eventually, he needed surgery, and Carrie accompanied him to Lackland Air Force Base in San Antonio, where surgeons performed a gastric resection.

While recuperating, he stopped by his mother's beauty salon and spied a new beautician, who a friend described as "a beauty."

Sharron Knight, a 1962 high school graduate[3] and one of four daughters of Fred Knight, a tapper at the Reynolds Metal Plant in Jones Mills,[4] and Pauline, a homemaker, became Frank's latest fascination.

However, Sharron confided to a friend, "I didn't want to date him, but his mother pushed him on me."

Regardless of how pushed on him she was, Sharron soon returned Frank's affection, despite their age difference and his marital history.

Frank's third wife Carrie was unaware of his affair. One evening, she told him, "We're going to have another baby!"

"Well that's tough," Frank said. "My girlfriend's pregnant, and I'm going to divorce you and marry her."

Frank kept his word. On September 13, 1963, he received a phone call from his attorney that his divorce from Carrie was final. Wasting no time, he called Sharron.

"Go put on a pretty dress," he said. "We're getting married today!"

The thirty-nine-year-old rushed over to pick up nineteen-year-old Sharron, then drove her to Murfreesboro, Arkansas, for a quickie marriage.

Frank and Sharron set up house while his ex-wife Carrie moved with her son into a rental home on Woodlawn Avenue, inconveniently close to Irene Davis's home in the Oaklawn neighborhood. Carrie's parents lived not far away on Trivista Right and became handy babysitters after she gave birth to a daughter and went to work as a receptionist for a new dentist.

Dr. Joe Little was a hometown boy who grew up hefting crates at his father's produce company and married a daughter of David Whittington, the Garland County prosecuting attorney. Joe thought his first hire was sweet, quiet, and kind of meek, which caused him to believe he was much older than she. But in reality, it was the reverse. He was a "lowly sophomore" at Hot Springs High School when she was a "lofty senior."

Joe knew Carrie was terrified of Frank Davis—literally scared to death of him. "She never went into much, and in hindsight, I would have been much more concerned," said Joe.

She once told her employer, "I know enough about different things Frank has done that I'm afraid for me and my children."

"What she knew, she never said," Joe told me. "He had a horrible reputation back then. I felt so sorry for her."

One day, Carrie told Joe that Frank had warned her that she and their children would pay if she filed for child support.

"She was totally devoted to those two children," he said. "Her mother kept them while she was at work. When she wasn't working, she was with her kids. She was closed mouthed about her personal life."

Carrie was so afraid of Frank that she left town without telling anyone but her family where she was headed. It was around tax time, and Joe needed to mail a W2 income tax form to her. He contacted her brother, who wouldn't give him her address—only the town where she had gone. With no other alternatives, he mailed the tax forms to Carrie's brother.

"I never heard another word about her after the income tax incident," he said.

Joe's story was corroborated by a Hot Springs woman.

"Carrie took the children and moved away from here so that he [Frank] could not find them," she said. "As far as I know, a high school friend was one of the very few people outside her immediate family who knew where she was or kept in contact with her."

With his third wife gone and no child-support obligations, Frank was free to concentrate solely on his fourth wife and their son, who was born ten months and seventeen days after their marriage. He and Sharron bought a farm and ranch house May 16, 1965, for $10,000 with a monthly payment of $75 due on the sixteenth of each month. They signed the purchase agreement two weeks later, with Frank being designated "first party" and Sharron "second party." Frank had great plans for his new family and business at Blacksnake Ranch. But how was he to know that it would all come crashing down a year later on June 24, 1966, and that he'd be scrutinized by the law for the accidental death of a minor at his ranch?

THE MOTHER

Regardless of what he did, Irene Davis never criticized her son. Their close relationship grew even stronger after the death of his father—her husband, Ray—in 1954. Seven years earlier in 1947, Ray moved the Davis family to

Arkansas, where he was born, and bought acreage in Bismarck, fourteen miles south of Hot Springs.

Ray Davis saw promise in the resort town, and similar to his earlier career changes from barber to liquor store owner, he decided to become a real estate salesman and rancher.[5] Irene extended her lucrative beauty salon career that began in Texas with the backing of her husband, who was working eighty hours a week to her sixty.[6] She soon was hired as an "operator" at Virginia Gigerich's beauty shop in Hot Springs.[7]

Ray worked just as hard in Arkansas, became ill, and died on December 18, 1954.[8] Irene held his service at Gross Mortuary Chapel with Elder Samuel D. Moore Jr. of the Latter-day Saints officiating. Ray's body was sent for burial to Big Springs, Texas, where his father was buried, and his mother and sister still lived.

After Ray's death, Irene moved from Bismarck into Hot Springs to be closer to work.[9] She found a home on Lakeshore Drive with enough room to accommodate Frank and his first wife, Naomi.[10] It was an ideal location for her son, only two miles west of the Garland County Fairgrounds, where he would become very active in the local rodeo club.

Irene built her clientele as a hairstylist at Virginia Gigerich's beauty salon and enhanced it by patronizing her customers' businesses. She would drop by Tom's Barbecue, which was owned by the husband of her customer Lee Ella Athanas and was across the street from the Oaklawn (thoroughbred horse) racetrack on Central Avenue.

Athas Athanas, known as Tom, had immigrated from Greece in 1906 when he was only fourteen years old.[11] On his entry through Ellis Island, his surname was shortened from Athanasopolis to Athanas, and he made his way to Hot Springs. His relatives were living in a boardinghouse filled with Greeks and Italians and working at his uncle's confectionary.[12] A decade later, he was a proprietor of Liberty Confectionary along with cousins, John Paulus and Sam Kaghelaus.[13]

Athas married Lee Ella Wallace,[14] and by 1930, they had two daughters, a son, and what the U.S. Census described as "a servant."[15] He now owned a sandwich shop. By 1946, no one was calling him "Athas." Instead, he was known as "Tom," the name he was using for his barbecue restaurant.

Lee Ella died of a heart attack in December 1953, and Irene Davis continued to patronize Tom's. Less than three years after Ray's death, Irene and Tom were married in Greenville, Mississippi, where her parents, Mr. and Mrs. H. C. Chapman, and sisters lived. Elder Wesley Ray Burr performed their wedding service on May 12, 1957.[16]

Tom and Irene returned to Hot Springs after their honeymoon. She soon opened Irene's Beauty Salon, a few doors down from his restaurant on

Central Avenue. Tom's home, where she now lived, was conveniently located on the corner of Henderson and Bell streets around the corner from both of their businesses.

A year later, a vehicle filled with teenagers rammed into Tom's automobile, causing it to roll over. The driver was rumored to be an underage girl in a car owned by her boyfriend, a jockey from Oaklawn racetrack.

Frances Gabriel Forsberg, whose Greek father was a close friend of Tom's, remembered the difficult days for Tom and Irene.

"He had so many broken bones in his back that Tom ended up in the hospital from then on, for the rest of his life. But the thing that stands out in my mind is what a kind person Irene was. He was in the Veterans Hospital in Little Rock, and she had an ambulance go over, pick him up, and bring him back to St. Joseph's Hospital, so his friends could come see him for a few days over the weekend. And, I just thought that was the most thoughtful thing I had heard of anybody doing."

While Irene was going back and forth to see Tom at the hospital in Little Rock, Frank and Naomi were living in her Lakeshore Drive home. The owners of Carter Dairy were distant neighbors on the rural road that went from the fairgrounds to Lake Hamilton. Nan Carter, whose husband was a second-generation dairyman, said, "I remember seeing Frank's wife. She was really pretty, had long dark hair, and wore blue jeans and cowboy boots and lots of makeup."

Nan also recalled her husband and father-in-law laughing one night as they told her a story about Frank Davis.

"If he wanted something, he'd bang his plate on the table and point— and his wife would get up and get him something."

Irene continued to care for her invalid husband, who spent four and a half years, the majority of their marriage, as a paraplegic at the Veterans Hospital. Tom succumbed to his injuries on Friday, July 5, 1963, and Irene Davis Athanas returned to Gross Mortuary to plan her second husband's funeral.[17]

The same as her first husband, Irene enlisted elders of the Latter-day Saints to preside over Tom's funeral service in the Gross Mortuary Chapel. But this time, the American Legion, Warren Townsend Post 13, conducted the graveside service at Greenwood Cemetery, where Athas was buried next to his first wife, Lee Ella. On his death, Tom's adopted name was removed, and he was acknowledged and buried as "Athas J. Athanas."

Another difference between Irene's husbands' interments was the pall-bearers. Athas's funeral included nineteen well-known Hot Springs business-men, neighbors, and leaders of the Greek community. His son-in-law, L. A. Vaught, served as an honorary pallbearer, and less than three years later, he and Athas's daughter divorced. Vaught remarried Faye Rader, moved next door to Sarah Ward on Prospect Avenue, and was one of Cathie Ward's pallbearers in 1966.

Irene continued to live in Athas's home on Henderson Street and kept busy at her beauty shop on Central Avenue, a few doors away from her late husband's barbecue restaurant on the corner. Sometime before his death, the business was sold to Herman Searcy, and by 1963, the name of the restaurant was changed to Shamrock Cafe.[18]

Pat Hogan, owner of the Little Rock Stockyard, became Irene's third husband and moved into the home she inherited from Tom. By the Fourth of July 1966, Irene and Pat were concerned about Frank. He was out of sorts because his business had disintegrated.

His wife Sharron was the only member of their household contributing to their family income. She graduated from Irene's Beauty School and landed a full-time beautician's slot at Vanity Beauty Shop in South Hot Springs near popular Cook's Ice Cream. Frank was staying busy on the ranch with the cattle and horses, but the carloads of kids coming out to ride horses had halted in the few weeks since Cathie Ward's death.

THE MUTUAL DISLIKE

The only parents driving their children to Blacksnake Ranch were Charles and Dollie Fager, Sharron's aunt and uncle. Dollie and Pauline Knight (Sharron's mother) were sisters, each of whom had a household of girls but no boys. Although they lived in different parts of town and didn't attend the same church, they were very close.

The Fagers would take their thirteen-year-old daughter, Debby, to visit her "favorite cousin," Sharron. Each time Debby arrived, the house would be bustling with young hired hands coming in and out to receive chores from Frank. Sharron, whose quiet demeanor matched her subtle beauty, would be working in the kitchen, making "a big ol' pot of soup," as Debby described it. Two-year-old Allan Ray was often playing with his toys on the living room floor while the baby slept in a bassinet nearby.

Debby could see how much Frank enjoyed being around teenagers, joking with them and grabbing his guitar to sing. He would make her feel special and was always polite. Even though she didn't think he was good-looking, she thought he was "a pretty cool guy."

Debby knew that what she called "a family feud" existed. Frank didn't like his mother-in-law, and the feeling was mutual.

"She didn't want her daughter to be with him, probably because of the way he appeared to her—a tall, rough old cowboy who wore boots, jeans, and a hat," Debby said.

She also witnessed underlying tensions in the Davis household. When the toddler would become boisterous with his toys, Sharron would rush to hush him. Then Frank would scream, "Let the kid be a kid! He just wants to have fun!" A squawking baby, however, caused a different reaction. Frank would become unhinged, jumping up from his perch on the couch and pacing the living room floor until she calmed the crying four-month-old.

⌒⌒

Frank may have been feeling the pressure of the ongoing investigation of Cathie Ward's death. Maybe the authorities roaming his ranch concerned him—what they might discover and if it matched his account of the accident. Maybe he felt squeezed with a wife and two children at home, or it could have simply been his ongoing stomach issues that frayed his nerves.

Although Sharron abhorred his behavior, she tried appeasing him in the kitchen with his favorite meal—pinto beans and corn bread with buttermilk. The next year, he would mention his food preferences to a psychiatrist but not his sexual proclivities.

Sharron confided to her mother, "He ties me up to the bed and sexually abuses me."

THE INVESTIGATION RULING

Frank's fretting over the unknown was thwarted on July 14, 1966, when the *Sentinel-Record* announced, "Girl's Death Resulted from Riding Accident."[19] David Whittington, the prosecuting attorney, confirmed, "The investigation into the death of 13-year-old Catherine Ann Ward here June 25 resulted from her being dragged by a horse in a riding accident."

Whittington stated, "None of the facts established in the investigation, autopsy report, or in statements taken from law officers, insurance officials, or members of the girl's family showed any evidence of the death having occurred in any manner other than having been dragged by a horse."

The county coroner, Dr. William Mashburn, and deputy coroner, Dr. W. R. Lee, performed the autopsy and reported to Whittington that the cause of death was due to "severe trauma to the head and brain." Whittington acknowledged that their extensive and complete autopsy was conducted, and the findings were consistent with the history that the trauma to Cathie resulted from being "dragged by a horse with a foot hung in a stirrup."

Whittington backed up his decision after reviewing the numerous statements of witnesses taken by his office and the evidence based on the investigation of certain details by the Arkansas State Police. He also considered insurance company investigators' statements and several conferences he'd held with law enforcement officials and members of Cathie Ward's family. The rumors of rape and murder flying around Hot Springs were not addressed, and a rape test was never mentioned.

The authorities completed their investigation of Cathie's death in eighteen days—the equivalent of one and one-third days for each year of her short life. The ruling was legal and in print, but among those who didn't agree with it was Cathie's father, Hiram Ward.

"The state police investigation ruled it an accident to start with, and I told them at the time, 'I don't believe this is an accident,'" he told me. "But there wasn't anything you could do about it."

· 6 ·

Mental Health and the Getaway

$\mathcal{C}$athie's death ruling had loosened the public noose around Frank's neck, but it didn't change his emerging paranoia and erratic behavior. He would hear voices at night and people walking in his house. So he'd jump out of bed, grab his gun, and look through the entire house, only to find nothing. Sharron and Frank's mother, Irene, held a family conference to encourage him to see a psychiatrist. An appointment was scheduled at Lackland Air Force Base in San Antonio, Texas, and Irene paid for the trip.

They sold it to him as a treat to take the kids and enjoy a short vacation. Frank dutifully met with the doctors and afterward informed Sharron and his mother, "They told me I didn't need a psychiatrist but only need to take care of my stomach."

THE GETAWAY

Frank was still very active in his rodeo club and had become a member of their competitive riding academy's guitar-playing group, which was scheduled to appear at an election-night rally on Tuesday, August 9, 1966. Frank was a big supporter of circuit judge candidate Robert "Bob" Ridgeway, an attorney and the current municipal judge.

The primary election in June ended in a runoff, and by August, the race had turned mean. On Sunday night, June 7, Ridgeway's campaign workers were distributing 10,000 circulars containing matter not carried in newspaper advertisements while workers of his opponent, former prosecuting attorney Walter J. Hebert, stole and replaced them with cartoon circulars aimed at

Ridgeway. When one of Hebert's campaign workers protested the Ridgeway circulars late that night, someone called the police.[1]

Lieutenant Norman Hall contacted city attorney Curtis Ridgway Jr. (no relation to candidate Ridgeway), who advised, "Persons found distributing such material at that late hour on private property could be arrested for trespassing."

Robert Ridgeway also called the police to complain that his workers were being molested. The altercation occurred in the Sixth Ward when one of Hebert's workers tried to grab a batch of Ridgeway's circulars from his worker and tore his shirt in the scuffle. Ridgeway asked the police for their protection.

Residents near Ridgeway's campaign headquarters at the Ramada Inn, less than a block from Hebert's headquarters at the Avanelle Motor Lodge, reported they were disturbed by loud talking and name-calling. Lieutenant Hall stopped by to check out the complaints but made no arrests. However, Police Chief John Ermey became involved, and the whole nasty affair wound up on the front page of the newspaper on election Tuesday, making the circuit judge's contest the hottest race on the August 9 ballot.

Staunch supporters headed to their respective candidate's gatherings that night, including Frank and Sharron, who stopped beforehand to leave the boys at the home of Sharron's parents. Walking into the rally with his guitar, Frank joined the rodeo band while Sharron found a seat by one of the wives. Throughout the night, the music was interrupted with announcements of voting tallies from the different wards, followed by cheers or boos from the raucous crowd. The circuit judge's runoff race was still undecided when the rally was scheduled to end, and Virginia, a rodeo club member, invited Sharron and some others to her home for a post-rally party to watch the election results on the 10:00 news. Since it was summer break, Virginia probably thought her thirteen-year-old daughter wouldn't be bothered by the late crowd.

For some reason, the subject of dirty diapers came up while Frank and Sharron were leaving, so he offered to drop her off at Virginia's and take care of the chore and then return by 10:30 p.m. Running late, he called Virginia's house and asked for her but was told she wasn't there. Next, he asked for Sharron and was given the same answer: "Not here."

Startled, Frank asked to speak to Virginia's teenage daughter, Madelyn, who helped around his ranch (and had invited Cathie Ward to ride horses at Blacksnake Ranch the day she died). The thirteen-year-old came to the phone, and when he asked about his wife, Madelyn answered, "She's not here. Her sister came for her."

The evening had been filled with overt emotions for the political candidates, but now it had taken a very personal turn for Frank. Frantic thoughts overcame him. *Why did Sharron's sister come get her? Are the boys okay? Did something happen to one of them? Why didn't Sharron call me?* Soon, he would have the answers.

⌒

Frank hung up the phone with Madelyn late that Tuesday night and began dialing his in-law's number. The evening had been chaotic. He was unsure if his candidate, Ridgeway, had won, and now he was puzzled why Sharron had left the watch party and gone to her parents' home.

Used to having a thumb on his wife, he may have thought he'd merely tell her, "I'll be right there to get you and the boys." But when he called, Sharron said, "I'm not coming back to you."

He asked her again and received the same answer, which wasn't at all what he was expecting. Frank was confused. He didn't understand what had happened. When they left home that evening, nothing was wrong.

To add to his misery, he learned his candidate, Ridgeway, who'd led the primaries, lost the runoff by a margin of fewer than 600 votes.[2] The night Frank had expected to be fun and jubilant wasn't.

No amount of alcohol could soothe his nerves and emotions from Sharron's bitter betrayal. That night, when he finally made it to bed, he cried while tucking a picture of Sharron and the boys under his pillow. Later, he would admit, "I've been at the point of tears ever since."

⌒

History was repeating itself. Now Frank was a two-time loser. He dumped his first wife, Naomi, after fourteen years of marriage, and then married Shirley on November 8, 1958.[3] She was twelve years younger and a member of his rodeo club.[4] An acquaintance of hers said, "Shirley pretty well held her own with him. She was a big, tall girl and had grown up rough, so Frank didn't mistreat her as much as he did some of the other women in his life."

But behind closed doors, Shirley watched him beat his favorite guitar into a million pieces across a coffee table. Once, she told her sister-in-law, "He put a gun to my head and threatened to shoot me!"

Shirley asked Frank to go to a psychiatrist several times, but he always refused. When she'd had enough, she told him, "I'm leaving you!"

"Oh no you're not!" he replied and then rushed outside and slashed her car tires.

She kept quiet on her next attempt and escaped when he wasn't at home.

"Shirley was a very smart lady," the sister-in-law told me. "She became a nurse and went into home health care. She's a Christian woman and very nice people."

The sister-in-law said Shirley wanted to keep her privacy after leaving Frank Davis. "I wish people wouldn't bring him up," Shirley told her. "It's over, and I want to get on with my life. It really disturbs me because that's behind me, and I'll never see him again and don't want to see him again. I want to forget it."

After Sharron left Frank in August 1966, her family wasn't surprised.

"There were several reasons why Sharron probably wanted to get away from him," Sharron's cousin Debby Fager said. "Number one, his cruelty, both physically and mentally. Number two, not really caring for the kids. And number three, him being a killer."

"Sharron didn't want to have anything to do with him," Debby added, "because she knew about the killings, the hired hand, and the girl and wanted to get away from it. He drowned one of his hired hands in the same little area that us kids used to go wade in when we were out there."

⌒⊃⌒

Frank woke up Wednesday morning, August 10, 1966, with a knock at his front door. When he opened it, there stood the same men he'd played guitars with at the political rally the night before. He might have thought they heard of Sharron's desertion and had come out to console him or to encourage him to go retrieve her and the boys. But that's not what prompted their visit. They'd driven out from town with the sole purpose of gathering Sharron's clothes.

Frank was furious. He'd been double-crossed. Later, he would call his rodeo club "the Mafia from Hot Springs" and describe them as "the thieves that control everything over there."

It was only a matter of time before the Garland County Public Welfare Department showed up and removed all the foster boys who had served as ranch hands.

Now that Frank was home alone, he began a daily pattern, which started with licking a lemon sprinkled with two tablespoons of salt and then swigging a half-pint of whiskey. Next, he would call Sharron and ask her to bring over the boys.

Her response was always, "I can't. I'm busy right now."

Then he'd demand, "Call me back!"

Frank sat by the phone most days, waiting for the call that never came. At times, she would tell him she'd bring the boys for a visit, so he would get dressed and wait all day into the night, but she would never show up.

Sometimes he'd call her at work, and they'd tell him she was busy and would have to return his call. So, once again, he'd wait hours on end. Occasionally, he received a call, but most of the time, he did not.

For some reason, the short time period between Cathie Ward's death and Sharron's escape—forty-six days—didn't cross his mind. He never made that connection. Blaming all his problems on others, he told someone, "Everybody's been so damn hateful about it. They said I only need to straighten up and quit drinking. I'll never drink another drop. I'd not take a drink for a million dollars. But I don't think drinking is my problem."

Frank was lonely and distraught. He'd always been the one who called the shots. Now, with that status changed, he was spinning out of control—smoking three or four packs of cigarettes a day, drinking heavily, and eating and sleeping poorly.

He started hitting the bars, as he had in years past, and one evening, while eating a steak at what he called "a gambling hall," he felt as if he were about to pass out. Recurring blackouts had haunted him many times since his days in World War II, but during this particular episode, he had the feeling that maybe somebody had slipped something into his drink. He'd had only one, but it felt like several. The odd sensation disappeared by the time he finished dinner, and he was able to go home, where Sharron and the boys were waiting for him—in the photo under his pillow.

· 7 ·

The Rumors

$\mathcal{L}$eslie Tracy, Bettye Jo Tucker, Mary Claire Atkinson, and I returned to school on September 6, 1966, without our friend Cathie Ward. But she was with us everywhere—in the classroom, the gym, and the cafeteria, where hushed conversations and rumors revolved around her tragic accident.

Thus, we and others were surprised when the first issue of Central Junior High School's newspaper, *Spartan Spirit*, came out in October and not a word was mentioned of Cathie.[1] Not a memorial. Not a remembrance. Nothing.

Plenty of stories about teachers with photos and catchy captions filled the pages. The music teacher's headline read, "A New Note in School, Mrs. McLarty." The band even ranked a lengthy article on the third page with the musicians' names in their various instrument sections, and although they were a closely knit group, the article, "Strike Up the Band," had not even a sentence of sympathy for Cathie Ward.[2]

The junior high school teachers didn't utter her name in our classrooms, but that didn't keep us from feeling the loss in their hearts. Clyde Covington, the seventh-grade English teacher, had taught Cathie the previous year. That summer, when he read the front-page story about her death, he thought, *What a terrible accident. Isn't that awful?*

Covington remembered Cathie when his new students started filing in for the 1966 fall semester. "She was the kind of student that teachers really liked to have in class," he said. "A very nice girl, who made good grades and was well behaved."

Years later, Covington explained his feelings of Cathie's death to me. "When a young person dies of normal natural causes, it's very upsetting, but this was even worse. There was a lot of talk in the community that she'd been murdered."

Pam Johnson and her fellow Spartan Band members remembered Cathie as a very likable, beautiful, and funny bandmate. As they grieved for her, their director, Joe Smith, decided they should play a special musical dedication for Cathie and chose *The Shadow of Your Smile*.

Covington, the seventh-grade teacher, was sitting in the school assembly the day the band played the popular song in her honor.

"It was very, very sad," he said. "Then afterwards, whenever I would hear the song, I would always associate it with Cathie."

The grade schools weren't exempt from rumors either. A little girl named Cathy Browne, a Jones School sixth grader who loved riding the fast, little horse at Blacksnake but stopped going after Cathie Ward's fatal accident, was on the playground one day when a boy approached her. "Did you hear about that girl who was drug to death at the ranch?" he asked.

"Yes. She fell off a horse," Cathy replied.

"I heard she was drug through a crystal field," he said.

"What?" Cathy asked.

"Yeah," the boy told her. "He put her on the horse after he killed her and put her foot in the stirrup to make it look like it was an accident and hit the horse and drug her through the crystal field."

Cathy Browne was horrified. Many times, she'd ridden through the big pasture with crystals and rocks—lots of rocks. Even as young as she was, she knew anyone would die a horrible death if they were dragged through a field with hard rocks and jagged crystals.

Students at Southwest, the other junior high school across town, were also affected by Cathie Ward's death. Some of the ninth-grade girls enjoyed strolling through downtown Hot Springs. Because it was too far for them to walk from their homes, they would go to the bus stop at Oaklawn and Central Avenue, where they would catch the bus to Como Square, the gateway to downtown shopping and the movie theaters. Years later, one of them told me, "It all changed when that happened to that girl. Our parents pulled in the reins on our treks around town after that."

Another Southwest Junior High School student, Debby Fager, experienced a more personal connection to Cathie Ward's death. She remembers hearing talk at home about her cousin, Sharron, and Sharron's husband, Frank Davis.

"He [Frank] made her [Sharron] go with him to take her [Cathie] into town," she said. "I think that's what I was told. He had Sharron get in the truck with him and take her into town. He put her in the back of the truck. Why, I don't know. He didn't want to take the girl in by himself, and he made Sharron go with him. Don't know where he took her. I was a silly ol' kid, and I didn't ask."

(It's doubtful this scenario actually happened. The local newspaper reported the sheriff's department being called at 3:48 p.m. A statement was also made that Cathie was transported by ambulance to Gross Mortuary. However, it didn't identify the starting point of the ambulance that took Cathie Ward to the mortuary. Frank Davis and his wife very well could have rushed her to a hospital emergency room. But again, it's a huge stretch of imagination that any young woman would load up two small children into a truck to help her husband drive a limp, bloody body into town in the back of his pickup.)

Grief and fear surrounding Cathie's untimely death were felt and expressed by her schoolmates, but it was taboo at home. Next-door neighbor Gail Rader, told me, "No one talked about Cathie."

Cathie's brother, Dick Ward, said, "She never came up in conversations at home. Mother didn't take us to visit her grave site. I've never been to her grave."

Later, he retracted his statement. "You know, I might have been to her grave, once," he told me, "when I was young, there in Murfreesboro. But I don't remember it for sure."

Dick's memory returned while mentioning his grandmother's funeral. "I remember when my grandmother died, my father's mother," he said. "I went back for the funeral [in 1992]. I might have seen Cathie's grave then. I don't have any remembrance of it. I had forgotten she was buried in Murfreesboro."

Years later, Cathie's father told me, "Except for the fact of losing a daughter, it had little or no effect on me. It didn't affect anything I would do. But you know, you think about her still. I was very busy with a medical practice at the time, and I did not have depression like other people would."

· 8 ·

The Sprees

*F*rank had good days and bad days but was in an upbeat mood while driving along the highway in September 1966 when he ran into the back of a woman's car. She was carted off to the hospital, and he was given a field sobriety test after saying, "I wasn't drinking at all! My head was on cloud nine, and I just wasn't noticing my business."

Well known in the enforcement community for repeatedly speeding and/or driving while intoxicated, Frank had finally exceeded their good graces (or whatever means had kept him out of trouble—mainly his mother's checkbook). The authorities yanked his driver's license. But he didn't care. That wasn't going to stop him from driving.

He also had no plans to quit phoning Sharron. Every morning, he would call her and ask, "Will you bring the boys out for a visit?"

Her response was always, "I'll see how things are going and let you know."

Frank was accustomed to getting whatever he wanted from his mother, her money, and his egomaniacal force. He always had the upper hand, but it wasn't playing out that way with his young, stubborn, fourth wife.

To counter Sharron's standoff, he packed up and moved into town to live with his mother. The only time he returned to the ranch was to feed the animals or, on a rare occasion, go out and wait if he thought there was a remote chance Sharron might bring the boys to visit.

Now that he was residing in town, Frank had a busy daily schedule. After waking and taking Meprobamate, a medication for the short-term relief of anxiety,[1] he'd ritualistically perform his morning regime—bite into a lemon covered with two tablespoons of salt and then slug a half-pint of whiskey. Later, he would go to the Blue Bell Cafe on Central Avenue, where

59

he ordered soup. He'd then take off to the bars for happy hour and stay until closing time. Back at his mother's home, he'd be unable to sleep, so he'd pace the floor and drink some more and, finally, go to his room and pass out.

Frank befriended Howard Hawthorn, a younger man half his age whose family owned a meatpacking business located by their home. Hawthorn Meat Company had a modern equipped plant that processed all types of meat products and custom butchering for businesses in other counties, but their mainstay was to supply the local hotels, hospitals, restaurants, and the popular fast-food restaurant Burger Chef, which was selling fifteen-cent hamburgers to most every teenager in town.[2]

Howard's younger sister, Margie, knew that Frank sold cattle to her father and that he would stop by to pick up Howard from time to time. She didn't know where they went or what they did, but she knew her brother didn't drink and thought he might've been Frank's designated driver.

One day, Frank stopped by to visit while Margie and her sister were in the business office. Her father turned to them and quietly said, "You girls stay away from that guy!"

Margie Hawthorn Golden told me, "Why my dad said that, we never questioned it. We'd head to the house if he came in, and we kind of steered clear of him."

Frank was soon spiraling out of control, neglecting the cattle at his ranch, and partying in town. But somehow he pulled it together and sought a helping hand from his friend Teddy Hill. The two men went out to Black-snake and cut a bunch of poles to build a corral by the big, deep-blue hole of clear water on the Bull Bayou Creek. Frank put out feed for the cattle and trapped almost twenty-five inside the corral. Later, Teddy went back out to the ranch with Frank to haul them away, but the cattle had trampled the fence down and took off.

"Have you been out to feed them?" Teddy asked.

"No," Frank replied.

Teddy knew that's why the livestock left—to search for food. He watched Frank throw a fit. "He started cussing and becoming so mad that he went and squatted down close to the spring, sat there for a few minutes, then jumped in," Teddy said as he shared this story with his wife, Margie.

Teddy and Margie Hill agreed that Frank would go berserk and do "off-the-wall things" that normal people just didn't do. To substantiate their claim, Margie shared a holiday story about Frank.

"He'd gone home after Christmas and threw a fit when he saw the Christmas tree still standing in the living room. His wife hadn't taken it down, so he grabbed the tree—trimmings and all—and threw it into the fireplace that was full of burning hot logs!"

Frank met a young man during the race meet earlier in the year and offered to cosign his loan for a truck. A few months later, the boy quit paying the monthly note and skipped town for Denver, Colorado. Frank flew there, repossessed the truck, and drove it back home. Now that he had two trucks, he decided to visit the Ford dealership while they were conducting their fall showing of new 1967 models. He walked around the showroom with a salesman and stopped by a blue Thunderbird.

"I'll take that one right there," Frank said.

"It's yours," the salesman replied.

"Tell you what I'll do," he said. "I've got two trucks I'll trade you one, and whatever's the difference, I'll pay you."

After dealing back and forth, the two men came to an agreement. But Frank didn't have a valid driver's license and couldn't insure the car, so he negotiated again. "Let's put this in my mother's name, okay?"

That same week, he decided the Thunderbird wasn't his style, so he gave it to his mother and returned to the Ford dealership. He walked around the car lot and looked at two different cars: a red Ford GT Coupe sports car and a Ford Fairlane convertible.

"I'll take them both," he told the salesman.

Frank paid the sales tax for the two new cars, but he never went to the courthouse and had them licensed. He kept the GT for himself and gave the convertible to Sharron. Frank told his mother, "I don't want Sharron driving her mother's old car. I want her to have a new car so she can come see me. She liked it!"

Soon, however, Sharron didn't like it and returned the convertible to Frank.

Everett Brown rented a small wooden building in Irene's backyard that served as his home. From his close perspective, he could see Frank swapping cars throughout the day. He saw him take off in the convertible late in the morning, switch to the Thunderbird for the afternoon, and wind up driving the red GT Coupe at night.

Brown witnessed other odd behaviors. "Frank busted in and out of the house a lot. Seemed like he was always in a hurry," said Brown. "He'd go out and leave the doors open, scatter their yard with empty glasses and bottles and stuff. He never put anything in the trash can or took any glasses back in the house."

What topped all these quirky behaviors happened one Saturday night around 9:00 when he saw Frank back up his GT Coupe against a tree with the rear jacked up on blocks and the motor running. It ran all night long into Sunday, and then around 10:00 Sunday night, Frank went out and turned it off. Curious, Brown had to know why. He knocked on Irene's back door and asked to speak to Frank.

"I saw your car up against that tree all night and was wondering what you were doing," Brown said.

"I burned twenty gallons of gas to check the gas mileage," Frank answered.

(The story of Frank's outrageous testing would be discredited two years later by twelve men. When they heard this story, they believed Frank did it because he was a spoiled adult man who disliked the new car so much that he tried to burn up the engine.)

⌒

The new cars had been Frank's temporary diversion. His main focus remained on his wife and boys. He thought about his oldest son, who, before he was even one year old, had ridden in the rodeo with him. Frank had him sitting in the saddle with him as he'd done with Cathy Browne's teenage friend, and off they'd gone in the Garland County fairgrounds arena. After the youngest son came in March 1966, Frank bought both of them matching black ponies and saddles along with a wagon and then gave each a dog, a horse, and a cow. He wanted his boys to grow up right, but Sharron put a kink in his plans, leaving him thirty-six days shy of their three-year wedding anniversary.

Now, Frank wanted her and the boys back, and he wouldn't stop calling her. He believed people had a plot against him. He knew his rodeo friends, stepfather Pat Hogan, and Sharron's mother, Pauline, were all trying to break up his marriage. He never imagined Sharron would leave him under her own volition.

· 9 ·

The Stalker

$\mathcal{A}$ little more than a month after her escape, Sharron was shopping in downtown Hot Springs, where the ethnic diversity of the retail/business district was like the United Nations. Central Avenue was lined with businesses either owned or managed by men and women with German, Greek, Russian, Irish, Italian, or English heritages, such as Schweer Cadillac, Searcy Pharmacy, Steigler's Bookstore, Lauray's Jewelers, Stonecipher's Photos, Schrader's Men Store, Mollie's [Kosher] Restaurant, and Gartenberg's. Shoppers frequented popular clothes or department stores Pfeifer's, Kempner's, Elta Ruel, Eleanor Harris, Hubert Mendel's, and J. C. Penney and bought shoes at Rosenthal's, DeMars, Sidney's, and Butler's.

Sharron was enjoying the day, going from each store to the next, when she noticed a vehicle driving slowly beside her as if on purpose. She turned to look at it and saw Frank glaring at her. Then she heard him yell, "I'm gonna kill you!"

She ran to her car and drove straight home to tell her parents. This wasn't the first time he'd stalked her.

"She got a restraining order," her older sister Cheryl later told her friend, Margaret Fulbright Gates. "But it didn't help any. He hadn't done anything. Everywhere she went, he'd drive along beside her in his car, and holler, 'I'm gonna kill you!'"

By mid-October 1966, Sharron had had enough and met with attorney M. C. Lewis Jr. She explained the history of her marriage to Frank Davis, and together, she and Lewis built a list of issues she wanted addressed in a divorce lawsuit. Lewis spelled them out in a "complaint in equity," describing two "causes of action."

The first complaint was against Frank, whom Lewis claimed "treated her with such indignities as to render her condition in life as his wife intolerable from his studied neglect, unmerited reproach, mental cruelty and physical abuse." Lewis interpreted Sharron's complaint, saying, "Without any just cause or provocation, he frequently embarrassed and humiliated her in the presence of other people. FRANK DAVIS has failed to furnish support and has threatened SHARRON DAVIS, and as a result of FRANK DAVIS' conduct, so habitually and systematically pursued, it finally became impossible for SHARRON DAVIS to live with FRANK DAVIS."

Lewis claimed the cause of action existed within five years before the institution of this action, which provided legal grounds for a divorce in the state of Arkansas. He also noted the couple's two children were living with their mother, whom, he stated, "is a proper person to have custody of said minor children."

Sharron felt Frank should be required to divulge the extent of his holdings. She acknowledged they owned a home under a purchase contract and that "he threatened to let [the home] go back if she will not do as he wants."

Attorney Lewis said, "[Frank] should be ordered to make the payments during the pendency of this cause and the property ordered partitioned and sold."

Sharron and her attorney were either unaware or ignoring the fact that it was not Frank's property to partition and sell. It wouldn't be until the contract was paid in full. From the property owner's account, Sharron and Frank had paid only $485 in sixteen months, which was $31.31 a month, far lower than their agreed-on $75 a month.

Sharron felt the real and personal property that his mother, Irene Davis, held in title was to defeat the interest of her and others (the children). She asked that Irene "be declared to hold the property in trust, and Frank and his mother divulge the full extent and amount of this property and give her the corresponding interest."

Sharron thought Frank should be ordered to pay a reasonable amount as support to her and the children. She also requested he be ordered to pay the attorney's fees and suit money.

Ending the first cause of action, Lewis insisted that "the bonds of matrimony between Sharron and Frank [should] be dissolved, canceled, set aside and forever held for naught through an 'absolute divorce.'"

He summarized the previous requests and asked that both Sharron and Frank "be restored to all the rights, privileges and immunities of a single and unmarried person."

Attorney Lewis addressed diversions of property and finances in the second cause of action, claiming that "Frank transferred the title to various properties, including livestock, horses, and real estate to his mother, Irene Davis, in order to defeat creditors and the interest of Sharron."

He asked that "Sharron be granted discovery as to the nature, value and extent of this property."

He noted Irene Davis held the title to this property in trust for Frank Davis, who "had the management, use, control, possession, and benefit thereof."

Lewis asked the court to "decree Irene Davis hold titles to both the real and personal property in trust for Frank and that he be declared the actual owner thereof; a dower and interest to the property and the property ordered partitioned and sold, be awarded to Sharron; and Irene Davis be restrained from selling, disposing, or encumbering any of the property during the lawsuit."

The complaint in equity was filed in the Chancery Court of Garland County, Arkansas, at 11:31 a.m., October 19, 1966, and became case #37,232.[1]

By 3:28 p.m., Joann Newkirk, the deputy clerk, sent a summons to the Garland County sheriff, commanding him to summon Frank and Irene Davis within twenty days. It stated, "[A]nd warn them that upon their failure to answer, the complaint will be taken for confessed. And you will make due return of this Summons within twenty days after the issuance thereof, to the June term, 1966 of said Court."[2]

Newkirk sent individual summonses to Frank and his mother. Beside Irene's typed name, Newkirk had handwritten her home address, a practice common at the time. And on Frank's, she also wrote two addresses: "163 Henderson or Royal Vista Inn."

(The Royale Vista Inn was a high-rise hotel and motor lodge with a busy restaurant and bar on Central Avenue near the entrance of the Trivista neighborhood and Oaklawn racetrack. The Royale Vista Inn was only a few blocks from Irene Davis's home.)

On November 28, 1966, a typed notice that included Frank's dual addresses was delivered to him. It stated the following:

> You are hereby notified to be present in the Chancery Court of Garland County, Arkansas at 10:00 A.M. on Tuesday, December 13, 1966, at which time the Plaintiff, Sharon [*sic*] Davis, will ask the Court:
>
> 1. To grant her temporary custody of the minor children.
> 2. To order you to pay a reasonable amount as support for herself and your minor children during the pendency of this case.
> 3. To order you to pay temporary attorney's fees and costs.
> 4. To restrain and enjoin you from disposing or encumbering any of the personal property while this case is pending.

5. To order you to divulge the full extent, location and nature of all of your property and property interests.

Frank Davis and his mother, Irene, hired attorney Robert "Bob" Ridgeway to fight Sharron's accusations and demands. He was the same man Frank supported in the circuit judge runoff election the evening Sharron left Frank.

Ridgeway filed a "Separate Answer by Frank Davis to Plaintiff's Complaint in Equity" along with a "Separate Answer of Irene Davis" in the Chancery Court of Garland County on December 15, 1966. He conveyed Irene's response by saying, "She denies each and every allegation . . . and prays that this Court exact strict proof from the said plaintiff, Sharon [*sic*] Davis, of some trust agreement prior to intruding into her privacy, and prior to allowing any individual to delve into the privacy of her private holdings and estate."[3]

He maintained that "Irene Davis believed Sharron Davis was on a fishing expedition to pry into her private and personal estate because she knew of the many loans she'd given Frank. Sharron knew about the cash monies she'd given her son for the down payment on the purchase of his home, as well as some monthly payments." Ridgeway said, "This defendant [Irene] has done nothing that any mother would not have done for her son."

Attorney Ridgeway stated that "she specifically denies that she holds any property or titles for the benefit of Frank Davis and states any type of restraining order on her would be unjust."

He said, "Irene Davis prays that said complaint of the plaintiff, including both causes of action, be dismissed as to her and that the plaintiff take nothing by her complaint."

Ridgeway addressed Sharron's complaints in Frank's "Separate Answers" and noted he denied all claims in the first cause of action, where Sharron described Frank's mistreatment of her.[4]

Then he said, "The defendant [Frank] states the separation was occasioned and caused by the unreasonableness of the plaintiff [Sharron] resulting from interference by outsiders." He added, "The defendant does not now nor has he ever desired a separation or divorce and is now ready and willing to provide a home with and for the plaintiff."

In Frank's denial of Sharron's belief that she was the proper person to have custody of the children, Ridgeway said "that he [Frank] is now and always has been ready and willing to support both of said children." Yet, Ridgeway later stated Frank denied all allegations pertaining to his being ordered to pay support for Sharron and the boys and her attorney's fees.

Frank claimed that he was purchasing the home Sharron mentioned and that he intended to continue paying for it but denied all the other allegations, such as his letting the house go back if "she didn't do what he wanted, and those charges against his mother."

Ridgeway acknowledged Frank's revelation that there was another parcel of property, but by agreement and with the full knowledge of Sharron, the property was sold, and she was given the entire proceeds from the sale. Frank said that the sale occurred after they'd separated and that the proceeds given to Sharron were more than any interest she was legally entitled to from any property division. He claimed she was not entitled to any further interest in his real property.

Ridgeway denied all allegations by Sharron that concerned Frank's real estate and personal property holdings through his mother. He said, "Any and all property titles held by Irene Davis was in her own separate right," which he "had no interest other than to aid his mother, Irene Davis, in the preservation thereof."

Ridgeway added, "This defendant is indebted to his mother for money borrowed from her. She holds mortgages on his personal property for money loaned to him; other creditors who have loaned him money also hold mortgages on his personal property and all such transactions are within the knowledge of the plaintiff or are a matter of public record."

Ridgeway ignored Frank's pride by declaring, "The defendant does not now nor has he ever had any considerable amount of money of his own but has depended on loans from his mother and other people to keep from being broke. Irene Davis should not be interfered with in the use, sale or enjoyment of her property."

Both Frank's and his mother's separate answers to Sharron's complaint in equity ended with a dramatic prayer of dismissal. It stated, "Wherefore, defendant, prays that the plaintiff's Second Cause of Action be dismissed along with the plaintiff's First Cause of Action and that she take nothing by her complaint."

Ridgeway provided a "Certificate of Service" to certify he had delivered Sharron's attorney, M. C. Lewis Jr., a copy of the "Separate Answer of Frank Davis" and "Separate Answer of Irene Davis." The two attorneys' offices were a block apart and the same distance to the county courthouse. Ridgeway stated he mailed the documents in a properly addressed envelope with five-cent postage to Lewis on December 15, 1966.

II

REDBIRD

· *10* ·

The Redbird

*L*ess than ten days before Christmas 1966, Sharron Davis was informed by her attorney that Frank had denied all her divorce allegations but still wanted to make a home for her and the boys. However, if they divorced, he would not take financial responsibility.

Considering Frank's unyielding attitude, it's doubtful and unknown if Sharron allowed him to spend the holiday with their two sons, now two and a half years and nine months old. Nevertheless, on Sunday, January 15, 1967, Frank genuinely believed Sharron and the boys were coming home to live with him. That weekend, his original plans were to meet some friends and go deer hunting in Prescott, Arkansas. But because he thought Sharron and the boys were returning, he canceled his trip. He waited the entire Sunday at the ranch and called her three or four times, but she never arrived.

Frank's hunting rifle was in his truck, but after Sharron's no-show, he transferred it to the Thunderbird. In anticipation of the reunion, Irene Davis had come to the ranch that day and on her drive home that night was unaware of the rifle behind her on the floorboard. Once Frank was back in town, he began driving the Thunderbird because his driver's license was invalid and the only legally licensed car his mother owned was that vehicle.

Sharron's Sunday slight festered, and by Thursday, January 19, Frank woke up full-throttle mad. That morning he kept his usual routine—a salt and lemon with a half-pint of whiskey, followed by a call to Sharron, which resulted in the same response: "Maybe." Next, he popped his anxiety medication Equanil (contraindicated with alcohol) and drove to lunch at the Blue Bell Cafe as he'd done almost every day in the past.

Occupying his usual table, he ordered soup and pulled a pint liquor bottle out of his coat pocket. Billy Tom "Stubby" Franks, the owner of the

Blue Bell, kept a bottle of Mountain Valley Water on every table and turned a blind eye on Frank when he slipped the booze into his water glass. Emptying his pint before the soup bowl, Frank left and walked a few doors down in Freeman Center to a liquor store for another bottle. He then returned to the Blue Bell, where he wound up spending a good portion of the afternoon. Between his drinks, he used the restaurant's phone to call Sharron at work. During his last call, he asked, "When will you be home?"

"I don't know," she told him. "Call me back around 5:30."

He hung up and dialed another number. "I need you to help me feed the cattle," he told his teenage friend Terral Adcock. "Meet me at Mother's in an hour."

Around 3:30 p.m., "Stubby" waved good-bye to his frequent lunch customer.

∾

Close to 4:00, Elza Young, a thirty-two-year-old insurance salesman, walked into the Frontier Club and Grill on Central Avenue, a half mile from the Blue Bell Cafe, and noticed all eyes were on him. His cousin, Ev Young, the bar owner, shouted, "Frank Davis just left thirty minutes ago. He came in all wild-eyed and was looking for you with a 30-30 rifle. He was going to kill you!"

Sitting down at the bar, Elza ordered a drink from Ev as he'd done every day on his way home after work. Elza and his business partner, Jack Everright, sold Washington Standard/Reliable Life Insurance, the most popular policies available in 1967. They'd built an organization that included three agents and sales so impressive that the company decided to award them a new territory in Arkansas and Louisiana.

As Elza remembers it, "Frank Davis was also an agent of my company and felt like he would be the one they would choose for the new territory. But that's not the fact. They chose us, and he was very upset about it. I didn't even know we were vying for it. It was an advancement. I had no idea there were other people in line for it until I heard he'd come by looking for me with a rifle, and I immediately put two and two together."

"I had previously read about this young girl that died as a result of being drug by a horse at one of Frank Davis' projects," Young said. "He had a lot of things that went on, so, I was aware of some other problems he had, plus I'd met him a time or two at meetings with the insurance company. I knew his reputation was a go-getter cowboy-type person. Most of the time I saw him, he had on blue jeans, more or less western gear. He was friendly to everybody, but he was narcissistic. He wanted to be in charge. That's what

I got from being around him. He wanted to be the leader and the person everybody looked up to."

With his missed opportunity at the Frontier Club, Frank must've snapped out of the rage and continued with his plans to feed the cattle. Terral Adcock was late, but they were able to make it to Blacksnake Ranch, where the young man drove the truck and Frank tossed the hay out for the animals. After rushing through the chore, they hurried back to Irene Davis's house in time for Frank to call Sharron sometime after 5:30 p.m.

"I'm still busy," she said. "Call me back at the house at 8:00."

"I didn't like that shit!" Frank later told a psychiatrist.

A double strikeout in one week with Sharron didn't sit well with Frank. He went outside his mother's home and started moving cars around. It was her sixtieth birthday, and he wanted to buy her a present at K-Mart. Before leaving, he received a phone call from Terral Adcock, who was following Sharron as a favor to him. Adcock told Frank she was at her job at the Vanity Beauty Shop across the street from Arthur Cook's Ice Cream and Dairy Company.

After the call, Frank drove off in the Thunderbird and stopped at Big J Liquor Store. He walked inside for a bottle and waited in line behind Prince "Bubba" Cook Jr., whose father had owned the local Ford dealership, Prince Cook Motors, and sister, Princella, who had stabled her horse at Blacksnake Ranch. Frank and Bubba spoke, purchased their liquor, and left with two very different destinations.

Unsure of Frank's whereabouts, Adcock called Irene Davis's home a second time and was informed by her that he'd just missed him. Adcock abandoned his lookout and drove around looking for Frank. When he couldn't find him, he returned to Cook's Ice Cream, where he saw Frank sitting in his Thunderbird.[1] Adcock joined him while they watched the beauty shop and Frank drank from his pint liquor bottle.

Before long, they saw Sharron's mother, Pauline Knight, drive up in front of the beauty shop across the street. They watched Frank's mother-in-law sitting in the car as she waited for Sharron to get off work. If they'd turned around to look the other way, they would've missed Sharron dashing to the car and jumping behind the steering wheel as her mother scooted over to the front passenger seat. They watched them leave. "You go to mom's house and wait for me. I'm going to follow that car," Frank instructed Adcock.

Frank wound up at the Redbird Service Station and Laundromat on Central Avenue, less than half a mile from Irene Davis's home. The Redbird's front and back doors were full-pane glass, which allowed anyone to see straight through the building, from the gas pumps in front to the laundromat parking in back.

He had gone to get some gas and happened to look through the building, where he spied his mother-in-law's car parked by the laundromat's back doors. He drove around the building and pulled up beside her car. He was close enough to see Allan Ray, his two-and-a-half-year-old son, grinning at him from the backseat. Pauline, who was sitting in the front passenger seat holding baby Fredrick Allan, got out of the car, turned to Frank, and screamed, "You no good SOB! Leave Sharron and the boys alone!"

"I want to see my boys," Frank shouted back.

"I'm going to have you placed under a peace bond so you can't bother them and Sharron," Pauline yelled.

She got back into the car and picked up the baby. Frank slowly started to drive away but stopped when he saw Sharron walking out of the laundromat's back door. He backed up and shouted, "I want to see my boys!"

Sharron ran to the car and jumped into the driver's seat. Frank backed up, and they began arguing. She cranked her window down halfway when he reached behind him, grabbed his hunting rifle that had been on the back floorboard since Sunday, stuck it out his window, and shot Sharron.

Pauline placed the baby in her seat, jumped out of the car screaming, and ran toward the laundromat full of people. Frank aimed his rifle at her and downed Pauline just as she entered the back door.

Hearing the gunfire, one man crawled behind the dryers to get out of sight.[2] Earl Peake, the Redbird owner, saw the pandemonium inside his busy laundromat and rushed out to see the shooter driving away. He recognized the man immediately—the son of his neighbor Irene Davis, who lived on Henderson Street only a few doors away.

Peake ran to the phone and made two calls: to the police and his son Glen. Living only two and a half miles away on Buena Vista Road, Glen rushed to his family's business.

"Frank Davis came in here looking for her," Glen Peake told me fifty years later while sitting inside the still standing but vacant Redbird Service Station and Laundromat. "He drove in on the north side of the building and went around, heading right back south. I mean, he's in a car, and she's in a car. The baby was beside her. The little boy was in the backseat, and her mother was in the passenger seat. Basically, they're close, and she's sitting sideways. Frank Davis backed up, and both drivers are side by side. He sticks out a 30-30 and shoots Sharron. Why the bullet didn't go through her and kill that little boy, I have no earthly idea, but it didn't. I don't know exactly where he shot her, but a 30-30, and she was a little lady. Her mother jumped out, and just before she got to the building door, he shot her, and it glanced off the back of her head. It didn't kill her, but it killed Sharron. I don't remember who got the kids after the ambulances came and got Sharron and her mother. It was just a bad, bad, bad thing."

⌒⌒

Lois Aicholz was on her way to wash clothes and stopped to eat some fried chicken. Otherwise, she would have been standing right there in front of the washers. "Davis was tearing out of there in his pickup and his wife was dead and mother-in-law severely wounded. I'll never forget the sight of all the blood and two small children being comforted [by a laundromat customer] by the dryers," she said online in a social media public discussion about the murder.[3]

The Crime Scene Photographer
and the Cousin

*B*ill Dever heard the police dispatching cars to the shooting at the Redbird Laundromat on Thursday, January 19, 1967. The twenty-year-old was a mile and a half away at the Williamson Apartments, his grandparents' two-story red brick building at the intersection of Greenwood and Central avenues.

Three years earlier, Bill trudged up and down the neighborhood streets, picking up empty cigarette packs people had tossed from their cars. A tobacco company was offering different levels of prizes for redeemed packs, so Bill saved enough for a camera. He mailed his packs, and after his "prize" arrived, he heard some sirens blaring all the way out Central Avenue and realized he had a gift and an opportunity. He was in a prime location for the endless automobile accidents that happened up and down Central Avenue (the main north-to-south thoroughfare in Hot Springs) and *now* possessed a camera to record them. During his senior year of high school, his first submitted accident photo made the front page of the *Sentinel-Record* and impressed one of his teachers.

Bill wanted to expand his hobby after graduating from high school and began saving money for a police radio, an old tube-type radio. He started building up his radios and used his Volkswagen as a "news vehicle" loaded with five radios and four antennas. By 1967, Bill was working days as a U.S. Postal Service worker and nights and weekends as a freelance news photographer. He always kept his radios tuned to the police band and his camera in the car, ready to go.

When he heard the police transmit the alarming news of the Redbird shooting, he jumped into his mobile news car and headed south on Central. Arriving around the same time as the emergency workers, he quickly took a photo of Gross Mortuary's white Pontiac ambulance. Then he walked around to the back of the building, where several men surrounded a 1964 two-door Chevrolet Impala. Bill went up to the car and saw a young woman (Sharron) lying in the front seat, her head and upper body slumped toward the passenger side door. A long, plaid winter coat with a fringed collar covered her white beauty shop uniform. He saw her right arm poking out from underneath her body and the left arm extending over the left hip, nearly touching her knee.

When he looked down at her left hand, he saw her wedding band on the ring finger. Her lower legs were still in the sitting position under the steering wheel, and the white shoes on her feet were propped on the floorboard next to the gas pedal and brake. Shards of glass were scattered on the floorboard where the rifle bullet exploded through the driver's side window.

Bill tried to stay out of the way of the crime scene but knew it would be hard to do if he wanted to get some good pictures. He shot continuously while the police investigation was being conducted and got what he could, knowing they'd need evidence.

Walking inside the laundromat, Bill saw an older woman (Sharron's mother, Pauline Knight) on the concrete floor with her head lying in a large pool of blood that contained a piece of scalp. She'd made it through one of the two glass back doors before being struck down by a bullet. Her head was facing toward the car, which was visible outside where it had been parked close to the back of the building. She was wearing a dark winter coat and appeared to be sleeping on her right side. Her right arm was under her body, and her left arm was bent so that her hand was almost touching her face. Her left leg was bent at the knee and lying above the extended right lower leg. Pointed dark shoes were on both feet.

As Bill began taking photos of her, he saw a man in a white shirt and dark suit walk in and look down at her. Then the man turned to look at a second man in street clothes and a uniformed officer as they walked through the left back door, none of them paying any attention to the woman on the floor.

He watched the men stepping around her and later noticed a flat army-type stretcher—canvas stretched across a steel-tube frame—placed next to her. The entire time he shot photos of her, he didn't see anyone attending to her or trying to stop the flow of blood from her head wound.

Bill went back outside just as two Gross ambulance attendants were lifting the young woman out of the car. A group of men were standing behind the driver's-side door. They included Lieutenant Detective Grover Douglas, Municipal Judge Earl Mazander, Detective Bobby Digby, and three unidentified men. Earl Peake, the Redbird owner, was standing outside the two back doors, watching her being transferred from the car to the stretcher. Once she was placed flat on the wheeled stretcher, the men could see her white uniform stained with a large patch of blood over her right breast and reaching almost to her waist. The ambulance soon sped away from the Redbird, siren blaring, toward the downtown hospital.

Another ambulance arrived for the older woman. Watching them leave, Bill then looked back at the laundromat and began taking photos of the right back door where the bullet came through and hit the woman. He walked around the building and saw another bullet hole in the front of the building and realized it was the bullet that had passed through her head and then flew through the laundromat, missing the people inside before exiting through the front window.

He returned to the rear of the building and took an exterior shot of the dramatic hole left by the bullet that whizzed through the building. Customers could now be seen clustered in groups near two double banks of washers. Some were talking, some were staring, but they all looked frightened.

Remembering that evening, Bill Dever said, "Basically, all I did was click the camera shutter. I shot the scene and the bullet holes and things like that. They show, step-by-step, what happened after the shots were fired, and it shows the dangerousness and the seriousness of the situation in regards to Frank Davis's actions. In other words, without the pictures, there's nothing there. My plan was to use the photos for legal purposes and photographic evidence for my collection. I knew the court and the city would want the photos but not the newspaper—they didn't want bodies or blood."

THE COUSIN

When the shooting was taking place, Sharron Knight Davis's teenage cousin, Debby Fager, was at Oaklawn School, a few doors away from her home. Debby and her friend Karen were attending a concert by the New Beats in Oaklawn School's auditorium. Afterward, they strolled to Debby's house as she excitedly clutched an autographed photo of the group who'd become popular after their 1964 hit "Bread and Butter."

As soon as her mother met them at the front door, Debby's postconcert euphoria changed. "Mom? What's the matter?" Debby asked, when she saw tears in her mother's eyes.

"I'll tell you later," Dollie replied.

She tried to smile at her daughter. "Here, you girls go sit in the living room while you wait for Karen's father to come get her. The little ones are asleep, so be quiet, okay?"

"Well, uh, okay," said Debby, concerned about her mother's sad demeanor.

When Karen's father arrived, Dollie was courteous but quiet, never mentioning the violent scene at the Redbird that involved her older sister, Pauline Knight, and her niece, Sharron Knight Davis.

As soon as Karen and her father were gone, Dollie took Debby to the kitchen. She explained the shootings to her daughter and how her father had rushed to the hospital to be with her uncle, Fred Knight.

"Sharron lived long enough to tell who did it," she said, and Debby started to cry.

· *12* ·

Evil Personified

*H*ot Springs residents woke up to frightening news on Friday, January 20, 1967. The *Sentinel-Record*'s front-page headline shouted, "Woman Fatally Shot, Mother Wounded at Laundromat Here."[1] The newspaper stated, "A young Hot Springs woman was fatally shot at a Central Avenue Laundromat here Thursday night, and her mother was critically wounded as she apparently ran for help. The younger woman's two small children witnessed the shooting."

The article said, "The husband of the dead woman was charged with first-degree murder," and said, "Sharon [*sic*] Davis, 22, was dead and her mother, Mrs. Pauline Knight, 49 [*sic*], was in critical condition at Baptist Hospital in Little Rock late Thursday night."

The paper went into detail, telling how Sharron Davis "was shot in her car at the rear of a laundromat at the Oaklawn Redbird Service Station, 3034 Central Ave.," and "died less than an hour later in a hospital here." It said her mother had been shot inside the rear door, and a witness heard her screaming, "Call the law, call the law," before she "was struck down."

It reported the incident occurred around 7:05 p.m. and noted, "The chief said both women were shot with a 30-30 rifle. The bullet entered Mrs. Davis' left shoulder and collapsed her lungs. Mrs. Knight received a head wound." The article described how the driver's-side window had been shattered and a bullet hole was in the glass rear door and front window of the laundromat.

No one started putting two and two together until they reached the fourth paragraph, which announced, "Police Chief John Ermey said Frank Davis, 39, had been charged with murder in the death of his wife. Davis operates a ranch on Blacksnake Road . . . arresting officers and investigators had found a 30-30 rifle in the backyard of the house."

81

Now it was obvious to them that Frank Davis was involved in yet another death, but this time, they knew he couldn't talk his way out of murder. There were too many witnesses.

People throughout Hot Springs began discussing the frightening shooting. "I didn't think he would go that far," said Harold Tankersley, Frank's bar buddy. "He had promised her that he was gonna kill her. The talk was all around town. They said, 'Frank's gonna kill his wife because she was taking the kids.' And that was all there was to it. He made up his mind what he was gonna do and went there and did it. Yeah, he didn't beat around the bush about it. He just went and killed her!"

Elza Young, the successful insurance man, was surprised to see Frank had murdered his wife at the Redbird only hours after trying to kill him at the Frontier Club.

"I suppose I would have been the one before her," he said. "He must've had a list. I knew if I had been there, I would've probably been shot at, at least. So, I thought I got lucky."

Prince "Bubba" Cook Jr. was sitting at the kitchen table when he read what Frank had done the night before. He looked at his mother, Mary Ella, and said, "I saw Frank last night before this happened, and for all I know, he could've shot me right then and there. Glad he wasn't mad at me!"

Phyllis Davis Spahn (not related to Frank) was devastated when she saw the story of Sharron's death. Her parents owned Davis Shoe Store on Albert Pike close to where Sharron Knight Davis was employed. The two young women met at the beauty shop and became friends. Sharron would often come over to hide out at Davis's store. The first time Sharron approached Phyllis and asked to hide, she said, "My husband won't think to look for me here."

Phyllis looked at the newspaper account of Sharron's murder and thought of the previous day, the last time she had seen her.

"Sharron rushed in, literally scared to death, wanting a place to hide until her ride arrived. I feel like I, my mother, and my sister should have done more," said Phyllis. Decades later, she could still hear Sharron begging, "Can I hide here? My husband's trying to kill me!"

Hot Springs residents were in shock. People who actually knew Frank Davis, such as James Tucker, Bettye Jo's father, or those like Gaby Forsberg, who knew him only by reputation, may have felt this gruesome murder was proof positive of Davis's killer gene and because of that the authorities should reconsider their previous decision on Cathie Ward's death ruling. They couldn't have known evidence to substantiate their beliefs was hidden away in a lockbox, courtesy of the now-departed Sharron.

The Picture in the Casket

$\mathcal{D}$ollie Fager was distraught over her niece's death and her sister Pauline's critical gunshot wound. Dollie's husband, Charles "Charlie" Fager, a respected trust officer at Arkansas Bank and Trust and deacon of Second Baptist Church, had been a pillar of support not only for her but also for the Knight family. The day after the shooting, he drove Dollie and their fourteen-year-old daughter Debby to the Knight's home, where they gathered two of Pauline's four daughters, although with Sharron's murder, there were now three. Cheryl, the third daughter, lived in Little Rock.

Charlie then headed east out of town toward Little Rock to check on Pauline. The carload arrived at Baptist Hospital's intensive care unit waiting room, where Pauline's husband, Fred Knight, had kept a constant vigil. Pauline was still unconscious from surgery. A plate had been placed in her head, and the surgeons had given her a fifty-fifty chance to live.

Like all intensive care units, visiting times were strictly upheld, allowing only one or two family members per visit at scheduled times throughout the day. That left endless hours spent sitting and talking in the waiting room. Debby Fager heard her cousin Cheryl say she was ready to go after Frank Davis for what he'd done to her mother and sister. Her Uncle Fred claimed he was ready to get him, too.

Debby, who had been one of Frank's biggest admirers, was also upset and ready "to bite his head off for what he'd done." She never thought Frank would have been that kind of person. With what little time she'd been around him, the way he was with kids, she always thought he was a nice guy.

Debby sat with her family, remembering when she was at the ranch with her cousin Sharron and how hateful Frank had been to her. She thought about how bossy he was to Sharron, telling her to do something, and if she wouldn't, he'd say he was going to do something to her.

Fourteen-year-old Debby remembered his threats to kill Sharron and thought, "And of course, he ended up doing it."

The family continued their watch over fifty-year-old Pauline, who hadn't awakened from surgery. When she finally came to, she asked, "How's Sharron?"

Pauline's question was skirted, and the family held a discussion in the waiting room. With her condition so precarious, they didn't want to upset her with the news of Sharron's death. *It could kill her*, they thought. Making a pact, they chose Charlie to deliver a little white lie at the next visitation hour. He walked in, and when she once again asked about Sharron, he said, "She's okay, Pauline. Now, we've just got to get you better."

Sharron's obituary appeared in the *Sentinel-Record* on Monday, January 23, 1967, four days after her death. The headline read, "Funeral Rites Set for Local Woman Killed in Shooting."[1] It noted her service would be held at 2 p.m. on Tuesday, January 24, at the Tigert Memorial Methodist Church (three blocks from her parents' home) with Reverend William T. Dunker officiating. Frank Davis was mentioned, saying he was "being held on a charge of first-degree murder by the Hot Springs police in connection with the shooting."

Burial was planned at Greenwood Cemetery, and the paper stated that "the family will be at 201 Oaklawn." The Knight family chose to receive mourners at Dollie and Charlie's home. Their house was on the corner of Oaklawn and Bell, a block south of Irene Davis, who lived on the corner of Bell and Henderson, just a few doors west of Earl Peake, the owner of the Redbird Laundromat. Eerily, an imaginary triangle could be drawn, connecting the three families involved in the tragic Redbird shooting—the victim, the murderer, and the crime scene property owner.

Charlie continued driving his family and the Knight girls from Hot Springs to Baptist Hospital in Little Rock, an hour drive each way. By Monday afternoon, Pauline was seventy-two hours postop, and her condition was changed from critical to serious. This prompted the family to finally tell her the truth. They felt she was over the hump and could handle the devastating news of Sharron's death. Once she heard it, Pauline immediately said, "I want a picture of Sharron in the casket."

Charlie was once again given the task. The next morning, he and his eldest daughter, Debby, went to Caruth Funeral Home, where Sharron's body was ready for visitation. Debby stepped up to the casket and leaned over to look at her favorite cousin. She scanned her from head to toe but kept returning to Sharron's hands. She couldn't stop staring at them. She thought they looked awful, all shriveled and discolored from makeup that didn't hide black-and-blue bruises. While Debby fixated on the hands, she became light-headed and began to faint. Her father saw her grab the casket railing, and as her legs began to buckle, he rushed to catch her before she collapsed.

"Are you okay, Kusher?" he asked, calling her by the nickname she was given as a child when she pronounced "sugar" as "kusher."

"Yes sir," said Debby. "Her hands—," she added as she came out of the spell.

"Uh huh, what about them?" he asked.

"Daddy, her hands can't be shown," Debby said.

He looked at Sharron's hands and realized what his daughter was trying to explain. Charlie found one of the funeral directors and asked him to put gloves on his niece's hands. After they were in place, he took the picture of Sharron in the casket and later gave it to Pauline.

Even as an adult, Debby Fager can't forget Sharron's hands. She remembers the funeral director saying, "She gripped the steering wheel so tight with her hands when she was shot that her fingers had to be pried from the steering wheel."

(However, Bill Dever's crime scene photographs prove that to be untrue, or at least not when he snapped the photo of Sharron after the shooting. Her right arm was poised under her body, and the left arm and hand were hanging over the left hip. Also, Debby didn't remember seeing a wedding band on her cousin's hand in the casket, although it was prominent in one of Bill Dever's crime scene photos.)

Margaret Fullbright Gates was married and living in Little Rock when she received the disturbing phone call about Sharron's murder. She rushed over to Baptist Hospital and consoled Sharron's older sister, Cheryl. Margaret recalled meeting her as a teenager at a Hot Springs skating rink in the mid-1950s.

"Cheryl was there, and her younger sister, Sharron, was with her. I thought she looked like a little angel with all her blond hair, and she had on a white fluffy-looking blouse," Margaret said. "Just a beautiful young girl."

Cheryl and Margaret stayed friends after Margaret graduated in 1959 and Cheryl in 1960. They tried to get together when they could, and Cheryl invited Margaret to go horseback riding at Blacksnake Ranch. When they arrived, Margaret was pleased Sharron had joined them. She explained how she'd met Frank at his mother's beauty shop, where she worked, and how Irene kept after her to go out with him.

"She didn't want to particularly, but she did," Margaret said.

Recalling that day at the ranch, Margaret said, "I saw that he was a lot older than Sharron, and he was abusive toward the horses. I did not see him abuse her at that time, but he just treated the horses like I didn't think you were supposed to treat horses, like hit 'em, and whack 'em, and stuff that wasn't necessary to get them to do right. But he said that was the only way he could keep them in line."

After Sharron's murder, Margaret remembered sitting with Cheryl in the hospital waiting room and listening to her talk about Sharron and Frank. She explained how he'd stalked and threatened Sharron and said, "He finally did what he said he would do!"

• *14* •

The Post-Murder Meltdown

$\mathcal{I}$rene Davis was preparing her sixtieth birthday dinner party on Thursday, January 19, 1967. Pat Hogan, her third husband, who owned the Little Rock Stockyards, was with her, while her son, Frank, was having an emotional breakdown in one of the bedrooms. She heard a knock at the front door.

Police Lieutenant James Holt, Patrolman Wayne Seal, and Patrolman John Gibson were lined up three deep on the tiny front porch and steps.[1] They informed Irene of the shooting at the Redbird Laundromat and their beliefs that Frank was the shooter. Then they asked to search her home and property. They were soon accompanied by Lieutenant Detective Grover Douglas and Detective Sergeant Bobby Digby. Meanwhile, prosecuting attorney Walter Wright was questioning witnesses at the crime scene with his chief deputy, William R. Mitchell, the law partner of M. C. Lewis Jr., who had represented Sharron in her recent divorce suit against Frank (and his mother).

Detectives Douglas and Digby soon found a 30-30 rifle with the barrel stuffed in a Levi's jacket out in the dog yard behind Irene's home. They brought it with them as they walked back into the house to arrest Frank. Finding him passed out across a bed, they called an ambulance to take him to the hospital.[2] Emergency room doctors determined he'd taken "some sleeping tablets." They revived him, then released him so he could be taken to the city jail.

Police Chief John Ermey decided Frank was groggy and couldn't be thoroughly questioned, so he let him sleep it off.[3] The next morning when Frank woke up in jail, he started screaming, "What in the hell. The mattress is on fire! My clothes are on backwards!"

Frank jumped up, saw the jailer on duty, and asked, "How'd I get here?" The man didn't reply.

Frank began yanking on his clothes and then walked up to the jail cell door and screamed, "Why am I here? I want out of this son of a bitch!"

"Don't you know?" the jailer asked.

"Sure don't!" said Frank.

"You killed your wife and your mother-in-law!" he said.

Frank glared at him. "No!"

"Yes, you did!"

"I don't believe it!"

"Well you did. Then you took a bunch of sleeping pills, and they took you out on a stretcher to the hospital," the jailer told him.

Frank still didn't believe he'd murdered anyone or taken sleeping pills. He later told a psychiatrist, "Hell, I hadn't taken any sleeping pills. They said I was out about four hours."

Frank watched people coming and going. When his attorney appeared, he knew something serious might be up because the lawyer usually didn't come when he was thrown in jail. He'd just call the jailer and get him released.

Frank wasn't allowed to read the newspaper, but on Monday, three days later, that status changed.

"They let me see a paper and I read what I'd done. I began to believe it then, but it didn't seem it could be so," he later claimed.

⌒

Handcuffed to Police Lieutenant James Holt, Frank was taken from the jail to the Municipal Court for a preliminary hearing on Tuesday, January 24, 1967—the same day Sharron was buried.[4] Judge Earl Mazander, who'd been at the murder scene as they were placing Sharron on the ambulance stretcher, presided over the preliminary hearing.

Frank was being represented by Jack Holt Sr., who during his mid-thirties served three terms as Arkansas attorney general and now at sixty-five was a powerful and unyielding Little Rock lawyer.[5] His cocounsel was a Hot Springs attorney, Robert "Bob" Ridgeway, the same man Frank supported in the recent political runoffs and the attorney he'd hired to combat Sharron's divorce lawsuit.

Still handcuffed to Lieutenant James Holt, Frank sat in the courtroom and watched Ridgeway stand before the judge to enter an "innocent by reason of insanity" plea.[6]

The State called Officer John Gibson and Detective Sergeant Bobby Digby, two of the investigative team who found the 30-30 rifle at Irene Davis's home, to testify. Digby explained the whereabouts of the murder weapon, saying, "It was identified at the police station as looking like one

Davis owned, and has been sent to the State Police headquarters in Little Rock for examination."

Lloyd Love, an employee of the Redbird Service Station, testified next. He said he knew Frank Davis as a customer and saw him riding around outside the station before the shooting. "I saw Mrs. Davis in the laundromat, saw her walk out back and get into her car. I saw him drive up beside her car but in the opposite direction and heard two shots." Love said he didn't hear them talk because there were two glass walls between him and them.

Thomas Mehalic followed and said, "I was washing clothes in the laundromat and heard Mrs. Davis tell her husband, 'I do not want to have anything more to do with you.'"

Mehalic told the judge, "I didn't know any of them. After I had gotten into my car to leave, I heard one shot and dropped into the seat of my car and heard a woman say, 'Call the law.' I saw Mrs. Davis's mother shot from a car and saw her fall. Then I heard him say, 'How do you like that, Sharron!' I went over to the car and took the two small children out. The gun I saw looked like a rifle."

Under cross-examination, Mehalic said, "Davis didn't leave his car. He and his wife were arguing before the shooting, but I couldn't make out their conversation."

Terrall Adcock was called to the stand.

"I've known Frank Davis around three months and have worked for him, without pay, to watch Mrs. Davis, a beauty operator at an Albert Pike shop," he said. "I worked for him out at Blacksnake Ranch, and I've been watching her four or five weeks."

Adcock went on to describe the guns Davis owned and said, "I identified the 30-30 Winchester rifle the police had as looking like the one Frank owned."

He said he and Frank were together near the beauty shop before the shooting. "Frank had been drinking and told me to go to his house on Henderson Street because he had something to do."

Adcock was in Irene Davis's home when Frank came back after doing "the something he said he had to do." Adcock said he watched Frank go into a bedroom with his mother and then saw her come out later with a cocked pistol, which she said Frank had dropped when he collapsed onto the bed.

During cross-examination, Adcock said it was fifteen or twenty minutes after Frank came home that police arrived. He then added, "Mrs. Davis said Frank had the pistol to his own head when he collapsed and dropped it."

Jack Holt called Officer Gibson to the stand.

"Officers obtained the cocked pistol from the mother and had tried unsuccessfully to arouse Davis before calling the ambulance and sending him to the hospital. I did not personally examine the pistol and don't know if it was loaded," Officer Gibson said.

The defense, aside from recalling one police officer, presented no testimony at the preliminary hearing. Jack Holt made a motion to reduce the charge to second-degree murder on the grounds the State's evidence, presented by Deputy Prosecutor Phil Crume, failed to establish necessary premeditation and deliberation.

Judge Mazander said, "Overruled," and explained the evidence was sufficient. He then charged Frank Davis with first-degree murder in the fatal shooting of his estranged wife, Sharron, and bound Frank over to the Garland County grand jury. Since first-degree murder is nonbondable, he was whisked off to the Garland County Jail, still handcuffed to Lieutenant James Holt.

• 15 •

The State Hospital

$\mathcal{A}$week later, on Monday, January 30, 1967, Frank was sent for psychiatric evaluations at the Arkansas State Hospital in Little Rock. The facility had originally been known as the Arkansas Lunatic Asylum.[1] Then it became the Arkansas State Hospital for Nervous Diseases, and by 1967, people simply called it "the state hospital." He was under the care of Dr. Shelton F. Fowler, psychiatric examiner, who would build a nineteen-page patient file containing a psychiatric history and mental status reports, progress notes, a psychologist's report, and the diagnostic staff conference report.

Dr. Fowler watched Frank Davis "quietly" enter his office on February 3, 1967, and felt he "acted and appeared extremely suspicious." Frank asked if the door could be closed before they talked, and he then asked Dr. Fowler if he could trust him.

Dr. Fowler explained his function as a psychiatric examiner and how he would present him to the Act 3 staff, where they would, as a group, decide his diagnosis. After the doctor further described the routine for a psychiatric examination, Frank accepted his explanation.

A letter from prosecuting attorney Walter G. Wright, dated February 4, 1967, was inside a file. It stated, "Frank Allen [sic] Davis is charged with First Degree Murder of his wife, Mrs. Sharon [sic] Davis, on the 19th day of January 1967, at a Laundromat in Hot Springs. Mrs. Davis was shot with a 30-30 rifle about 7:00 p.m. at close range in the presence of her mother, Mrs. Pauline Knight, who was also shot in the head as she attempted to run inside the laundromat for protection."

Dr. Fowler asked Frank about the shooting and charges. Claiming no memory of the events, Frank said, "The Hot Springs paper said I shot my wife about three weeks ago at a laundromat." He continued with an explanation of his incarceration and waking up with his clothes on backwards at the jail.

"Were you drunk?" Dr. Fowler asked.

"I'd been drinking that day [January 19, when he murdered Sharron], but I wasn't drunk," Frank responded. Changing the subject, he added, "They won't let me have my boys. All I ever wanted was to have lots of boys and teach them to be cowboys. I wanted only boys, cows, and horses. They took them away from me. Everybody works against me. I had some fine boys, and they took them away, and I can't find them. I don't know why I can't have my boys. That's all I ever wanted."

Frank then gave a history of his four marriages, saying he had no children with his first two wives (Naomi and Shirley). "Married the third time and had a son and daughter," he said. "But she [Carrie] took them about four years ago. Haven't heard from them since. About a year ago, I tried to take them presents, but couldn't find them." He paused. "I think someone spirited them away from me. Then I married the fourth time [Sharron], and we have two sons. She left me about six months ago and has been living with her parents in Hot Springs. I had visiting rights with them when she'd bring them over. But I'd call, and she would say, 'maybe,' then wouldn't show up."

Explaining his recent visitation problems with his sons, Frank added, "I don't like a lot of people, but mostly I hate my mother-in-law [Pauline Knight]. She always screams at me on the telephone when I call Sharron. She says, 'You sorry yellow-bellied SOB!' That's how they talk over there at their house, and I don't like my boys being raised around all that vulgarity. She's the one who was trying to keep me away from my boys. The rest of them did, too."

Frank felt people involved with his wife, including her family, had joined together in an effort to keep his boys away from him. He shared other personal experiences that bordered on paranoia.

"I've seen people watching me and peeping around. I've been followed for five or six years. Sometimes, these people would follow me in town and flash lights in my eyes. Twice, they put knockout drops in my drinks. They've stolen my money, cattle, and horses. Me and the sheriff haven't been able to identify them, but the people are definitely against me. I know it."

"Who are they?" the doctor asked.

"Everyone," he said. "I just don't see why I can't have my boys!"

Dr. Fowler kept quiet as Frank gave a history of his education, service in the armed forces, medical visits and results, and not being allowed to see his sons after Sharron's departure.

At the end of the session, he said, "I've always been high-strung. I get angry real easy, and I've gotten mad at a lot of people because they harass me—my wives [he named them], my mother, her husband Pat [Hogan], my grandfather, some of my employees, and many others." Frank remembered a few fistfights and explained that although he felt like tearing people up, he'd rarely been assaultive. He claimed most of his fights were what he called "cuss fights."

After the session ended, Dr. Fowler wrote his impression of Frank on a note: "Paranoid—probably schizophrenic."

Five signed statements were sent to the Arkansas State Hospital from February 3 to February 7, 1967, describing Frank's previous behavior. They began with Frank's second wife, Shirley, who described him destroying objects.

"He was insanely jealous and sometimes acted crazy." Shirley also said she'd tried several times to get Frank to see a psychiatrist, but he always refused.

"His general behavior is what caused me to leave him," she stated. "I've seen him several times in the past year and thought he'd changed. He had a wild look in his eye and couldn't be still."

The next correspondence was from P. C. (Pat) Hogan, Frank's second stepfather. Hogan described Frank's "unreasonable spells" when he brought cattle to sell at his stockyard. He said, "He was never satisfied with the prices he got. He would go into cursing and raging attacks against his best friends, saying everyone was mistreating him."

Ethel Greenberg, a beautician at Irene Davis's beauty shop, said, "I've known Frank and all of his wives for twelve years, and I noticed a change in him in the past five years. I've seen the wild look in his eyes and have seen him throw tantrums in his home, which I consider unnatural."

Glynn Reynolds of Clark County said he'd known Frank since 1951 and described personal scenarios that happened during the past three years. Dr. Fowler interpreted Reynolds's accounts as follows: "The patient displayed spells of extreme mental discomfort to the point of becoming highly irrational."

Frank was confused at his second interview on February 8, 1967, and questioned the doctor, thinking his previous session was after an electroencephalogram (EEG) was conducted. Dr. Fowler listened to his concerns and explained the tests were requested *after* their initial meeting. Frank seemed amazed and said, "I can't see how it had happened in that order."

"Do you remember the date of the examination?" Dr. Fowler asked.

"No. All this medicine I'm taking makes me talk a lot, after I've had an ounce and a half, but it doesn't make me sleep," he said.

Frank was taking Butisol, a barbiturate sleep aid with a fast onset of effects and short duration of action, used to treat insomnia and anxiety.[2] Dr.

Fowler later heard that after being given the Butisol over in the observation area, Frank said, "Wish I had a gallon of this!"

The medicine was working overtime on Frank, prompting Dr. Fowler to note, "He was extremely hyper-talkative, expansive, and at times grandiose. There was evident a flight of ideas and some confusion in time sequence. The patient said he had figured out the date of the alleged crime was on January 19, 1967, because this had been his mother's birthday. The patient wanted to go into extreme details in describing everything that he talked about, and it was extremely difficult to keep him on one subject. I asked him to give the details of January 19, 1967, as he now recalled it and he made an effort to do so."

Frank explained his recent car purchases and previous automobile accidents before Dr. Fowler could rein him back to the original subject. Trying once more, he asked, "You say you figured out that the alleged crime was on January 19, 1967. Can you tell me what you did that day?"

Frank explained his daily "whiskey routine" and how he waited for Sharron to bring the boys over. "She didn't come on Sunday. She said she might come, but she didn't."

"Was January 19 on a Sunday?" Dr. Fowler asked.

"I don't know what day it was on," he replied. (Frank had referred to Sunday, January 15. He murdered Sharron four days later on January 19.)

Detailing his movements on Thursday, January 19, Frank arrived at the point where he'd gone around 5:00 to his ranch to toss hay to the horses. He said, "I can't tell which came first, the chicken or the egg."

Dr. Fowler noted, "He complains of his inability to organize his thoughts and to concentrate and to recall all the events of the evening in sequence."

Frank refocused and then reached the point where he had driven to the Redbird Service Station and Laundromat on Central Avenue. He said, "I don't know what possessed me to drive to that laundromat. These people [the owners] had been friends of ours for years. When I got there, I saw my wife's mother's car and drove beside it. Her mother and the two boys were in the car. The boys grinned at me. My wife was not in the car, so I guess she was inside. You know, I never hit or spanked any of my boys. My dad used to beat me every day, and it did no good. It only made me meaner. I use psychology on them."

Frank repeated himself: "I don't know why I drove to that laundromat." He said, "I was sure surprised to see the old lady and the boys." Then he recalled the backdoor scene where his mother-in-law called him a no-good SOB, Sharron walked out of the laundromat, and he shouted at her.

"She ran into the car and shut the door, and I don't remember a thing after that until I woke up in jail," Frank said.

He continued to explain events at the jail. "There were about twenty drunks in jail. They just piled them in. Then they had a plea day about the day I came up here. I don't know what day. My attorney got up and said I was insane. And the judge said the state law required me to come here for examination. So, I'm in the chicken-coop bughouse! When are you going to let me out?"

Dr. Fowler didn't note his response to Frank's question but instead listened to his patient. "You know, when I first got here, they put those wires on my head. Then after that, you saw me."

Dr. Fowler again explained that he had seen him before he had had the EEG.

"I must be confused," said Frank. "But I've told you everything, even more than I've told my lawyer. Things are becoming a little clearer."

Dr. Fowler made a note in parentheses. "This would have been approximately twenty days since he had been taken to jail."

Wanting to continue, Frank said, "I'm not going to lie about anything. I don't have to lie. If you tell one lie, you'll have to tell ten to correct it. I wouldn't bring harm to my mother or my children or my children's mother. It was just that she kept calling me a yellow SOB over the phone, or if they saw me out in town, she'd say, 'There goes that damn SOB.'"

Frank interrupted himself and said, "There's a noisy SOB *here* who yells and stomps his feet all the time. If I could get to him, I'd kill the SOB! There's nothing wrong with him, just a mean n——er. If they'd let me, I'd stop all of his shit in a minute!"

He continued, "Mr. Fowler, there's nothing wrong with me. I hurt all over, all the time, and especially in my stomach. Have for fifteen years. There's only one thing that will stop the pain, and that's enough whiskey. I can drink a fifth a day, and I don't get drunk."

Changing the subject, Frank said, "But, you know, it's terrible, my boys being raised with all that filthy talk at the table! Damn, and every other four-letter word they use are as common at the table as salt and sugar, and that's no place for children."

Dr. Fowler sat quietly, letting Frank talk.

"I'd just about gotten Sharron's language cleaned up. She loved being a married woman and having children. I wanted more children. I don't know why people won't let me have my children. I never laid a hand on my children and never spanked their butts. I had my older son riding in the rodeo before he was a year old. I bought all them ponies and saddles. They had a matched team of black ponies and a wagon. I've been offered five hundred dollars for them, and I wouldn't take ten thousand! I wouldn't sell anything that is theirs.

I must have four or five thousand dollars in ponies and saddles. I only wanted them to grow up right. I had each of them a dog, a horse, and a cow."

Frank added, "You know many people don't know anything about a ranch. It takes four or five generations to build a big ranch, and you have to keep working and constantly improving it over a long time. Twice, I have had this pretty well under way for my boys. They would never have had to worry in their lives about a job. I had it fixed for them. Now, I've sold the cows and the ranch. You lose interest when things break up. We'd have started again if she had come back, and that damn old lady hadn't interfered."

He told the doctor, "Often dozens of people dropped in to eat at the ranch. I had twenty children following me around, and I had to teach everybody's children to ride, but my own! I can size up a horse just by looking at him and judging by his conformation. I'm a psychiatrist!"

Dr. Fowler waited for him to say "horse psychiatrist," but he didn't.

"A horse is ten times as smart as a dog, and a Brahma cow is the smartest of all cattle," he said.

Then he jumped to religion. "I don't believe a just God would have given the Bible only to the Jews in the Holy Land. I figure the Bibles over here are just as good as those over there."

Dr. Fowler tried to end the interview but found it difficult. Frank kept going, then finally seemed to be all talked out.

"Well, I really enjoyed our visit today, Mr. Fowler! You know I can handle any boy, of any kind, in ten days, and have him completely straightened out. Adults too, if I can get them to work properly. Bring me a boy from the Boy's Training School so I can prove it." He stood up. "But I'd have to have a horse to do it."

Frank returned for his third interview on February 9, 1967, and just like the second, he was still in the "expansive mood" Dr. Fowler described from the previous interview. He told of his father's (Ray Davis) death and then broached his mother's problems.

"She's had several nervous breakdowns. She's had a lot of hell to go through in her life. She's a softhearted person," he said lovingly.

He discussed the car wreck and hospitalization of his mother's second husband ("Tom" Athanas) and her marriage to third husband Pat Hogan. Dr. Fowler wrote, "Two years ago, they [Irene and Pat Hogan] had a serious car wreck, and he said both are still recovering from it. His mother owns two beauty shops around Hot Springs."

Dr. Fowler later stated, "There is the question of mental illness of his mother, but he is not sure of any others. He says many of his relatives were very intelligent."

Frank told Dr. Fowler that his father, Ray Davis, was very strict and "saw to it that I got an education." He stopped and then added, "This was a mistake. With an education, you have to think and drive too much, and you develop ulcers and heart trouble. If you don't get an education, you can just plow a mule and forget it. I guess I never had very good guts. They always hurt me."

Frank spent a while reminiscing about his childhood and then reached his military service and health.

"In 1953, I had undulant fever, and it still bothers me today. I've taken 2,500 Aureomycin capsules, 2,500 Terramycin capsules, the maximum of Streptomycin, and all the Chloromycetin the doctors could give me, and none of these helped. I've also had skull fractures in the past two or three years and three jaw fractures when I was beat up by policemen [in another Arkansas town]. Years ago, my blood was positive for malaria and typhoid," he said.

Dr. Fowler inquired about his friendships before delving into his socialization skills.

"I've always been outgoing and have had lots of friends," Frank said. "It's hard to judge friendship, but I find it easy to make friends."

When the doctor summarized this visit, he stated, "The patient's personality features appeared to be cyclothymic with overuse of alcohol and drugs. There appears to be much overt hostility."

Frank seemed more nervous and anxious at his fourth interview on February 13, 1967. He told Dr. Fowler that he'd complained of being extremely cold in the observation area, but everyone else said they were warm. He felt chilly and sweaty all over and said his feet were freezing. He stuck them out to the doctor. Dr. Fowler leaned over to feel Frank's feet and agreed they were cold.

Frank said, "I wish the temperature was about twenty degrees higher."

Dr. Fowler thought Frank appeared somewhat more depressed and flatter than he had on previous occasions. His voice was "quite low," he was somewhat slow in "his productions," and "every now and then, he would sit and hesitate a while before talking," the doctor observed.

Frank's moods ranged from mild irritability to affability, which Dr. Fowler thought also included evidence of some depression as well as expansiveness. "He shows most affect when talking about his ranch or about his boys," the doctor wrote. "There appeared to be no genuine remorse or sincere regrets that he had killed his wife."

Covering Frank's orientation, a common medical assessment, Dr. Fowler stated, "His understanding and comprehension of why he is here seemed to be vague. He knew he was here for mental observation but had no feeling that this examination was for any other purpose than to determine if he needed treatment. He was unable to say that this had something to do with his responsibility for his crime and, after talking about this for a while, remarked that he couldn't see why mental illness would make any difference about responsibilities. 'If a person did something, he did it whether he was mentally ill or not, and whether he was out of his mind made no difference.' He appeared to be aware of his situation but said he had no desires one way or the other and didn't care what happened to him."

Frank's memory appeared fairly well preserved, but he changed subjects and discussed remote events containing irrelevant details. Dr. Fowler said, "He recalls several occasions when he has fallen off a horse while stunting and trying to exhibit for a crowd and momentarily feeling stunned and unable to tell why he had fallen off the horse since he is such a good rider. The patient remarked that there was a high bluff near his farm that he used to ride horses up, that it was practically straight up. For a while, the horses attempted to do this, but after a while, they got to where they wouldn't go up this steep bank, and he would jump off the horses about halfway up." Dr. Fowler added a parenthetical comment, "I don't know what the meaning of this was, but it sounds a little bizarre."

Considering that Frank's retention and recall seemed restricted in some areas, Dr. Fowler said, "He bragged that he had a photographic mind and that things he learned stayed on his mind for a long time."

Frank showed extreme obsessions of cattle, ranching, and horses, which the doctor related to his chronic compulsion to be active. He told the doctor that he was somewhat of a showoff with his trick riding, which "he did for the pleasure of others." He said he'd ruined several good horses just because of his own compulsion to break them regardless of what the outcome might be. He constantly battled others from cheating him and, from what Dr. Fowler understood, "did things for his own personal pleasure." (However, a dichotomy existed between Frank's wish to pleasure others through his trick riding while conducting his life solely on self-satisfaction.)

"There is a compulsion to talk and also to do certain things and never give up on what he intended to do, such as conquering a recalcitrant horse [killed some] and recalcitrant cows. He said he had always outwitted any dumb animals," Dr. Fowler stated.

Frank told the doctor how he "felt men should always be in control of women, especially their wives." He talked obsessively about the problems of bringing up boys correctly and was concerned with their development, education, and welfare.

Unlike his previous interviews where he felt education was detrimental, this time he was "a little bit ambivalent about the question whether education is beneficial or harmful to people."

Dr. Fowler noted, "He said he always felt he could do anything he wanted to and that he would have made a good astronaut."

Frank later explained he would have weird feelings that "he was going to explode." He didn't know if these were not natural feelings but said occasionally that they occurred with a migraine-type headache, and he didn't know if this was migraine or not.

"His judgment was questionable in many areas," Dr. Fowler sensed, "especially about himself in interpersonal relationships and the use of drugs and alcohol." Frank claimed he didn't think drinking was his problem. He said, "There was always a bunch of old women trying to lead me off and get me into trouble."

Asked if he heard voices or experienced auditory hallucinations, Frank said, "Yes, I sure damn have, Dr. Fowler. They are not clear. I can just hear the rumbling, but I can't figure out what they are saying. That's been going on a long time, about twenty years. It doesn't last too long. I always figured it was something else, like the wind or the trees."

Frank couldn't distinguish whether the voices were male or female. He thought they were both but couldn't tell what they were saying to him. Dr. Fowler noted, "He went on to say he had heard the bastards walking up and down the halls at home at night and that sometimes his wife heard them too. He said that someone told him the house was haunted before he moved there."

Frank couldn't recall having dreams but said, "I see my two boys sitting in the swing at the house that I own, where they've never lived. I'm sitting in between them, and we sit and swing for about ten minutes. Then we all fall out." Frank said he could see this nearly anytime by looking at the wall for a while and had seen visions like this off and on all his life.

Dr. Fowler felt Frank's "hypochondriacal ideas appeared actual products of extreme anxiety and tension, his judgment was questionable, and his insight was almost entirely lacking." His summary noted Frank's "severe affective disturbance, expansiveness in thought processes, grandiosity, perceptual distortion, and projection of a pseudo-community aligned against him."

The four sessions resulted in Dr. Fowler's two diagnoses: "(1) manic-depressive reaction, manic type (hypomanic) and (2) psychophysiological reaction of the gastrointestinal system manifested by history of peptic ulcer disease." His recommendation was "treatment."

· *16* ·

The Psychiatric Team Diagnosis

$\mathcal{D}$r. Fowler referred Frank for psychological testing with clinical psychologist Dr. Bernice Burns on February 16, 1967. She administered six tests, which included the Full Range Picture Vocabulary Test, Bender-Gestalt, Rorschach, Word Association, Draw-A-Person, and the Minnesota Multiphasic Personality Inventory.

Dr. Burns found Frank's associations to the Rorschach test, which dealt with personality factors, to have a number of features found in the records of individuals who were evasive and reluctant to express themselves. She said he "gave little or no justification of his percepts other than form and was unable or unwilling to comment or elaborate on his meager and inadequate associations." She added, "For the most part, his responses consisted of derogatory remarks about the cards—looks like a bucket of paint was thrown at a canvas or somebody's weird idea of art."

Her focus on his inability to form associations in the Rorschach test reinforced Dr. Fowler's intrasession observations of Frank's lack of correlation between the murder of his wife Sharron and his current psychiatric hospitalization.

Dr. Burns considered that his "general card criticism" represented an expression of hostility and possibly fear and apprehension. She observed him frequently commenting on "the symmetry of the cards," such as "it's the same on both sides" or "there's always two of everything."

"Remarks such as these point to a means of ordering things spatially and represent an attempt to control unacceptable feelings," she noted.

His validity scales on the Minnesota Multiphasic Personality Inventory seemed "representative of either moderate psychopathology or a more or less deliberate attempt," she stated, "to 'fake bad.'"

Looking back at Frank's childhood, "bad" always seemed to exist in his DNA. He claimed to have burned down a jailhouse when he was seven years old. He also said his father gave him daily whippings. He was not the perfect child or adult. He frequently brawled in bars, treated his mother like she was an ATM machine, badgered his many wives, and divorced his pregnant third wife in order to marry his much younger girlfriend.

Dr. Burns claimed six of the ten clinical scales were elevated, which she said "tended to support an assumption of some attempt to appear in an unfavorable light." Three of the six elevated scales were Hs (for bodily health), Ma (showing hypomania), and Pa (for paranoia).

She noted a lack of significant elevation for the K scale, which measured psychological defenses, and Sc, the schizophrenia scale. She said this would limit him from the likelihood of a delusional and confused state, and she believed the combinations of some of the scales, such as Ma, Si, and Pa, indicated a socially outgoing, gregarious adjustment, possibly to the point of expansiveness, high impulsivity, and distractibility.

With this observation, Dr. Burns substantiated Dr. Fowler's findings of Frank's "expansiveness." She found evidence of his paranoia, which he indicated earlier in sessions with Dr. Fowler as he described the voice he heard in the night and people following him and shining lights in his eyes.

She described that his general behavior during the testing contained hostile comments that seemed directed toward the tests in general and said that "on several occasions when a question was asked by the examiner, he would talk incessantly about his past life."

Frank had exhibited the same behavior with Dr. Fowler, going off on a talking jag and having to be reeled into the original subject of discussion. His "estimated IQ," she determined, "was 102 to 105, which is well within the average range of intelligence."

⌒

On Monday, February 27, 1967, Dr. Fowler presented Frank's case history to the Arkansas State Hospital, Act 3 diagnostic staff, which consisted of eight physicians, a social service worker, two senior medical students, and a psychologist (not Bernice Burns). The group discussed the contents of Fowler's evaluation report, which included the psychiatric history and mental status report, progress notes, the psychologist's report, the electroencephalogram interpretation, and a physical assessment.

The members of the Act 3 diagnostic staff agreed on the psychiatric diagnoses of "manic-depressive reaction, manic type," and "psychophysiological reaction of the gastrointestinal system" and proposed he be retained for treatment.

The diagnostic staff team felt Frank, "in their opinion, was mentally ill to the degree of legal irresponsibility at the time of this mental examination and that he was probably mentally ill to the degree of legal irresponsibility at the time of the alleged commission of his acts."

Their evaluation form contained an all-or-nothing question, stating whether the patient "is" or "is not" competent to receive and discharge funds judiciously for the welfare of himself and dependents. They circled "is not."

The Posthumous Birthday Gift

*C*athie Ward would've celebrated her fourteenth birthday on April 21, 1967. No doubt, she would have gone to the Y-Teen dance that night and may have, by then, been the prettiest coed on the dance floor. We'll never know.

Her father and his wife Pat may have visited her grave that Friday afternoon. Hiram said, "I've been out there on her birthday. My second wife and I went several times. She was more a grave visitor than I was. I see enough people die and this kind of stuff. The fact where a person's buried, it's not where they are. That person is already gone wherever they're going. It's memories."

Cathie received a posthumous birthday gift eight days earlier, when a grand jury indictment charged Frank Davis with first-degree murder in connection with her death. A bench warrant had been delivered the day before to the jailer of Garland County, commanding him "to arrest Allen [*sic*] Frank Davis and bring him before the Garland Circuit Court to answer in that court against him for the offense of murder in the first degree."

At the time, Frank's attorneys were probably confused. The bench warrant didn't designate *whom* Frank had murdered. He'd already been through the same process for the murder of his wife Sharron, so they were probably scrambling to learn the name of this victim. They might have thought Pauline Knight's shotgun injuries had finally taken their toll.

Bob Ridgeway, the father of a junior high school–aged daughter, may have overheard the school kids' rumors of Cathie Ward's rape and murder and put two and two together. But Jack Holt, a Little Rock resident, was probably unaware. Frank had pretended Cathie's death was an accident and had more than likely never discussed the subject with his out-of-town attorney.

Frank's attorneys soon learned the victim's name when they held the actual indictment in their hands. Garland County prosecuting attorney Walter

Wright filed the document, which accused Frank Davis of "murder in the first degree." It declared, "Allen [*sic*] Frank Davis . . . on the 24th day of June A.D. 1966 did feloniously, willfully and with malice of forethought and after deliberation and premeditation, by then and there assault, kill and murder the said Kathy [*sic*] Ward, by striking the said Kathy Ward in the head with a rock, in violation of Ark. State. Ann (1947) 41-2205 and 41-2227."

A grand jury had met for three days during the first week of April and then reconvened Wednesday, April 13. The jury foreman, O. M. Young, [1] vice president of Guaranty Title Company,[2] said their decision was based on information that alleged Davis attacked Cathie with a rock, causing her death, and they "felt there was enough evidence to warrant a trial in the case."[3]

The next day, a newspaper headline announced, "Man Indicted in Death of Resort Girl." The startling news of Frank's second murder charge was not only disturbing but also confusing to Cathie's family and friends and many Hot Springs residents. How, they may have wondered, in the thirty-nine weeks it took to investigate Cathie's death at Blacksnake Ranch, did they come across a rock that Walter Wright claimed was Frank Davis's murder weapon?

Cathie's father soon learned the basis of this accusation. "When Frank Davis killed his wife and his mother-in-law in front of the washeteria," Hiram said, "his wife had what he had done in the past, written in a letter, and she put it in a lockbox. She said he'd killed my daughter and a little colored boy that was in a pond in the front of their house. The authorities drained the pond, and there he was. I don't know if any of these are true. The letter was in the papers. And I don't know what happened to it. Of course, a lot of people that lived up there in Hot Springs talked to me about it. This is just what I was told, and it's been too long ago to remember who told me."

The Ward family had Sharron Knight Davis to thank for the new death ruling. She'd come back from the grave with retribution against her husband for Cathie's death. It's unknown if the actual rock was in the lockbox where Sharron had placed her letter or if she had simply documented the weapon that he had used to murder Cathie. The newspaper account Hiram referred to could not be located.

Hot Springs residents, whose gut feelings were "he murdered Cathie Ward," had waited ten months for their beliefs to be validated. Others, who never suspected the man who'd recently murdered his wife at the Redbird was also responsible for murdering a thirteen-year-old girl at Blacksnake Ranch, were shocked.

No one expected this resolution, but many suspected Frank Davis had done it. Now that it had been confirmed, an avalanche of emotions was released.

Bettye Jo Tucker, whose father would not allow her to join Cathie, Madelyn, and Peg at Blacksnake Ranch that terrible day, was frightened when she heard Davis was charged with Cathie's murder. She remembers talk about her body being drug by the horse with her foot in the stirrup, making it appear as if she'd had an accident rather than having been murdered.

"Through listening to people talk, because they did it behind my back because no one wanted me to know, I figured out she had been raped," Bettye Jo told me. "The best I could understand in my brain at that time is that that's what had happened to her, and that's all I knew of what happened. I always thought about that because my skin is dark like hers. My hair was dark like hers. My eyes were not dark. They're blue green. But I just always thought if I'd gone, that could've been me. You think selfishly, which I did, and it scared me so bad."

Cathie's father told me he remembered that a girlfriend was supposed to go horseback riding with her that day.

"And for some reason, she could not go," he said. "And this girl was upset because she thought if she had gone, it wouldn't have happened." (Although Ward couldn't remember "the girl's" name, he was referring to Bettye Jo Tucker.)

Bettye Jo also recalled how the murder charge affected her neighbor Peg, who'd been given permission and was at Blacksnake Ranch when Cathie died.

"We were not allowed to talk about it. I don't know whatever her dad or mom said, 'Don't talk about it,' but I know they were afraid of this guy! They were terrified, absolutely terrified of something happening and Frank Davis not being convicted, not being held in jail. She and her sister were home a lot by themselves because their mother was a waitress at a large restaurant in town. I know she was scared to death. Peg and I were still good friends. Don't get me wrong, we still talked about stuff—but we didn't talk about that."

Paula Seay, who lived in Bettye Jo's and Peg's neighborhood, recalled her connection to Cathie's murder. "Madelyn had invited me, and Mother wouldn't let me go. I told her I hated her and thought she was the meanest mother in the world! Then Cathie died, and I thanked her. I said, 'Mom, thank you. It could've been me.' Several of us had the same experience and feeling." (Cathie's boyfriend, Mike, would later date Paula in high school.)

Clyde Covington, one of Cathie's seventh-grade teachers, had been shocked by her accident and death, but now with this new revelation, he was totally upset.

Mary Ellen Cook was a quiet and refined matriarch, and most considered her the finest example of a true southern genteel woman. With three generations living together in a lovely home on Garland Street, she nurtured her granddaughters while trying to keep a tight rein on her son and daughter,

Bubba and Princella. Mary Ellen paid Frank Davis's stabling fee for Princella's horse, Rusty, and never interfered when her eight-year-old granddaughter, Delia, wanted to ride at Blacksnake Ranch.

Mary Ellen was a churchgoer and rarely had a bad thing to say about anyone, but the morning she heard about Frank's latest murder, she held court in her kitchen. "This could've been you," she said to Delia and Princella. "He could've killed you as easily as he killed that girl and his wife! I never liked that man!"

Lorna Garner, who encountered the man in the truck she suspected was Frank Davis, said, "Kay, Babette, and I would sit and talk about that and how somebody could do something so horrible."

Gary Jackson, two years older than Cathie, recalled hearing his mother when the details of Cathie's death came out. "I remember my mother being so livid, if she could of gotten a hold of him, she would have killed him! I remember her talking about it. I think she casually knew them. Don't think she knew them well, but I think it was just the brutality that he did it to a child. And her reaction probably wasn't any different than any other mother at the time. I didn't know her, but I remember feeling scared when it happened because things like that didn't happen that often in those days, and I can remember thinking *never heard of such a thing*. Scary!"

Frances Forsberg, who was friends with Sarah Ward through the Fine Arts Center, said, "Everybody thought he had in some way violated the Ward child and then rigged this business of her being dragged by the horse to make it look like she'd been in an accident rather than murdered. I think there were people who knew about his violence because I think it was suspected from the day that that child died until the day he actually killed his wife, and it was documented, and everybody really knew that's what happened. Everybody just said, 'Uh, huh. We thought so!' I think Sarah thought so. I just remember knowing it was Frank Davis, and he was the one everybody suspected. And he'd killed the Ward child. It was like, 'Yep, we knew he was a bad person!'"

Cathie's father said, "I would have killed him, I guess, if I had seen him at that time."

Cathy Browne-Robbins, the ten-year-old girl Davis would chauffeur to his ranch for a day of horseback riding, remembered being disturbed about Sharron's murder. Then, six months later, the sixth grader learned that Cathie Ward had actually been murdered.

"I didn't know Cathie, but I heard she had fallen off the horse, and they figured that was what killed her," she told me. "Then they found that she had had a blow to her head. I remember this because it shocked me so much when I heard it out on the school playground. Then Mother showed it to me in the paper. I was just in shock that it happened. I kept saying, 'Mr. Frank, no.'"

Cathy Browne had difficulty believing the man who was so kind to her at the ranch had murdered his wife and now this young woman. The rumors Cathy heard on the Jones School playground had come true—one of them at least: the murder.

↶

Now that Frank had been formally accused of Cathie's murder, the foundation of her murder case was being laid while the upcoming trial for Sharron's murder was being built piece by piece. Garland County Circuit Judge Henry "Hank" Britt issued a court order on May 19, 1967, stating, "The defendant [Allen (*sic*) Frank Davis] has entered a plea of Not Guilty by Reason of Insanity."

Judge Britt said the Arkansas State Hospital furnished a letter opinion diagnosis of manic-depressive reaction, manic type. To prepare the State's case, he said, "further examination by expert medical witnesses be made of the Defendant." He requested Frank Davis be "made available for observation and examination by such witness or witnesses as the State may designate."

A brief letter from M. T. McMurry, registrar of the Arkansas State Hospital, was mailed to Judge Britt on June 15. "[They] Requested, on May 3," McMurry claimed, "a commitment that would give them legal authority to hold Frank Davis for treatment and asked that it be furnished as soon as possible."

Four days later, on June 19, Dr. Charles Yohe, a Hot Springs psychiatrist and diplomate of the American Board of Psychiatry and Neurology, fellow of the American Psychiatric Association, and certified mental hospital administrator, mailed correspondence to Garland County prosecuting attorney Walter G. Wright of his examination of Frank Davis on June 14 at the state hospital. Yohe explained that he was also given access to his "available records" and discussed the case with Dr. Walters, his physician, after which he made a decision and conclusion that "Allen [*sic*] Frank Davis is at present sane and competent."

Dr. Yohe saw Frank as being quite able to understand the charges against him and to aid his attorney in his defense. Yohe said, "From what his personal physician, Dr. Walters, related to me, I do not imagine the Little Rock State Hospital will in any way dispute or contest my statement and opinion in this regard."

Based on these interviews and the examination of all available hospital records, Dr. Yohe went on the record saying, "Allen [*sic*] Frank Davis was sane and competent on January 19, 1967, at approximately 7:00 p.m." (the time of Sharron's murder). Dr. Yohe said further details and rationale to "back up" his opinions "were available from his office upon request."

Two days later, on June 21, Frank was promptly returned to the Garland County Jail. The same day, a letter was sent from Judge Britt to Little Rock attorney Jack Holt. He wanted to know if Holt would also represent Frank Davis for Cathie's murder since he was already representing him for Sharron's murder.

Judge Britt said, "If you represent him in this case, his arraignment may be held on any Monday morning. If you have any preferred date for arraignment, please let me know."

Then, on July 11, 1967, Walter Wright, prosecuting attorney, mailed correspondence to Holt, informing him of the postponement of Frank Davis's arraignment for Cathie's criminal case. Wright said, "That arraignment will be deferred . . . until Garland Criminal No. 12, 827 [Sharron's murder] is deposed, or by the jury on August 10, 1967."

This meant the formal murder charge for Cathie Ward was in limbo while Frank waited a month for the murder trial of his wife, Sharron.

• *18* •

The Foreclosure

$\mathcal{M}$r. and Mrs. J. A. Culberson hired Hot Springs attorney Clayton Farrar Sr. on June 20, 1967, to begin foreclosure proceedings on Blacksnake Ranch.[1] Four months earlier, Frank Davis told Dr. Fowler during a session at Arkansas State Hospital that he'd sold his cattle and Blacksnake Ranch, but that wasn't true. The Culbersons owned the property, and Frank (or his mother, Irene) hadn't paid them a dime since the beginning of the year. Frank had also been late with the 1966 annual taxes of $19.64, which had been due in February 1967.

Culberson's attorney, Clayton Farrar Sr., filed a judgment against Frank in the Garland County Chancery Court for $9,377.40 with interest at the rate of 6 percent per annum from December 9, 1966. Summonses were sent to Frank at the state hospital in Little Rock and to his two sons in Hot Springs, who were in the custody of their maternal grandparents, Fred and Pauline Knight. For some reason, a third summons was sent to Frank six days later, on June 26.

Noting that Frank Davis was a patient at the Arkansas State Hospital from January 30, 1967, to June 21, 1967, Clayton Farrar Sr. filed an "Application for Appointment of Guardian ad Litem." He claimed that neither Frank Davis nor his two sons had a guardian, nor had a "guardian ad litem" been appointed to appear and defend them in this action.

Farrar's strategic move prompted Frank's reliable Hot Springs attorney, Robert Ridgeway, to offer his services as Guardian ad Litem for Frank Davis "if appointed by the court," and Sam L. Anderson stated the same for the minors.

Twenty days later, neither Ridgeway nor Anderson had made applications for the appointment of a guardian ad litem, which prompted Farrar to

111

enact an "Order Appointing Guardians ad Litem" on July 18, 1967. With this legal move, he was making a motion to order the appointment of Ridgeway and Anderson as guardians ad litem for Frank Davis and the minors.

Ridgeway and Anderson finally gave the same answer for their separate clients on August 16. Both attorneys claimed "to have neither the knowledge nor information sufficient to form a belief of the truth of any allegations of Plaintiffs' Complaint." They also "denied each and every allegation" Farrar presented in his clients' foreclosure litigation.

Farrar followed the legal process, filing a "decree," then a "judgment of rem" (against a piece of property, not a person). The Culbersons wanted the entire monies owed them with interest and the 1966 property taxes due. If that wasn't satisfied by July 28,1967, the court was instructed to appoint Sherlon Hilliard, the court's clerk, to sell the property to the highest bidder in a public auction at the Garland County Courthouse after first advertising the terms and place of sale for a period of twenty days in a local newspaper. It declared that "the sale would constitute a perpetual bar to all right of redemption and all other right, title and interest of the defendants, Frank Davis and his two sons."

The Culbersons went to the public auction at the Garland County Courthouse on September 21, 1967, and purchased their own property for $9,914.66, which was $45.02 shy of the amount Frank Davis owed them, including the 6 percent interest and property taxes due. Now they owned the property free and clear of any future claims or interference by Frank Davis (or his mother, Irene) and his minor sons. The Culbersons could resell the ranch to someone who could either buy the property outright or make monthly payments on time.

The ownership of automobiles, wives, and Blacksnake Ranch was very important to Frank. It's unusual he'd let something so important, such as his property and the requisite monthly mortgage, go unattended. He missed the January 9, 1967, payment ten days before he murdered Sharron, so he couldn't use her as an excuse. Maybe Sharron's estrangement and his continued cover-up of Cathie's murder had caused him to start unraveling.

· 19 ·

The Trial *Stay* to *First Day*

$\mathscr{F}$rank Davis spent the majority of his 189 days of incarceration in the Arkansas State Hospital at Little Rock. Although he'd lost Blacksnake Ranch during that time, he received something more valuable when the arraignment for Cathie's first-degree murder charge was temporarily shelved. Also, with Sharron Knight Davis's mother, Pauline, surviving her traumatic gunshot wounds, he'd escaped a third murder charge. He was getting one lucky break after another, and that momentum hadn't changed when the *Sentinel-Record* ran the July 27, 1967, headline, "Frank Davis Trial Gets Stay."[1]

The Arkansas Supreme Court stayed Frank's first-degree murder trial, which had been scheduled for August 10, 1967. Frank was now being housed at the Garland County Jail, and because he'd been judged insane by psychiatrists at the Arkansas State Hospital, Jack Holt Sr. wanted Garland County Circuit Judge Henry M. Britt, who handled the case in the lower court, to have Davis committed to the state hospital. Britt had earlier denied the state hospital's request to extend Frank's treatment, saying the question of insanity was for a trial jury to decide.

Frank Davis's expensive Little Rock attorney, Jack Holt, had earlier requested his client be sent for more testing at the state hospital. For any inmate awaiting trial for murder in Arkansas, if given the choice, daily confinement in a hospital rather than a jail would be preferred. However, Frank wasn't allowed that luxury and instead was forced to continue his detention at the Garland County Jail.

The Arkansas Supreme Court's stay delayed Frank's trial for almost a year. Then, on Tuesday, June 11, 1968, he left the county jail to walk upstairs to the Garland County Circuit Courtroom. For the first day of his first-degree murder trial, Frank was wearing a dark business suit, white shirt, and a tie the color of blood.[2] He sat down beside Jack Holt and cocounsel Robert Ridgeway of Hot Springs. The newspaper described Frank's demeanor the next day as "stoic" and stated, "He listened to the questioning of the jurors with an expression that changed little throughout the entire day. Most of the time he stared straight ahead."

The reporter, whose name didn't accompany the article, pegged Frank as being "in his late 40s." The newsperson was obviously unaware Frank's forty-fourth birthday had fallen on the first day of the trial of his wife's murder, which had been committed on his mother's sixtieth birthday.

Jack Holt Sr., a sixty-five-year-old with a linebacker's physique, queried forty prospective jurors individually. He asked specifically, "Do you have any scruples against the penalty of life imprisonment should the defendant be found guilty?" He also questioned their attitude toward a plea of insanity as a defense.

The prosecuting attorney, Walter Wright, who served as the chief deputy prosecuting attorney for five years before winning the recent 1966 fall elections, questioned many but not all of the juror candidates.

Wright would not say whether the state would seek the death penalty, but he did question them, asking if they might have any convictions against it.

"The significance of the death penalty questions in this murder trial hinged on the belief it was the first in Arkansas since the June 3, 1968 U.S. Supreme Court 5–4 decision, which held that the death sentence cannot be imposed by a jury from which persons with conscientious or religious scruples against capital punishment were automatically excluded," the nameless newspaper reporter noted.

"However, court attachés here who have read the complete opinion, interpreted the opinion, say that jurors may be excluded from service if their scruples would interfere with a fair and impartial decision in cases where the death penalty is involved," the reporter added.

Judge Henry M. "Hank" Britt presided over the Garland County Circuit Court. The forty-nine-year-old was the only Republican elected as a circuit judge in Arkansas during the recent November 11, 1966, elections.[3] Six years earlier, in 1960, Britt ran for governor of Arkansas against incumbent Orval Faubus, who'd made international headlines for blocking the 1957 Central High School desegregation. Britt lost, earning only 30 percent of the vote, and by 1968, his cousin Maurice "Footsie" Britt had become the state's lieutenant governor.

Judge Britt listened patiently to the jury, questioning and then excusing thirteen juror candidates for possessing scruples against the death penalty.[4] He also dismissed others who either had formed an opinion in the case or, as in one instance, had a physical disability.

Late in the afternoon, an all-white, all-male jury was chosen: retirees Oliver H. Craig, James Casey, James Jett, and L. G. Burrell; business owners Richard Clem, William Dacus, Charles Hughes, and Allen Kilby Jr.; and others in various occupations from clerks to construction workers Roderick Jewell, Luther Tackett, Martin Powell, and John Umphers. Frank Eckard was chosen as one of two alternate jurors along with the only female, Velma Welch.[5] The entire jury, men and woman, admitted to having no previous experience in a criminal case.

Judge Britt instructed the court clerk, Sherlon Hilliard, to administer the oath to the jurors, and then, at 4:30 p.m., an afternoon recess was called. Chief Deputy Sheriff Kenneth McKinney walked to the counsel's table, placed handcuffs on Frank, escorted him out of the courtroom on the third floor of the courthouse, and led him to the county jail on the second floor.

Deputy prosecuting attorney Ben Harrison gave instructions to the jurors before they were allowed to leave. "Do not discuss the case with anyone, and do not read the newspaper account of the trial, especially tomorrow's newspaper," Harrison instructed them.

At the time, two Hot Springs newspapers shared the same owner and offices on Central Avenue behind the Como Hotel. The *Sentinel-Record*, with editor Robert Dean, was distributed every morning, Sunday through Friday, and the *Hot Springs New Era*, with general manager Alden Mooney and publisher Walter E. Hussman, came out every evening, Monday through Saturday.

Had the jurors been allowed to read the Wednesday morning newspaper, they would have seen their names listed on the front page. In addition, they would have learned the state had twenty-one possible witnesses and the defense between twelve and seventeen. Furthermore, if they had been unaware of Frank's two separate murder cases, they would have learned he was an accused multiple murderer by reading the last, long paragraph, which stated, "He has also been indicted by the Garland County Grand Jury charging the same offense in connection with the earlier death of a 13-year-old Hot Springs girl at his ranch on Blacksnake Road, but has not been brought to trial in that case."[6]

· 20 ·

The Admission

The second day of Frank's first-degree murder trial began Wednesday, June 12, 1968, with opening statements. Walter Wright, a short man with dark hair and eyeglasses, stood in front of the jury to try his first criminal case as prosecuting attorney. The thirty-eight-year-old said, "If the court please, gentlemen of the jury and alternates, you will recall yesterday, that in questioning by myself, I asked you certain questions about the death penalty. Your answers were in the affirmative. That was done for a purpose. The State of Arkansas, represented by myself and Mr. Harrison, is asking the death penalty in this case of first-degree murder. The charge is first-degree murder against Frank Davis. This gentleman sitting right here." Wright stopped to point at Frank Davis, who was sitting at the defense counsel table between Jack Holt and Robert Ridgeway.

Wright wanted to win his first trial for Sharron's parents, who had visited him multiple times in his office. Continuing, Wright said, "The charge is not against the jury. It's not against myself. It's not against Mr. Harrison. It's not against Mr. Holt, and it's not against Mr. Ridgeway. It's not against the court."

He paused. "Mr. Frank Davis is charged with first-degree murder. He is the person here to be tried. Not any other person in this courtroom. Not any other witness who may testify from this stand. Not something that is imagined. Frank Davis is the person that's standing trial for first-degree murder. I want to make that clear at the beginning. I will not take up your time in the opening statement with details that the state hopes to prove. I would like to take just a small portion of your time this morning, in giving a brief outline of what the state will generally show."

Removing all doubts of his sole opponent's identity, Wright explained the separation between Frank and Sharron and described Frank's harassing phone calls to her and the surveillance of her by his "watcher." He detailed the evening of January 19, 1967, saying, "Sharron had driven her mother and two sons to the Redbird Laundromat with wet wash that needed drying."

Wright explained how Frank "had driven up beside their car where Sharron had positioned herself behind the steering wheel and her mother in the front passenger side when a conversation began. Then a shot, and another shot." He continued with the shooting aftermath and then concluded by saying, "I say to you the manner in which this killing, this cold-blooded killing, was perpetrated demands the highest penalty. The state is asking that you impose that penalty. Thank you." Wright waited a moment for the last statement of his opening argument to settle in before taking his seat.

Frank's lead attorney, Jack Holt, had become a successful lawyer after relinquishing his political ambitions after three bitter losses for Arkansas governor and U.S. senatorial races to popular postwar-era politicians Sid McMath, Francis Cherry, and John L. McClellan.[1] Holt's legal expertise had been obvious the previous year when he was able to secure a stay for Frank's trial, causing Frank and his mother to consider the intimidating yet down-home lawyer as the ace in their back pockets.

Holt's courtroom skills were evident as he addressed the jury.

"It is every man's right to a fair and impartial trial. Gentlemen of the jury and Mrs. Welch, you know fortunately the only thing that has made America great is the right of any person, regardless of who he is or what he might be charged with, to be permitted to come before a jury and there to have a fair and impartial trial under the law and the evidence, eliminating bias and prejudice."

He continued. "If we stop only because we're sorry somebody has been killed, we have no right to be here. We'll just go on and do what the prosecuting attorney says, 'electrocute the fellow and get him out of the way.' Now, apparently that old feeling brought down from the dark ages exists here today because 'somebody has been killed, we want the death penalty.' Not satisfied with anything less than that. But nothing was said about the law.

"But this country is not a country of man. That's why we seceded from England. This country is a country of law, and if and when you and I become so biased and so prejudiced and our mind so warped that just because someone is killed, we're going to ignore the law that governs the facts in the case, we're not only not good jurors, we're not good Americans," he said.

The courtroom spectators were in awe of Holt as he spoke with confidence. He continued, "Now, at the proper time, the attorneys for Frank Davis, the Honorable Cocounsel Bob Ridgeway, and myself, we're going to admit the killing. We're going to admit that Frank Davis killed his wife, Sharron. But we're going to turn around and do what any decent, ordinary citizen, you or me or anybody else, would do, that we say under the law, he's guilty of the killing, but under the law, he is not guilty of murder. There's a lot of difference between murder and killing. If that were not true, everybody that was killed in the world wars, whoever did it, is guilty of murder."

Holt explained his war scenario, the legal terms of insanity and reasonable doubt, the suffering of Frank Davis after having committed the crime, and his years of drug and alcohol abuse. "The unanimous findings by the psychiatric staff at the Arkansas State Hospital," Holt said, "found that Frank was a sick man at the time of the unfortunate incident."

Arriving at the crux of the accusations against his client, Holt said, "This defendant is charged with murder in the first degree, and to that, he has pled not guilty, number one. Number two, not guilty by the reason of insanity. And either one, if you believe is sufficient, it will be your duty to render a verdict of not guilty."

Holt then addressed the jurors' inexperience with a warning. "If I make any statement in this opening statement, which after all is only for the purpose, don't consider it as evidence at all. It's only to try to assist you, and if you've never been in a criminal case before, to get you in, or your son or some loved one, who would be unfortunate enough to be in the shape he's in, the court says, now look at him, he's presumed to be innocent."

Continuing, Holt said, "It will be in evidence that he is the only child of Mrs. Pat Hogan [Irene Davis's married name at the time]. Unfortunately, he became addicted to alcohol and drugs several years ago. His father died in 1954. He had a fairly good education. But even when he was growing up, he was moody, flighty, erratic, irrational, very impulsive, subject to temper and tantrums."

Holt followed this statement by a time line of Frank's college education, military service, marriages, children, and marital difficulties and then ended with his medical maladies and treatment.

"His condition has gradually grown worse during the past several years. This, I think, is unfortunate but very significant, especially when a man's life is at stake."

Frank hadn't budged while Jack Holt covered his crazed life in a few brief minutes. "At the time of the unfortunate incident, Frank Davis was a sick man. He was insane. There is only one God-fearing verdict you could give, and that would be that, 'we the jury, find the defendant not guilty.' Thank you," Holt said.

With the opening statements completed, witness testimonies began. The state was first to call two men who had seen Sharron at the hospital.

Dr. William R. Mashburn, deputy coroner, said he examined Sharron in the hospital's emergency room. Then Dr. W. R. Lee, coroner, who conducted the autopsy, said, "The victim died as the result of a gunshot wound."

Next on the witness stand were representatives of the Hot Springs Police Department, who had been at the crime scene location and later tracked down Frank Davis. They were Lieutenant Detective Grover Douglas, Detective Sergeant Bobby Digby, Police Chief John Ermey, Lieutenant James Holt, and Officers Wayne Seal and John Gibson. They explained their investigation at Irene Davis's home and Frank's arrest and then his hospitalization, which lasted "thirty to forty-five minutes" before he was "removed to the jail."

Officer John Gibson, over considerable objection by the defense, testified that Davis's mother had advised "a bottle of drugs found on the dresser in the home had contained capsules but that it was empty, with one lying outside the bottle," when officers arrived. "But he was coherent," in the officers' opinion, when taken from the hospital to jail and had voluntarily asked them coherent questions.

Captain Paul McDonald, officer in charge of the Arkansas State Police crime laboratory, testified to the processing and examination of evidence. The rifle, identified as the one officers found wrapped in a blue-jean jacket in the backyard dog pen at Davis's mother's home the night of the shooting, was introduced as evidence. A smashed bullet said to have been fired from the rifle, eight metal fragments allegedly removed from Mrs. Davis's body, one expended cartridge case, and three loaded cartridge cases were also given as evidence in the first-degree murder trial.

The state called Terral Adcock, a twenty-year-old factory worker, to the witness stand. Adcock said that, as a favor, he watched Sharron on January 19, 1967, the day she was fatally shot by Davis, and on several prior occasions reported her movements to Davis.[2]

Adcock told prosecuting attorney Wright, "Mrs. Davis attended Tigert Memorial Methodist Church where I go, but I've never seen her at the ranch."

He described how he "watched Mrs. Davis" the afternoon of January 19, prior to the shooting, at her place of employment, the Vanity Beauty shop across Beard Street from Cook's Ice Cream Company. He said he'd parked his car at Cook's and, after a time, had called Frank to tell him his wife was in the shop. He made two phone calls to Frank. On the second call, Frank's mother told him Frank had left.

Adcock said he drove around looking for Frank and then went back to Cook's. Frank drove up, and he joined him in his car.

"Davis drank some liquor there," Adcock said. "I've been with Frank when he was drunk, and he wasn't drunk on that day."

Adcock saw Pauline Knight and the Davises' two young children drive up to the beauty shop, pick up Sharron, and drive away. Adcock remembered that at the time, Frank said, "I hate Sharron's mother, but I love her cooking. Cornbread and beans!"

Adcock testified that Frank then said, "I'm going to do something I should have done a long time ago."

"He sounded normal, except that he sounded mad," Adcock added. "When Sharron and her mother left the beauty shop, Frank told me to go to his home on Henderson Street and wait for him. Frank said he was going to follow the car."

When questioned about the car, Adcock said, "I didn't know what car he was talking about."

Adcock said he did what he was instructed to do and joined Frank's mother and grandfather and "a girl" at Irene Davis's home on Henderson Street

He remembered Frank coming in later, waving, and saying, "Hello, Buddy-O, Buddy,' or something."

Adcock said he watched Frank ask his mother to go into another room. When questioned further, Adcock said he didn't notice a change in Frank's appearance or tone of voice. He said he later saw Irene Davis come out of the same room with a cocked pistol. "I heard her say Frank shot or killed Sharron and another woman." Adcock also remembered Irene saying, "He had the pistol and would finish the job, but I kept talking to Frank, and then he fell out."

Adcock said, "I saw Frank carrying a blue-jean jacket that stood up alone but didn't see a gun wrapped inside."

Wright asked Adcock how long he'd known Frank Davis. "Probably three months before the shooting. I helped him feed stock at the ranch. He's always been good to me."

⌒

Frank's attorney, Jack Holt, cross-examined the young man. Adcock admitted that he drank on several occasions with Davis but had not had any alcohol in the past two or three weeks. He admitted taking nerve pills, given to him by a physician, but denied having ever had a nervous breakdown, been hospitalized for this affliction, or that the reason for his friendship with Davis was to get liquor. He said he saw Davis almost every day, and most of the time, Davis was drinking.

Holt pointed out several discrepancies in Adcock's testimony given in municipal court shortly after the slaying, but Adcock said it was not his intention to lie about anything.

"I was confused then," he said. "But since then, I've had time to think things out."

Holt asked Adcock, "What time did you arrive at the Davis home to await Davis's arrival, and when did he return?"

"It was after *Dead or Alive* and about halfway through *Daniel Boone*," Adcock said, referring to the popular television shows. His testimony lasted one hour, the same length of time he watched television at the Davis house—while Frank was out "doing something he should've done a long time ago." At that point, Holt ended his cross-examination of Adcock.

The state called other witnesses who were onsite during the shooting. Earl Peake, the owner of the Redbird Service Station and Laundromat (with his son Glen), said, "I know Frank Davis and waved to him as he drove in."

Thomas Mehalic, the laundromat customer who removed the children from the car after the shooting, told the jury he heard Mrs. Davis tell her husband she didn't want to have anything to do with him, and as he (Mehalic) got into his car, he heard the shot and saw the barrel of the gun.

Lloyd Love, a gas attendant at the service station, said Davis was a customer of the Redbird, but he did not see the actual shooting.

Bill Dever said he rushed to the scene after hearing the report of a shooting on his radio at home and began taking pictures, later giving them to the prosecuting attorney's office. The court admitted into evidence only seven of Dever's eleven murder scene photos.

Pauline Knight, Sharron's mother, was the last person called before prosecuting attorney Walter Wright announced he was resting his case. He walked to where she was sitting in the courtroom and escorted her to the witness chair. The *Sentinel-Record* later described her as "a frail woman 49 years old, the time her daughter was killed." (Pauline was actually fifty years old, only seven years older than Frank Davis.)

Pauline Knight said, "Sharron and the children and I had gone from the beauty shop to the Redbird Laundromat to dry clothes. Sharron was driving, and she had gone inside the laundromat when Frank drove up in the opposite direction from where our car was parked, and he parked opposite to us. He asked me to roll down the window, and thinking he wanted to see the children, I got out and walked between the cars. He was smiling. Then he mumbled something, and I said, 'Frank why don't you leave Sharron alone?' Then he asked if Sharron would give him a divorce, and I assured him that she would. Then he left, but when Sharron came out of the laundromat and got back into the car, he drove back up and called 'Sharron.' She said, 'I am tired and do not want to be embarrassed,' and he shot her. I either put the baby I was holding on the seat or the floor of the car and ran into the laundromat to call for help when I was hit by a bullet and fell inside the door."

When Pauline Knight was finished, Wright escorted her back to her gallery seat. Jack Holt declined to examine Mehalic, Love, and Peake; a number of other state witnesses; and Pauline Knight. After she was seated, Judge Britt invoked the rule on witnesses, excluding them from the courtroom during the trial.

The evening newspaper was quick to get the story out after the witnesses' testimony. The *Hot Springs New Era* front-page headline read in boldface type, "Admits Wife's Slaying, Death Penalty Asked at Frank Davis Trial as Testimony Begins."

In this second day of coverage, the newspaper was already speculating on a quick trial. "The admission by the defense of the shooting, which came as somewhat of a surprise, is expected to shorten, to some extent the number of witnesses, but it is unlikely that the case will reach the jury today," it stated.[3]

Faking Bad

On the third day of the trial, Thursday, June 13, 1967, the defense questioned Frank's family and friends. Jack Holt called Frank's second wife, Shirley, to the stand.

"I was married to him from 1958 to 1961, and he was an insanely jealous person, which was a lot of our trouble," said the woman, whose friends thought she could handle his erratic behavior.[1]

"The jealousy started on our honeymoon, and he would make up things," she said. "My opinion, he's mentally ill. I was afraid of him. I've seen him destroy things and cry like a baby at times, but when he was acting normal, you couldn't have asked for a better husband. We were divorced because I was afraid of him. He was so unreasonable."

Other witnesses called by the defense to testify to Frank's unusual and erratic actions and drinking problems included the following: M. J. (Pat) Storey, vice president of Resort Ford; John W. Harmon, salesperson at Resort Ford; Fred Ingle, assistant manager at the Majestic Hotel, who said he prepared income tax returns for Irene and Frank Davis; Robert Glen Reynolds, a truck stop operator in Arkadelphia and former close associate of Frank's; Martin Bradley and Joe T. Smith, blacksmiths; Everett Brown, racetrack mutuels employee and renter at Irene Davis Hogan's Henderson Street address; Ethel Greenberg, employee of Irene's; Will Rogers, manager of the Farmer's Association Feed Store; and Troy Carter, dairyman.

Some admitted on cross-examination that Frank Davis's actions were probably no different than any other person under the influence of alcohol, but others told of witnessing his "fits" of temper and tantrums, which he called "cuss fights," with relatives and actual fights with others at his ranch on Blacksnake Road. Some of the witnesses claimed Frank would often fall on his face, paw the earth, and cry, and on at least one occasion, one of the witnesses said they saw him chase and throw rocks at a truck on the highway as it passed between cattle he was driving across the road.

Carter recalled seeing Frank Davis angry to the point where he tore up an electric blanket and the headboard of a bed. Then afterward, Frank told him, "You better not tell anybody." Carter wouldn't express his opinion of Davis's sanity but added, "I've seen no one else act like him."

Dr. Vernon Sammons (who coincidentally lived up the street from the family of Frank's third wife, Carrie) told the prosecutors, "I performed surgery on and administered treatment to Davis from November 1962 through June 1965. Although I had found him an unsatisfactory patient who could not be depended on to do what he was supposed to, at no time did I think it necessary to suggest psychiatric treatment."

The pace of witness testimony changed when Jack Holt opened the railing door that separated the gallery from the bar and welcomed his client's mother, Irene Davis Hogan, to the witness stand. Holt moved quickly through topics, such as Frank's education, military service, and health, arriving at his employment.

Irene talked of Frank's job as a cattle inspector and then answered other questions concerning her son's business acumen.

Standing in the well in front of Irene on the witness stand, Holt asked, "Did he later on go in business for himself?"

"Well, he's never been in a real business for himself, I would say, other than just ranching and farming," she replied.

"And what did the ranching and farming consist of?" he asked.

"Well, he had cattle . . . a herd of Black Angus and some Brahman . . . we had horses, and we had sheep before this together."

"Were you interested in this ranching venture with him?" Holt asked.

"Yes, I always managed things because I felt that I had to."

"You did what?" he asked.

"I always managed these because I financed . . ."

"Did you manage the financial end of it . . . because you thought you had to?"

"That's right," she said.

"Would you tell the jury why you thought you had to?"

"Because he was not stable enough to take care of it. I could not turn it over to him because his ideas were too large for our amount of money that we had control of. And I had to control it," she explained.

Holt may have stopped, wanting Irene's last statement to linger. He was establishing Frank's insanity case and needed the jury to remember her words.

After covering Frank's four marriages, Holt circled back to the second and asked, "Were you ever present when his wife at that time would beg the defendant to go see a psychiatrist?"

"Well, she talked with me about it," Irene answered.

"Did you talk to your son also about seeing a psychiatrist?"

"Oh, yes, many times."

"Now when did you first observe, if you did, the conduct of your son Frank and his actions that caused you to suggest psychiatric treatment?" he asked.

"When he was married. Well, I think that it's been at least twenty years I've known that he needed it," she replied.

"Twenty years?" he asked.

"Yes."

"Did this condition exist during the period of time that he was married to the four women we have talked about?"

"Yes."

Holt checked off each item on his insanity case list and now wanted to address Frank's addictions and irresponsibility. "He would drink every day?" he asked.

"As far as I know, he did."

"Where would he put the empty bottles, if there were any empty bottles?" he asked.

"Oh, he just threw them anywhere. I picked them up in the yard and—"

"Most anywhere?"

"Yes."

"What other?" he asked.

"I also found bottles of vodka and other liquor. Vodka especially. Hidden all over the house."

"What were some of the things, if any, that he did in your presence that caused you to think, if you did think, he wasn't acting normal?" he asked.

"Well, he wouldn't take care of his property or his cattle. He neglected them, and he always had big ideas of buying more land and more cattle. In fact, he was on a deal with Q. Byrum Hurst [a prominent Hot Springs attorney] to buy his home and cattle at one time, and he didn't even have the money to buy it."

Frank couldn't react to his mother's statements as he had in the past by throwing a punch if anyone assassinated his character. He had to remain silent as she revealed the embarrassing secrets about him.

"Well, that reminds me," Holt said. "Do you remember the time when there were three new cars bought almost right together?"

"Yes."

"Approximately when was that?"

"That was when the '67 models came out in late '66," she said.

"What need did he have for these three cars?"

"He didn't have any need for any of them. He needed a pickup."

"Is it true that Mr. Brown and the officials of the Ford Motor Company here refused to sell him the cars until they came out there and got your okay?" he asked.

"That's right. They called and asked me."

"What were those three new cars?" he asked.

"A Thunderbird . . . a Fairlane convertible, and then I don't know whether it was a GTO or whatever the sport model is of Fords. He bought that."

"Now, did he have a truck or two at that time also?"

"He had two trucks," she said.

"Did he at the time have dreams of grandeur? By that, I mean he just felt like he was a millionaire, and he could buy anything he wanted to?"

"Oh yes, he always . . . he's had that for many years," she responded.

"Did he at times seem depressed when he couldn't buy anything?" Holt asked.

"Oh, he was depressed that he didn't seem in need to go on living at all, wasn't anything to live for," she said.

Holt was pleased with Irene's answers and the positive direction his insanity case was taking. He was serving the jury a full-course meal and wanted it to be hearty enough to stay with them when they reached deliberations.

"This is your only son?" Holt asked.

"That's right," she answered.

"Your only child?"

"He's my only child."

"Were you home on January 19, 1967, when some young man came to your home, I believe by the name of Adcock, is that right?" he asked.

"I was home, yes. A boy by the name of Terry," she said.

"When did you get there?"

"That evening, I went home about six or shortly after."

"Now when you got home, was Adcock there?" he asked.

"Yes," she said.

"What was he doing?"

"He had a drink in his hand. He was drinking."

"Now, was your son, Frank Davis, there at the time you got home and found Adcock in your home drinking?" he asked.

"Yes, he was there because he went home to wait for a telephone call."

"All right, what happened then? What was the next thing—what did your son do? What was the next thing he did that you know of?" he asked.

"I went ahead preparing our dinner, and I thought he was going to be there, and he said, 'I've got to run some place.' And I said, 'Well, I pulled my car up.' I was driving the Thunderbird at the time, and I said, 'I pulled my car up.'"

"Yes."

"What color?" he asked.

"It's light blue," she said.

"You were driving it?" he asked.

"I had been driving it to work and back, and I pulled it in the carport behind the car that he was driving. He was driving the convertible."

"Now what color was the convertible?"

"Aqua," Irene said.

"He was driving that, and you pulled in behind him?" he asked.

"Yes, I did."

"All right, then what happened?"

"Then I told him, when he got ready to go. I said, 'Well, wait a minute, I'll move my car,' and he said, 'No, that's all right. I'll just take that car. It won't make any difference. I'll just run in this one.' So, he left in that car."

"When you got home, you parked behind the car he had been driving, which was the aqua car?"

"That's true," she answered.

"You were driving the Thunderbird?" he asked.

"Yes."

"When he got ready to leave, you told him his car was blocked but you'd move it, and he said, 'Well that's okay, don't worry, that's all right,' something like that?" he asked.

"Yes, that's right," said Irene.

"Do you know whether or not there was any gun in the Thunderbird at the time?"

"I do know that there was this old 30-30 he had in his pickup [that] he carried for many years. And when he bought the car down at the Ford Motor Company and traded his pickup in, he transferred this old gun over to the back of the Thunderbird, and there it stayed," she said.

"And it stayed there from the day he brought the Thunderbird home until this particular time when he drove off in the car you had been driving?"

"Yes, sir."

"He left. Now, approximately how long was it until he returned home, if he did?" he asked.

"Well it didn't seem very long, but I don't know exactly the time, but he came back in the back door," said Irene.

"He came to the back door?" he asked.

"Yes."

"All right, when he came to the back door, did he knock on the door or just come on in the house?"

"No, just rushed in. He looked very upset, and he walked or ran practically to his bedroom, and I followed to see what was wrong. And by the time I got there, he had already . . . he had the pistol at his temple. There was a pistol in the drawer, and he had it cocked, ready to pull the trigger, and I just grabbed it," she said.

"Did he ever say anything to you, that you could understand?"

"Not that I could understand," she said. "He just looked like he was just so disturbed that I—I'd never seen such a wild look in his eyes before. And I didn't know what—"

"You walked in, and he had this pistol to his temple. What did you do?" he asked.

"I grabbed him and the pistol at the same time, and I said, 'Don't do it! You'll kill me!' And then, he just fell."

"Where did he fall?"

"He fell right at the edge of the bed. He was standing at the edge of the bed, and he fell there. He was half on and half off the bed, and I took the pistol out of his hand because I was afraid it would be discharged, and by that time, the officers were there."

"When the officers got there, did you still have the pistol in your hand?" he asked.

"I did."

"What did you do with it?" he asked.

"I just handed it to them because I didn't know how to release it or anything," she said.

"Now, how long were they at the house before your son was removed, the law?" he finally asked.

"Well, I don't know how long. But he was, I thought, dying. And they worked with him. They worked his arms and kept trying to move him and to raise him up and keep him breathing because he was—"

"How did they take him out of the house?"

"On a stretcher. The ambulance came after him," she said.

"Did he ever say anything to you or in your presence that you could understand from the time he came in the house until they took him away on a stretcher?"

Downtown Hot Springs, Arkansas, circa 1966. *Courtesy of Garland County Historical Society*

The Southern Club, located in the middle of downtown Hot Springs, Arkansas, was the popular hangout of gangsters Al Capone and Lucky Luciano decades earlier. *Courtesy of Garland County Historical Society*

Cathie Ward and Bettye Jo Tucker side by side in their fifth-grade class picture, 1963–1964. *Courtesy of Bettye Jo Tucker Wilson*

Cathie Ward's seventh-grade (1966) photo hangs in her father's Murfreesboro, Arkansas, home. *Courtesy of Dr. Hiram Ward*

Cathie wrote in Bettye Jo Tucker's seventh-grade autograph book at the end of the school year. A month later, Bettye Jo penciled in Cathie's death date. *Courtesy of Bettye Jo Tucker Wilson*

Cathie forgot her skateboard at Leslie Tracy's house days before her death, and it became Leslie's lifelong cherished object. *Courtesy of the author*

Girl Killed In Horseback Riding Accident

Catherine Ann Ward, 13, daughter of Mrs. Sarah Ward of 1003 Prospect Ave., was killed Friday in an accident at the Davis Ranch on Black Snake Road.

The girl was apparently dragged to death by a horse she was riding when her foot caught in a stirrup, Garland County sheriff's deputies reported.

Allen Frank Davis, owner of the ranch which specializes in horse rentals, pursued the running horse but was unable to catch it before the girl was killed.

Deputies Talmadge Mayben and Marvin Teague investigated after being notified of the accident at 3:45 p. m.

Dr. William Mashburn, county coroner, said an official report giving the cause of death will be filed when an investigation of the accident is concluded.

The body was taken by ambulance to Gross Mortuary.

Cathie Ward's front-page news ends with a listing of her family members and information of her 1:00 funeral (less than twenty-four hours after her death). Hot Springs New Era, *June 25, 1966*

A 2018 photo of the ghostly Blacksnake Ranch tack shed where kids would mount their horses in 1966 and then head to the riding paths. *Courtesy of the author*

Frank would jump off a nearby cliff atop his horse into a deep pool of water at Bull Bayou Creek on the eastern border of Blacksnake Ranch. *Courtesy of the author, 2018*

Frank Davis kept an undated photo of himself in his personal belongings. *Courtesy of Fredrick Davis, Frank's youngest son by Sharron Knight Davis*

MAYOR DAN E. WOLF PROCLAIMS:
NATIONAL BEAUTY SALON WEEK, FEB. 10-16
Local Unit President Irene Davis, left, and Local Chairman Burla Love, are pictured with the Mayor.

Irene Davis (left) in a 1963 newspaper advertisement, the only known photo of Frank Davis's mother. Hot Springs New Era, *February, 1963*

KNIGHT, Sharon . . . Spring Graduate.
LACY, Robert Wayne . . . Student Council 1,3.
LANE, Vicky Carol . . . Cheerleader 2; Basketball Homecoming Maid 1; Student Council 1; Peppers 1; Thespians 3.

LEE, David . . . Golf Team 1,2,3; Student Council 1,3; Beta Club 2,3, Vice-President 3; Homeroom President 1,2; Old Gold Book 3; Junior Classical League, President 2;

Sharron Knight's 1962 senior class photo. Fifteen months later, she would become Frank's fourth wife hours after his divorce became final from his third wife. HSHS 1962 Old Gold Book, *courtesy of Melting Pot Genealogical Society*

Frank Davis spies his estranged wife Sharron Davis at the Redbird Laundromat on January 19, 1967, and an argument leads to a shooting. *Copyrighted photo by permission of Bill Dever*

Frank Davis's close-up rifle blast pushes Sharron across the front seat where her mother Pauline had just been holding baby Fredrick. *Copyrighted photo by permission of Bill Dever*

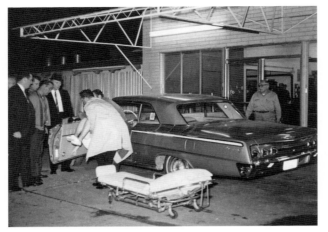

Sharron is moved to an ambulance stretcher under the watchful eyes of Lieutenant Detective Douglas (hat), Municipal Judge Mazander (tan sweater), Detective Bobby Digby (suit), and Redbird owner Earl Peake, standing by the laundromat's back door. *Copyrighted photo by permission of Bill Dever*

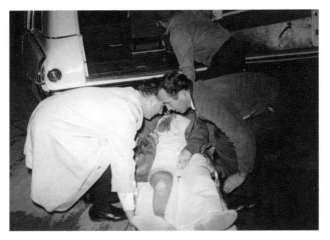

Blood can be seen on Sharron's white beauty shop uniform as she's hoisted into Gross Ambulance, which took her twelve blocks away to Ouachita Hospital. *Copyrighted photo by permission of Bill Dever*

Sharron's mother, Pauline Knight, screams as she runs for help into the laundromat, where she's felled by a bullet from Frank Davis's 30-30 rifle. *Copyrighted photo by permission of Bill Dever*

A 30-30 bullet hole view of Hot Springs police talking to Redbird Laundromat customers after the shootings. *Copyrighted photo by permission of Bill Dever*

Hot Springs residents are elated to read the June 18, 1968, news that Frank Davis will fry, but they don't know they're in for a big surprise. Hot Springs New Era, *June 15, 1968*

Frank Davis tools himself a prison briefcase. *Courtesy of Fredrick Davis*

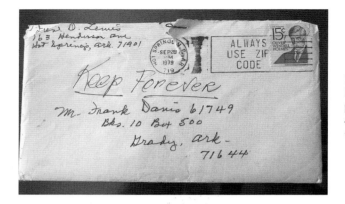

Frank stuffs an envelope with letters from his prison pen pals—his mother, his fifth wife, and a friend named Oran. *Courtesy of Fredrick Davis*

Arkansas Department of Corrections inmate #61749 inventories his personal belongings. *Courtesy of Fredrick Davis*

This tattered piece of paper, found in Frank's briefcase, proves that his guitar playing evolved into songwriting during his incarceration. *Courtesy of Fredrick Davis*

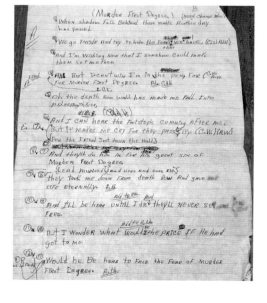

"No, not that I could ever understand. He was more or less groaning or just wasn't saying anything, and the officers told me when they came in what had happened."

"You were close to him all of that time?"

"Yes, I was. I was afraid to leave because I thought he was dying."

"Had he made any statement that was understandable? You were close enough to him to hear what he was saying?"

"Oh, yes, I was right by his side," said Irene.

Wanting the jury to understand the importance of his question, he once again asked, "And he made no statements?"

"No," she replied.

Holt maneuvered through every area of his insanity agenda but the obvious. He saved that for last.

"Now, prior to the time the officers got there, was there any, or rather when the officers got there, did they say anything about this rifle you're talking about, that you told about a few minutes ago?"

"No, the officers didn't say anything to me at the time about it. They later said they were trying to find the gun," she said.

"Did you give them any information about the gun?" he asked.

"I told them I didn't know where it was, but he ran through the backyard, and for them to search back there."

"And did they go back and search?" he asked.

"They searched back there and found the rifle."

"They searched and found the rifle back there?"

"Yes," said Irene.

Holt turned and looked at Walter Wright, sitting at the plaintiff's table. "You may take the witness."

Ben Harrison, the deputy prosecuting attorney, stood and looked at Judge Britt. "If it please the court, this is going to take a little time. Would you like to break for lunch or—?"

Britt replied, "What's the pleasure of both of you?"

Frank's attorney, Ridgeway, said, "We vote in favor of eating."

When the jury came back from lunch recess, they were digesting not only what they'd just eaten but also the substance of Irene Davis Hogan's morning session with Jack Holt. And now with deputy prosecuting attorney Walter Wright getting his turn with Frank's mother, they had more to consume.

Wanting to prove Frank Davis's sanity and knowing his mother might not be that helpful, Wright was brief with his cross-examination of Irene Davis Hogan. He asked only thirty-four questions, clarifying previous testimony on the automobiles, her finances in relation to Frank's businesses and home,

Frank's mental state the evening of Sharron's murder, and the rifle. Then he posed one of his questions—based on testimony of Frank being unstable during his four marriages, spanning twenty years—to help substantiate the state's sanity agenda. "During this period of time, it's my understanding that you didn't take any steps to have Frank committed. Is that correct?" he asked.

"The only step I took to try to get him committed, really sending him to a doctor, was when I sent him to San Antonio with his wife in July. And we talked it over and tried—thought we might get him in without his knowing what we were doing," Irene admitted.

Wright let her answer slide and then asked, "On direct examination, did I understand your testimony to be that when Frank entered, reentered the home after he left for a few minutes, that he didn't say anything you could understand, in fact made no statement?"

"No, he made no statement," said Irene.

"To you or to any person that you might—"

"No, he did not."

"Why then, when the officers came in, did you tell the officers that you did not know where the rifle was if it was supposed to be in the back of the blue T-Bird?" he asked, trying to discredit her testimony.

"I said that he didn't bring the rifle in, and they said it was not in the car, and I said, 'I don't know where it is, but search the yard. Search all around there, you have my permission.'"

Wright said, "I also understood your testimony to be, 'Frank looked so disturbed, had a wild look, ran into the bedroom, I knew something was wrong and went immediately to the bedroom, and Frank had the pistol cocked and to his temple.'"

"That's right," said Irene.

"Yet, as soon as you said, 'You might kill me,' Frank released the pistol and fell down and collapsed. Is that correct?"

"That's correct."

Wright, satisfied that he had driven his point home, looked at Judge Britt and said, "I have no further questions."

Dr. Sheldon Fowler, staff psychiatrist at the Arkansas State Hospital from 1961 through 1968, took the stand as Jack Holt's medical expert.

Dr. Fowler told him, "I examined him [Frank] in 1967 on February 3, 8, 9, 13, and 27 for a total of 10-1/2 hours."[2]

Dr. Fowler reported the state hospital staff was unanimous in its opinion that Davis was a depressive reaction, manic type, which he described in lengthy detail and as one of the major forms of psychosis. He said based on his examination and findings, he was of the opinion that at the time of the alleged crime, Frank Davis was very disturbed and psychotic to the point where he did not know the nature and quality of the act he was doing. The physician told of the many tests and laboratory work he had requested for Davis during the time he was at the hospital and said that Davis had been interviewed before the entire staff before its report was made.

When prosecuting attorney Walter Wright cross-examined Dr. Fowler regarding his medical evaluations and prognosis, he stated, "Specialists differ."

Wright then picked up two pieces of paper. "Here's a report by clinical psychologist Bernice Burns of Little Rock, and on the second page, it has two words I don't understand, 'fake bad.'"

Dr. Fowler waited a minute to respond. "*Fake bad* means a person might be putting on a show to make people think he was sicker than he really was."

Some gallery spectators looked at Frank to see his reaction to Dr. Fowler's statement.

Wright said, "Burns, the clinical psychologist, says in the summary, 'This patient seems to be functioning within the average range of intelligence. Current test results do not show unquestionable evidence that would support a psychotic reaction.'"

Dr. Fowler replied, "Some manic types can be productive citizens, can be normal five years at a time probably, and not need to be hospitalized."

He added, "Davis's failure to go to a psychiatrist even though urged to do so by his mother and one of his ex-wives was a 'normal reaction.'"

Fowler explained that "a man with psychosis is very resistant to change and will put up all kinds of excuses and be very disagreeable." He said Davis's medical history showed he had been taking drugs for his nerves, narcotics, barbiturates, and sleeping pills for ten to fifteen years.

Concluding his cross-examination with the clinical psychologist's summary of Frank Davis, Wright said, "There was no evidence to support a psychotic reaction."

⌒

Jack Holt hurried to get his next witness to the stand. He was counting on Dr. Robert F. Shannon to boost the level of the insanity plea with his medical authority.

The private-practice psychiatrist told him, "I've examined Davis on two occasions, the first on February 25, 1967, in the state hospital at the request of Mrs. Hogan [Frank's mother, Irene] and the second on January 20, 1968, in the Garland County Jail. I recommended in 1967 that Davis be confined for treatment and care of his emotional disturbance."

Dr. Shannon continued. "It was my opinion that, because of his disease of the mind, Davis was not responsible for his actions at the time of the shooting. I think at the time of the alleged offense, Davis was suffering from a mental disease. It's questionable that Davis would have known right from wrong or that he could control his impulses due to the alcohol and drug intake."

Holt asked, "What was your diagnosis?"

"I found the defendant with manic-depressive psychosis, severe and chronic and of a high type, and with an acute brain syndrome due to excessive alcohol and a type of tranquilizer. I have statements from a number of persons regarding Davis's condition and had talked with Dr. Fowler before forming my opinion."

"That will be all for the defense, Your Honor," Holt told Judge Britt.

Walter Wright then approached the witness stand where Dr. Shannon was still seated. "If proof were presented that Davis did rational and purposeful acts and that his behavior and conversation were normal immediately before, during, and after the crime, would that have influenced your evaluation?" he asked.

"I would have been surprised, but that would not have changed my feelings," Dr. Shannon replied.

Wright ended his cross-examination.

The trial kept a brutal pace that by Thursday, June 13, may have caused the jurors to experience what's known in judicial circles as the "third-day slump." It's like running a marathon and hitting the wall at mile twenty. It was time for them to go home and relax without reading the newspaper with the trial coverage or watching the evening news that might report the day's testimony. But the hardest task they had to endure while away from their jury seats was avoiding the prying questions by their family and friends.

· 22 ·

The Psychiatrists' Say

𝒯he twelve jurors and two alternates weren't privy to the *Sentinel-Record's* front-page headline on Friday morning, June 14, 1968, which announced, "Murder Trial Continues, Psychiatrists Testify Davis Suffering From Mental Illness."[1] The story lead stated, "The two Little Rock psychiatrists who'd testified most of yesterday afternoon said that, in their opinion, Frank Davis, because of mental illness, was not responsible for his actions the night of January 19, 1967, when he shot and killed his estranged wife, Sharon [*sic*], 22."

Prosecuting attorney Walter Wright had listened to the defense's psychiatric-medical experts from the Arkansas State Hospital give their opinions of Frank Davis's insanity. So today, on the fourth day of the trial, his plan was to prove otherwise with two practicing psychiatrists from Hot Springs.

Dr. Robert Lewis, employed by the Hot Springs Rehabilitation Center, was his first rebuttal witness. Wright questioned his medical and psychiatric education, credentials, and employment and then asked, "Did you complete a three-year psychiatry and neurology residency in 1965?"

"Yes," he said.

"Do you know Frank Davis?" Wright asked.

Jack Holt leapt out of his chair and walked up to the bench, where a conference was held out of the hearing of the jury.

Judge Britt called a five-minute recess for a conference in the chambers.

Inside the private room, Jack Holt explained his objections to Lewis's testimony. He said, "It would be inadmissible and in violation of privileged communication between client and between doctor and patient."

Deputy prosecuting attorney Ben Harrison then explained, "I believe this is a fact, that Dr. Lewis was employed by the defendant's mother through another doctor; however, I don't know whether it was a personal contact between Dr. Lewis and Frank Davis's mother, but at any rate, he was told to go see Frank by a doctor who said that Mrs. Davis had contacted him."

Harrison noted Arkansas Statute 43-2004, which generally provides that civil procedure would govern in the compelling of witnesses to testify.

He stated another statute that contained a provision providing the state the opportunity to use Lewis's testimony because the defense had also called a private-practice psychiatrist (Dr. Shannon) who was employed by the defendant (Frank's mother). In essence, the state blindsided the defense by calling Irene Davis Hogan's privately paid physician to cross over and testify for them.

A lengthy discussion ensued, resulting in Judge Britt stating, "The court is going to permit Dr. Lewis to testify, but the state will be precluded from asking Dr. Lewis questions he propounded to the defendant or responses from the defendant to Lewis. Your objections are noted, exceptions noted."

The four men returned to the courtroom, and Judge Britt went back to the bench.

Wright walked up to Lewis, waiting in the witness stand, and said, "I recall, Doctor, my last question was, 'Do you know Frank Davis?'"

Lewis said, "Yes," then pointed to Davis when Wright asked him to do so.

"Within the past two years, have you seen Frank Davis professionally?" he asked.

"I saw Davis twice, once on January 19, 1967, and again on the following day, both at the city jail for a total of something over an hour," Lewis replied.

"If it has been testified to here that Davis is manic-depressive, manic reaction type, at the time of the killing," Wright said, "would you observe anything in Davis's conduct and demeanor that would indicate manic behavior at the time?"

"No," said Lewis.

"Did you attend Frank Davis, or did you see Frank Davis for medical treatment or psychiatric evaluation? Which one?"

"I feel like it was both," said Lewis.

"Pass the witness," Wright said after making his point.

Knowing Wright won that fight, Jack Holt responded, "No questions. Thank you, Doctor."

Judge Britt asked Lewis to step down.

Walter Wright next called Dr. Charles Yohe, a staff consultant at the Benton unit of the state hospital with a Hot Springs medical practice located in the Medical Arts Building. Wright asked Yohe forty-seven questions in total concerning his education, medical training and residency, medical armed services experience, employment, and professional credentials before inquiring, "Doctor, do you know Frank Davis?"

"Yes, sir," said Yohe.

"Do you see him in the courtroom?"

"Yes, sir."

"Let the record show that Dr. Yohe pointed to the defendant, Frank Davis," said Wright to Irene Larsen, court deputy clerk and court stenographer.

"Doctor, were you asked by my office to make a psychiatric evaluation of Frank Davis?"

"Yes, sir."

"Was it with specific reference to the date of January 19, 1967?"

"Yes, sir."

"Doctor, with reference to that, did you have interviews and conversations with Frank Davis?" Wright asked.

Robert Ridgeway jumped up from his seat at the defense counsel table and approached the bench. He said, "I request a conference in your chambers, Your Honor."

Judge Britt, Frank's attorneys Ridgeway and Holt, and state prosecutors Wright and Harrison went to the judge's chambers, where Ridgeway objected to Yohe's testimony. He stated three points. The second, Arkansas Statute 43-101, he said, "is unconstitutional in that it provides for an invasion of the privacy of the defendant, as well as a violation of the provision against self-incrimination."

Harrison responded, "Stature 43-1301 specifically provides that the state and the defendant shall have free access, and I believe the words used, 'for observation and examination during the period of his commitment.' Now, that is the statutory law for the State of Arkansas. The prosecution for the State of Arkansas must recognize the constitutionality of its statutes. We cannot question it, and we therefore stand on this specific provision and authorization made and provided under the statutes."

Judge Britt conducted a discussion between both sides, with a last objection being presented by Ridgeway.

After a brief question-and-answer session with Ridgeway in the presence of the other three men, Judge Britt said, "Well, I'm going to hold the statute constitutional, and I'm going to overrule the objections, and exceptions are saved."

The state won this skirmish, and Wright now had the opportunity to emphasize his main objective to convince the jury Frank wasn't insane when he murdered his wife—beginning with Yohe's testimony.

The five men returned to the courtroom, where Wright clarified the process by which Yohe examined and evaluated Frank Davis. After the doctor was finished, Wright asked, "All right, sir. If you would, would you state what your psychiatric evaluation was on conclusions?"

"I didn't find him insane at the time of my examination a year ago, and from all I could gather, I didn't think he was insane at the time of the murder of his wife on January 19, 1967," he said.

Wright struck a home run, but no team had taken the lead.

"Doctor, if I may, I'd like to ask you some general propositions. Is it true that manic-depressive reaction is a mood disorder?" Wright asked.

"Yes, it's often referred to that way," Yohe told him.

"Is it true that a mood disorder such as manic-depressive reaction has nothing to do with external events?" Wright asked.

"Well, by and large, these things, manic-depressive psychosis, come about all by themselves pretty much independent of what's going on," Yohe said. "You can't rule out external events completely in some cases."

"Does heredity, or is heredity significant in this type of diagnosis, manic-depressive?"

"Very much more," Yohe said. "Probably more than any other common mental illness, this one is considered to have hereditary roots."

"Is it true that manic-depressive reaction does not often produce criminal acts?" asked Wright.

"That's right," Yohe said. "Usually, you don't associate criminal acts with manic-depressive psychosis."

"By criminal acts, would that include acts of violence?" Wright asked.

"Yes, with the one exception of suicide."

"Doctor, if there were facts in evidence, if believed that Frank Davis attempted to take his life immediately after the killing of Sharron Davis, would that mean to you that it was a sign of remorse, or would it mean to you that it was a symptom of manic-depressive manic reaction, considering the other matters you have in your psychiatric evaluation?" asked Wright.

"Well, I, I think remorse would be more, more it," Yohe said.

"If there were facts in evidence that immediately prior to, at the time of, and immediately after that Frank Davis had meaningful and purposeful conversations and actions, what would this indicate to you?"

"Well, it indicates that probably no psychosis of any type was present," Yohe replied.

Wright hit another home run.

"From your, for lack of a better word, let me use a layman term, 'investigation' or 'examination' of Frank Davis," said Wright, "all those things that you said you did and all those things you used in your psychiatric evaluation, would you say that Frank Davis on the evening of January 19, 1967, was under such a defect of reasoning from disease of the mind as not to know the nature and quality of the act he was doing?"

"No, I would say he was not suffering from any such defect," Yohe replied.

"If he did know it, meaning the nature and quality of the act he was doing, that he did not know what he was doing was wrong?"

"I think he knew it was wrong," said Yohe.

"Now if Frank Davis knew the nature and quality of his act and knew it was wrong," Wright said and paused, "that he was under such duress of mental disease as to be unable, because of the disease, to resist the doing of the wrong act." He stopped and then asked, "Was the result solely of his mental disease?"

"I do not believe that he was under any such duress, and I think he could have resisted the act," Yohe said.

Jack Holt stood up and said, "If the court [Judge Britt] please. I object to leading the witness. Let him ask him what his psychiatric evaluation was rather than telling him in advance what he wants to say."

Wright replied, "If the court please, this is an expert witness. The qualifications of Dr. Yohe have not been challenged, and leading questions are not prohibited with an expert witness."

Britt said, "Go ahead and ask him."

Holt added, "Note my exceptions."

Wright said, "In line with the question that I previously asked you, is it your opinion that Frank Davis did or did not on the evening of January 19, 1967, know the difference between right and wrong?"

"I think he did know the difference between right and wrong," said Yohe.

"Pass the witness," Wright said to Judge Britt.

Holt questioned Yohe regarding his qualifications, past employment, association with the Arkansas State Hospital, and experience with manic-depressive reaction cases. He scrutinized Yohe's review of Frank Davis's state hospital–provided medical documents and his participation in the testimony given by state witnesses.

Holt said, "Now you say that usually a man who has suffered manic depression, I'm going to change that so I can understand it. He's either insane or off his rocker, or he's nuts, or he's not competent. Now that I can understand that sort of thing, usually he doesn't resort to criminal acts. Is that right?"

"Usually, not in my experience—" Yohe said, as Holt cut him off with a quick question of his experience with manic depressives.

Deputy prosecutor Harrison said, "Now, let the witness answer the question, if Mr. Holt wants to examine him. The witness is trying to answer the question, and he interrupts."

Britt replied, "Mr. Holt, I think you're being argumentative."

Prosecuting attorney Walter Wright stated, "I would like to hear the answer. I know I didn't hear it, and probably the jury didn't, about his experience with manic-depressive reaction."

Holt said, "I'm talking about cases similar to this. How much experience have you had with cases similar to this, of this magnitude?"

"I think we all see manic depressives all the time in private practice," said Yohe.

"You are evading my question. I said with cases of this magnitude?" Holt snapped.

"Oh, I suppose—" Yohe continued.

Deputy prosecutor Harrison said, "If the court please, let him explain what he means by cases of this magnitude?"

Defense attorney Robert Ridgeway said, "He understood the question Your Honor. He started to answer it."

"If you mean murder cases, I suppose I've been in on forty or fifty of them in the last twenty years," Yohe replied.

"How many in Arkansas?" Holt shot back.

"Oh, I suppose this is the third or fourth one in Arkansas," Yohe replied.

Satisfied with Yohe's response, Holt asked him about his employment by the state for Davis's murder trial. Holt then highlighted the state hospital medical professionals' findings and questioned him of his time line and interpretations of those evaluations.

Holt asked, "Did you check the names to see who was on the staff, who voted that this man was suffering from a mental illness and that he wasn't competent for his acts and recommended hospital treatments?"

"Yes," said Yohe.

"You must remember that you saw the decision was unanimous?" Holt asked.

"I've heard that since, but I don't recollect that on June 14, 1967, I noted that fact."

"Well, as a matter of fact, whether the decision was unanimous or not, you were going to decide it the way you wanted to decide it, weren't you?" Holt asked.

"I made up my own mind, all by myself," Yohe replied.

"All by yourself. And in making up that mind, did you have a statement or the evidence of anybody from the Ford Motor Company here about the defendant buying three new cars within a short time and the condition in which he was at the time he bought them?" asked Holt. "Did you have that evidence?"

"I hear that he bought the cars in a rather short period of time."

"Did you have that when you were considering your psychiatric evaluation?"

"Yes, sir," said Yohe.

Holt brought up testimony from the first day, where his defense witnesses related stories of Frank Davis's unusual behavior.

"Suppose it's in evidence and that you had it at the time you made this evaluation, and if you believed it to be true, that Martin Bradley, a blacksmith who knew him well, shod a lot of horses for the defendant, and at times, for no apparent reason, he would get mad and fall over on his head, beat his head on the ground, and then get up and hit his horse with his fist?" Holt asked. "Would that tell you anything?"

"That would tell me that he had a violent temper," Yohe replied.

"If the defendant and some parties were out rounding up his cattle out in the road, and someone comes along in a truck eight or ten miles an hour, kind of drives through the cattle, and the defendant grabs up a rock and throws it at the truck and chases it, and then when he doesn't catch it, he comes back and falls down on the ground and beats his head in the ground and his arms and all. Would that have anything to do with your—" Holt asked.

"Again, it would indicate quite a temper, yes."

"Quite a temper. But that's all he'd have, just a bad temper, wouldn't mean anything to you?"

"Nasty temper is quite a thing to note," Yohe replied.

"Oh, temper," Holt said. "And in the medical phraseology, haven't you often said that the madder a man gets, the crazier he is? And he gets so mad that temporarily he's insane. Isn't that true?"

"No, I would not say that to be true."

"You wouldn't say it? All right, then if at another time, he was trying to get his cattle up, and the cattle would run, would outrun his horse, and he couldn't get them up, and he just got down on the ground and beat his head and his hands and cried like a baby, mad again, eh?"

"Frustrated. Mad," Yohe replied.

"Have you ever known anybody like that in your life, personally?"

"Quite a few. Frustration is a pretty universal phenomenon," Yohe said.

Holt continued to give examples of Frank Davis's temper tantrums on the farm, his dreams of grandeur, and his depressive crying jags, and then he asked if those were normal reactions.

"That word 'normal' is a very slippery word," Yohe said. "In a certain sense, none of us are normal."

"You don't—" Holt began.

"If the court please." Wright stood up while addressing the judge. "If Mr. Holt will let Dr. Yohe complete his answer."

"Well, if he wants to argue with me, I guess I can argue back," Holt shot back. "He can say, yes or no. Now, he says 'normal' is a broad word. So is a Mother Hubbard skirt."

"If Mr. Holt didn't like the prior answer, he could have asked that it—" Wright added.

"I want him to answer my question," said Holt.

"Then let him," Judge Britt shot back.

"In your experience, as a human being and as a doctor and a psychiatrist, the people you've known, if this behavior has existed with this defendant, with the people you have known, is that normal?" He paused. "That's what I'm asking you."

"So many of us are," Yohe began.

"I'm asking is that normal behavior of the people you have known?" Holt said.

"The vast majorities seem capable of losing their temper."

"Answer the question," Holt said without a hint of kindness.

"One could call it normal," Yohe replied.

"It calls for a yes-or-no answer," Holt said.

Judge Britt said, "Doctor, answer the question. If you need to explain the answer, you may then do so."

"Well, let's hear the question again, please?" said Yohe.

"During all of your life as a student, as a doctor, as a psychiatrist, as a person who goes from here to there, I don't know where, it doesn't make any difference. The friends you know, if the things that I have stated have actually happened, can you name a single, solitary person that would act like this, and, if so, do you call it normal? Is that normal behavior on anybody that you have ever known?"

"Yes," said Yohe.

"Who?"

"Take a great many children, for instance," he said.

"Take one," said Holt.

"My own son, when he was six years old."

"He beats his head on the ground, chases cattle, rocks the car, and all that?" Holt asked.

"At age six, he sure did."

"Is that normal behavior in a boy?"

"I think we could say it's normal from the four- to six-year-old range, but it also carries on into all too many adults too," said Yohe.

"Did you do that when you were a little boy?" Holt asked.

"On a few occasions."

"Do you still do it?" asked Holt.

"No."

"Who's going to pay you for your testimony? Do you know?"

"I suppose Garland County," Yohe said.

"You expect to be paid?" asked Holt.

"I hope so."

Holt looked at Judge Britt and said, "I think I've got good news for the court. I have no further questions."

Walter Wright stood up. "The state rests. Dr. Yohe may be excused."

A conference between the court and counsel for both sides was held out of earshot of the jury. The judge called a ten-minute recess after its completion and then instructed the jury to go relax in the jury room without discussing the case.

The courtroom emptied as spectators from the gallery stood in the hallway, talking or smoking and waiting to go back inside. They didn't want to miss a moment of the dramatic murder case that was the talk of the town.

Judge Britt entered the courtroom after the jury filed back in, followed by the prosecutors, the defense, and Frank Davis. Once behind his bench, Britt announced, "The statute of the case is that both sides of the lawsuit have rested."

Wright and Holt agreed with the judge.

"As far as testimony is concerned, there is no more testimony. Is that correct?" Judge Britt asked.

Both Ben Harrison, for the state, and Bob Ridgeway, for the defense, answered, "Correct."

Judge Britt then recessed the court until 2:00 and said, "At the conclusion of arguments, if the twelve jurors in the box appear that they are going to proceed, then we will, at that time, dismiss the alternate jurors. Counsel for both sides will meet with the court in chambers at 12:30. And at this time, the court is going to admonish the jury again, do not discuss the case among yourselves or with anyone else. No one is to talk about the case in your presence; you are not to express or to form any opinion about the case until the case is finally submitted to you. As before, I must ask you that if anyone attempts to discuss this case or express an opinion or anything else in your presence, tell them not to do so. You should not read any newspapers that relates to this case, listen to the radio or television. If anyone attempts in any way, after you have asked them to cease and desist, please report it to the court, the names and addresses. In a nutshell, leave the case here until you get back at 2:00 and until the case is submitted to you. Are there any questions about the admonition? If not, court will be in recess until 2:00."

The courtroom was silent when Judge Britt stood up to leave. The gallery spectators rushed out—some excited, others anxious about the conclusion to Frank Davis's murder trial. The man who had brutally murdered his twenty-two-year-old wife, injured his mother-in-law, viciously murdered a thirteen-year-old girl, and allegedly drowned a young ranch hand was now at the mercy of the hearts and minds of twelve Hot Springs men. Would they treat him like his mother who'd coddled him all his life or reject him as his rodeo-guitar-playing buddies had after Sharron escaped their marriage?

· 23 ·

The Jury Deliberates

$\mathcal{B}$y Friday, June 14, 1968, the *Allen Frank Davis v. State of Arkansas* first-degree murder trial had seen thirty-three witnesses testify over two and a half days.[1] Then at 1:30 p.m., Judge Britt asked Walter Wright, "The state is ready?"

Wright stood up and answered, "The state is ready."

Britt then looked at the defense table, where Frank Davis sat in a white short-sleeved shirt, black belt, and khaki slacks. "Defense ready?"

Jack Holt stood and said, "The defense is ready."

Britt turned toward the jurors, and said, "Lady and gentlemen of the jury, you have heard the evidence, and it is now the court's duty to give you the law in the case."

Judge Britt carefully instructed the jury of the law that applied in the case. He defined the degrees of homicide and insanity, pointing out the difference between positive and circumstantial evidence. Britt urged jurors to "exercise common sense" as they deliberated. Then he gave the jury five verdicts to choose from: (1) guilty as charged, (2) guilty but with life imprisonment designated as the sentence, (3) guilty but of second-degree murder with a penalty of from five to twenty-one years, (4) innocent by reason of insanity, or (5) innocent.

Britt said, "Now gentlemen, when you retire to the jury room, your verdict must be unanimous. If you find the defendant guilty of either murder in the first or second degree, whatever your verdict might be in that respect, it must be signed by one of your members as foreman, and at the appropriate time, I will hand you the proper forms of the various verdicts, which I have related to you. Gentlemen, anything further?"

145

No one responded, prompting Britt to say, "If you will give your attention to the attorneys, they will present their arguments in the case."

Wright stood before the jury and recalled how the killing had been admitted by the defendant, termed it "a cold-blooded murder, murder in the first Degree," and reiterated the state's request for the death penalty.

He told them, "Davis's plea of innocent by reason of insanity was like instant Sanka, the chief ingredient being a hope of escape of punishment. The state has proved the first-degree murder charge contained in the information and beyond a reasonable doubt." He then added, "Frank Davis is bad, not mad!"

Holt's words contrasted with Wright's in the two men's closing arguments. Holt's final plea for Davis contended that the witnesses' testimony had substantiated the insanity plea, maintaining that Davis's abnormal behavior had been present over a period of at least fifteen years. Holt accused the state of "not bringing the whole truth out" during the trial. He said, "Much defense testimony has been undisputed."

Holt emphasized the importance of Fowler's examination of his client and his findings as well as those of Shannon and was critical of Yohe, to whom he referred as "Dr. Yoyo" and "Dr. Yuhee."

Holt also had a great deal to say about the testimony of Terral Adcock, who had testified to watching Davis's wife's movements the day of the killing and reporting to her husband. He called Adcock the state's "star witness" and made light of his testimony. He also said that Yohe's evaluation of Davis's condition was a horseback opinion and that in all his legal experience, he had never seen more flimsy testimony than offered by the state. Holt was quoted by reporters as saying, "Davis has been nutty as a fruitcake for fifteen years."

Holt spoke more than ninety minutes, ending his plea to the jury with a quotation from William Cullen Bryant's eighty-line poem "Thanatopsis."

Wright, in rebuttal, told the jury, "If Davis's mother had been so concerned that her son was mentally ill, she would have taken definite steps to get him committed. Let the punishment fit the crime."

The alternate jurors, Velma Welch, who was the lone lady of the jury, and Frank Eckard, were excused by the court at the conclusions of the final arguments. The case then went to the jury at 4:25 p.m., and Frank Davis, who didn't testify, was handcuffed and taken to the county jail, two floors below the courtroom in the four-story Renaissance Revival–style structure.

Reporters rushed to make the Friday evening deadline while the jurors were sequestered in the jury room. The *Hot Springs New Era* came off the press that night with news of the final day trial news but no verdict. That would make the Saturday edition. They did, however, run a teaser headline: "Case Goes to Jury Today, Four Psychiatrists Split Evenly on Issue of Frank

Davis Sanity."[2] The story pointed out the polar differences of testimony given by the Hot Springs and Little Rock psychiatrists. The two from Hot Springs, who testified for the state prosecutor, were of the opinion Frank was sane and responsible for his actions when he shot and killed Sharron, and the two Little Rock psychiatrists, on behalf of the defense, felt he was not.

Jury deliberations were interrupted at 5:35 p.m., when the jury room became stifling hot. County employees solved the problem when they found the air conditioning was turned off elsewhere in the courthouse.

Twenty minutes later, the jury asked permission to view the report made by practical nurses and technicians during the time Frank was confined to the state hospital for examination. The jury then asked to return to the courtroom and was advised by the court that this report had not been introduced as evidence and could not be given to them.

Next, the jury asked to hear the portion of the transcript recording of the testimony by Dr. Sheldon Fowler, the psychiatrist who had conducted the major portion of Davis's examination at the state hospital. After a conference with counsel, the court told the jury it would not be permitted to hear this testimony again, and they would have to rely on what they recalled from the witness stand. They were told, "Some 12,000 feet of tape, or more than two miles, was used in transcribing the entire trial."

When the jury room door opened at 6:38 p.m., a little over two hours after the deliberations had begun, L. G. "Nick" Burrell, jury foreman, announced, "We are ready."

While Frank was being returned to the courtroom, he may have glanced at his mother sitting behind the railing near the counsel's table but probably never looked in the opposite direction at his dead wife's family.

Jack Holt waited as Frank walked toward him and then stopped next to him. When Ridgeway joined them, they walked together and stood in front of the judge's bench.

Twenty-five spectators sat quietly in the courtroom, watching Frank Davis's fate being passed from the jury to the judge on a small piece of paper. They knew that Frank admitted to the killing and that Judge Britt instructed the jury to choose between five different verdicts—three for "guilty" and two for "innocent." Now they were minutes away from hearing which way the jury leaned.

• 24 •

The Verdict

*C*entral Arkansas hadn't experienced a sensational murder trial since 1946, when James Waybern Hall, known as "Red," murdered four people across the state between 1944 and 1945.[1] He included his wife, who had deserted him, in the killing spree.[2] Hall was sentenced to the electric chair and on the way there laughed and joked with the guards. After they strapped him in and fastened the electrodes, he said, "Boys, I'm not afraid. I can take it."[3]

Twenty-two years later, Frank Davis replaced Hall in Arkansas' history as the newest multiple murderer. Although Frank had been tried on only one of his two murder charges, a third remained hearsay until a decade later when a *Sentinel-Record* editor initiated a crusade against Frank.

Hot Springs residents had heard the excited talk surrounding Frank Davis's verdict on Friday night, and they couldn't wait to read the details on Saturday, June 15, 1968. Most were happy to see the *Hot Springs New Era*'s front-page double headline: "To Be Sentenced Monday, Jury Finds Davis Guilty/Death Penalty Automatic."[4]

They read how Frank Davis "stood while the court read the verdict and showed no emotion either then or when he sat down at the counsel table with his attorneys." Then they learned this judgment was one of the first death penalties to be assessed in the nation since a U.S. Supreme Court ruling on the punishment the week before.

People such as Mary Sue and Frances Forsberg were probably glad to read, "Davis still faces a charge of first-degree murder in the death of a 13-year-old girl, prior to the time of the shooting of his wife, at his ranch on the Blacksnake Road." Those who'd believed from the onset that Frank Davis had murdered Cathie Ward were feeling vindicated with the death sentence and joined the Knight family in gratification of the guilty verdict.

"Mrs. Knight and her husband were deeply concerned and came by my office quite often. They were really good people," prosecuting attorney Walter Wright told me. "Very fine people, but very reserved, and Mrs. Knight's brother-in-law [Charlie Fager] was very helpful. They wanted Davis put away. What really concerned me about the violence, was the fact that two of the children were in the backseat when he shot the 30-30 [rifle] and killed his wife and shot Mrs. Knight in the back of the head. It was bright as daylight when he took that on and killed them with the kids in the backseat. During the course of the trial, Davis at one time was mentally ill. Supposedly, the defense attorney put on some witness that said Davis ran after a car and barked like a dog. To counterbalance that and other allegations of mental illness, I didn't have a budget, but I got the county judge to provide $1,500 for Dr. Yohe to examine and give an opinion. Yohe related it to a child's temper tantrum, and I think the jury picked up their ears when they heard that."

Hiram Ward, Cathie's father, didn't spend a day in the courtroom. Nor did he keep any newspaper clippings of the trial. He assumed his ex-wife went, but he didn't discuss the proceedings with her. He'd never seen Frank Davis, had no idea about his family, and had never heard of the man before Cathie's murder. However, afterward he heard gossip.

"I think a year before this happened, he was barred from the state fairgrounds for beating a horse with a chain," he recalled, adding, "and he was always jumping on somebody, gonna whip somebody, gonna kill somebody."

Sharron Knight Davis's family attended the trial and didn't miss a day. Pauline, Sharron's mother, sat silently in the front row just outside the rail when the verdict was returned. After it was given, she calmly walked over and talked to Walter Wright. She and husband, Fred, were pleased he'd come through for them and their daughter.

Sharron's uncle, Charlie Fager, was part of the Knight family, and since Sharron had been his eldest daughter's favorite cousin, he allowed Debby to attend one day of the trial. Charlie and his sister-in-law Pauline saw the dirty looks Frank Davis was giving them throughout the proceedings and noticed he included others, including the judge and court stenographer, Irene Larsen. They knew no one was spared Frank's mean glares. When he received the death sentence, they didn't return his wickedness by taunting him or displaying overt acts of glee but contained their huge smiles and were respectful of the jury's decision. Now, Frank Davis was lawfully scheduled for death, but they'd have to wait a few more days to find out how he would meet his maker.

· 25 ·

The Sentence

$\mathcal{F}$rank entered the courtroom for sentencing on Monday morning, June 17, 1968. His lead attorney, Jack Holt, immediately took him to an anteroom for a brief conference before the proceedings were to begin.[1] When they returned, Holt positioned Frank between himself and co–defense attorney Ridgeway in front of the counsel's table as their opponent, Walter Wright, stood adjacent to them.

Judge Britt sat at the bench in his black judicial robe with the verdict and the judgment of conviction in his possession. He took the verdict and began to read, "We, the jury, find the defendant guilty of murder in the first degree as charged in the information."

He stopped, placed the document on his desk, looked at the defense and state attorneys, and said, "Is there any reason sentence should not be pronounced at this time?"

"No, sir," said Wright.

"None," Holt added, and then turned around and talked with cocounsel Ridgeway.

"Your Honor, may we caucus in your chambers?" Holt asked.

After a quick meeting, the five men returned to the courtroom, and the judge asked, "Is there any reason sentence should not be pronounced at this time, aside from those recited in chambers?"

The jury was not informed of the private discussion before both state's attorney, Wright, and defense attorney, Holt, replied, "No."

Judge Britt grasped the judgment of conviction and began reading. "On this seventeenth day of June 1968 comes the State of Arkansas by Walter G. Wright, prosecuting attorney, and Ben J. Harrison, deputy prosecuting attorney, and comes the defendant, Allen Frank Davis, in proper person in

151

custody of the sheriff of Garland County, Arkansas, and by his attorneys, Jack Holt Sr. and Robert D. Ridgeway, for pronouncement of judgment of conviction and imposition of sentence upon the verdict of guilty found by the jury herein on June 14, 1968, against the defendant, Allen Frank Davis, for the crime of murder in the first degree of Sharron Davis on January 19, 1967, as charged in the information filed herein on January 25, 1967, by the prosecuting attorney.

"And, the court, having informed the defendant, Allen Frank Davis, that, after a trial by jury commencing on June 11, 1968, the jury did on June 14, 1968, find him guilty of murder in the first degree as charged by the information herein for the murder of Sharron Davis in this county on January 19, 1967, for which the penalty is death by electrocution, asked the defendant if he has any legal cause why judgment should not be pronounced against him, no sufficient cause to the contrary being shown or appearing to the court.

"Therefore, pursuant to the jury verdict returned herein on June 14, 1968, and in accordance therewith, it is the judgment of the court that defendant Allen Frank Davis stand convicted of the crime of murder in the first degree as charged and that defendant Allen Frank Davis be and is hereby sentenced to be put to death in the electric chair at the state penitentiary on August 17, 1968, a Saturday, between the hours of sunrise and sunset."

Frank, who was handcuffed to the chief deputy sheriff, didn't flinch, while the eighteen spectators in the gallery, barring Frank's mother and aunt, were probably also trying to contain their emotions.[2] Judge Britt continued to read the last two sentences pertaining to Frank's incarceration, but everyone was probably still at "electric chair."

The judge later complimented prosecuting attorney Walter Wright and defense attorneys Jack Holt and Robert Ridgeway for their presentations of the case. Then Jack Holt escorted Frank Davis back to the anteroom along with his mother and aunt. After their meeting, he was returned to the county jail for transfer to the penitentiary.

The *Hot Springs New Era* reporter rushed up to Walter Wright for a victory quote. "Within the rules as pronounced by the American Bar Association and the U.S. Supreme Court, the only statement that I can make is the jury faced a tremendous responsibility," Wright said. "I hope the community recognizes that the jury accepted that responsibility and discharged its duty."

Next, the reporter approached Frank's legal team. Holt said, "The case will be appealed. Between now and the date set for execution, we will file a motion for a new trial, which is the first step on the road of appeal to the Arkansas Supreme Court."

Arkansas' electric chair had been dismantled and stored at the prison after the 1964 execution of Charles Franklin Fields. However, it was understood by lawmakers that it could be reassembled within a short time.[3]

The Knight family once again showed no overt displays of pleasure that Frank Davis's electrocution would now be only two months away. After his sentencing, neither family was quoted in the newspapers. They kept their feelings to themselves. Frank's mother was silent as well—but she was accustomed to letting her money do the talking just as she'd done in the past. Now she needed to win an appeal for her son.

III

COWBOY CONVICT

· 26 ·

The Death Row Inmate

$\mathcal{F}$rank Davis was driven in handcuffs to Tucker Prison on Tuesday, June 18, 1968. Although the penitentiary was due east of Hot Springs, it was accessible only by taking a two-hour, roundabout trip on state roads. When the vehicle entered the prison gates, Frank could see the Wabbaseka Bayou that snaked through the 4,500-acre Tucker "State Farm" Prison.

After processing, he became "prisoner 61719" and a minority member of death row, which held fifteen men: three Caucasians and twelve African Americans.[1] Frank arrived at Tucker months after the corruption in the Arkansas prison system had been exposed and was now being reformed by Governor Winthrop Rockefeller.

Rockefeller, the grandson of Standard Oil founder John D. Rockefeller, came to Arkansas in 1953 at the urging of a World War II buddy who lived in Little Rock. His visit coincided with his attempt to escape the tabloid press in Manhattan, New York, where he'd become known as the black sheep of the prominent Rockefeller family.[2] A year later, in 1954, Rockefeller bought a large parcel of land near the Arkansas River on Petit Jean Mountain with picturesque waterfalls and an unusual flat top that would be perfect for an airport. He built a showplace home and named his property WinRock Farms. Rockefeller became familiar with statewide politics and entered the 1966 gubernatorial race, using his high-profile name to win and become the first Republican governor in 100 years.[3]

Before Frank Davis joined Tucker's death row in 1968, Governor Rockefeller had ordered their electric chair dismantled and placed in storage. Then he put a stop to the "Tucker Telephone," a homemade torture device that delivered electric shocks from a phone's electric generator wired in sequence to two dry-cell batteries.[4] When an inmate was brought to the prison infirmary, he was restrained on the examining table as a grounding wire was wrapped around the big toe, and the hot wire that delivered a current of electricity was attached to his genitals. The doctor would crank the phone, and an electric current would shoot through the prisoner's body. If he received a "long-distance call," it meant he was given a longer charge—just before he passed out.

"This inhumane torture device, invented by resident physician Dr. A. E. Rollins," the *Encyclopedia of Arkansas History and Culture* stated, "caused permanent organ damage, and for some inmates, insanity. The infamous phone was found in a shoebox in the closet of Tucker superintendent Jim Bruton, who was eventually convicted in the 1970s of violating prisoners' civil rights. The judge suspended his sentence, feeling if he did serve time, it would result in his execution at the hands of vengeful inmates."[5]

Frank dodged the Tucker Telephone but still felt the threat of "Old Sparky," the electric chair that could be reassembled. He sweated out his execution for forty-four days until his lawyers fulfilled their posttrial pledge on July 31, 1968. But, in true honesty, they weren't responsible for that feat. An *Arkansas Times* story by Andrea Ringer reported, "In a 1968 meeting with local leaders he [Governor Rockefeller] announced that all inmates on death row in Arkansas would be granted a stay of execution until the U.S. Supreme Court ruled on the constitutionality of capital punishment."[6]

This stay of execution, signed by Jimmy H. Hawkins, the clerk of the Arkansas Supreme Court, was another lucky break that came Frank Davis's way. They seemed to happen at the most opportune time for the most hated murderer in Hot Springs.

Frank's lawyers kept the momentum going by following the stay with an appeal that contained eight points of contention:[7]

1. Frank Davis had been deprived of his rights under the Fifth Amendment of the U.S. Constitution.
2. The trial court erred in excluding jurors who had conscientious scruples against capital punishment.
3. The trial court abused its discretion in admitting in evidence pictures taken by William Ralph Dever Jr. (Bill Dever).
4. The verdict of the jury ignored the overwhelming evidence of insanity, and their verdict was contrary to the evidence and to the law concerning insanity.
5. An argument concerning trial court instructions.
6. The trial court erred in excluding the appellant and/or permitting his absence during trial.
7. Appellant refers to conferences in chambers between the court and counsel.

8. The imposition of the death sentence constitutes cruel and unusual punishment.

On May 5, 1969, Arkansas Supreme Court Justice Conley Byrd delivered his opinion of the appeal. He noted that points 1, 2, 3, and 5 were without merit. He said, "The appellant waived the privilege he may have had a right to claim under the statute [in points 4, 6, and 7]," adding, "Point 8 should be addressed by the legislature instead of the courts."

Justice Byrd concluded, "In his motion for new trial, appellant raised other issues. We find all such issues to be without merit."

The next day, May 6, the local newspaper ran a front-page story saying, "Little Rock attorney Jack Holt, told the *Sentinel-Record* he thought 'the decision of the Arkansas Supreme Court is erroneous, and the case will definitely be appealed in the U.S. Supreme Court.'"

While Frank waited for the higher court's decision, a rehearing in the Arkansas Supreme Court for June 2, 1969, was denied. Frank had lost his appeal but not his death row cell. Nine days later, though, he earned a consolation prize—another one of his lucky breaks. On July 11, the Garland County Circuit Court filed a motion to dismiss (case no. 12,846), which accused Frank of "murder in the first degree of Kathy [*sic*] Ward by striking her in the head with a rock."

The motion became an order to dismiss on January 8, 1970. Garland County Circuit Judge Henry M. Britt signed the document, which announced, "Comes the State of Arkansas by the prosecuting attorney for the 18th Judicial Circuit and moves the court to nolle prosequi and dismiss the above styled criminal action on the ground that the defendant was convicted of murder in the first degree in State vs. Davis Garland Circuit No. 12,827, is presently in the Arkansas State Penitentiary under sentence of death."

Frank's first-degree murder charge for Cathie Ward would never be tried in a court of law by a judge and jury. Walter Wright, the prosecuting attorney who signed the original first-degree murder indictment, explained the reasoning behind Cathie's murder case dismissal. During a 2014 phone interview, Wright said, "The thirteen-year-old's case couldn't be proven that he killed her."

Walter Wright had been assisted by deputy prosecuting attorney Ben Harrison in convicting Frank Davis for Sharron's murder. As the many coincidences continued to mount in this story, another one involved Harrison. He was the father of Jan Harrison, who'd been invited by Cathie Ward to a bunking party/sleepover at her home the night she died. Jan recalled her father later explaining the "rock," which was designated as the murder weapon in Frank's murder indictment for Cathie.

Jan told me, "Supposedly, when the horse threw Cathie, she hit her head on that rock and then was drug by the horse. I remember Daddy explaining as well as he could the importance of whether Cathie hit her head or was hit in the head [with the rock]. My biggest shock, though, was when I saw the saddle at the courthouse and saw the bloodstains. I was spending the day with Daddy, and he specifically told me I was not to go into that room. Wish I had listened."

Remembering the dismissal of the first-degree murder charge for his daughter's death, Hiram said, "He was already on death row for the other crime, and there was no need to have another trial."

After Frank was sentenced to death, no one in Hot Springs ever imagined his sentence could change. They knew it was a sure thing.

• 27 •

Rockefeller's Goodwill and
Peace to Prisoners

$\mathcal{F}$rank went back and forth to the Arkansas State Hospital in Little Rock, where a procedure at its surgery clinic was scheduled on March 12, 1970, along with follow-up appointments on March 19, April 9, and May 7. Months later, on December 29, 1970, a commotion began on death row. It was tainted not with hatred but with glee—the inmates were being evicted from death row by the governor![1]

With the governor's goodwill and peace to the prisoners, Frank would no longer be facing execution. He and his death row mates were being moved to the general prison population, and once again, he'd received a lucky break. The first one was the stay of postponement for his August 1967 trial for Sharron's murder. The second came a month after he arrived on death row when Governor Rockefeller placed a moratorium on death row executions. The third was on January 8, 1970, when the Garland County circuit judge dismissed Cathie Ward's first-degree murder charges because Frank was already in prison, serving a death sentence. Now, the fourth lucky break topped them all by removing his death sentence on December 29, 1970.

Governor Rockefeller's term was ending, and as a lifelong opponent of capital punishment, he chose to commute the sentences of all fifteen men on death row to life imprisonment. Nine had been convicted for murder and six for rape. Twelve were black, and three were white. Robert Sarver, Arkansas commissioner of corrections, told reporters, "This is the first time in history that a governor has commuted all death sentences at once."

On Christmas Eve, Rockefeller had appointed a five-member committee to study the situation of Arkansas' death row and make recommendations. After his commutations, Rockefeller admitted he would have acted purely from conscience, but the committee approved his action. His hope was that the U.S. Supreme Court would clear up the question of whether the death penalty was constitutional. When the Court did not do this, he felt compelled to follow his conscience and commute all the pending death sentences in Arkansas while he still had the chance.

Rockefeller explained his stance on the commutations. "The records, individually or collectively, of the fifteen condemned bear no relevance to my decision," he said. "It is purely personal and philosophical. I yearn to see other chief executives throughout the nation follow suit so that as a people we may hasten the elimination of barbarism as a tool of American justice."

Winthrop Rockefeller carried out his last-minute executive order on December 29, 1970, and then left office on January 11, 1971. He and his second wife, Jeanette, a Seattle-born socialite,[2] separated on February 19, 1971, and she sought an amicable divorce.[3] He was later diagnosed with pancreatic cancer and passed away on February 22, 1973, in Palm Springs, California, at the age of sixty.

୧──

Hot Springs residents were disturbed to read the *Sentinel-Record*'s December 30, 1970, article about Frank's status changing from "death" to "life in prison." The front-page article with the headline "Arkansas Death Row Is Emptied" explained Rockefeller's beliefs and gave vignettes of the prisoners affected by his kindness. The story said that Lonnie B. Mitchell, "a Negro who arrived at the prison April 11, 1959," when he was twenty-three years old, was the senior prisoner on death row and had been sentenced for the rape of a seventy-six-year-old white woman in Union County.

"Another of the reprieved," it said, was "William L. Maxwell, 30, who was convicted in 1962 for the rape of a white woman at Hot Springs." Maxwell's case had been before the U.S. Supreme Court months earlier, but they passed up an opportunity to rule on the constitutionality of the death penalty.

Frank's name appeared at the end of the article, fourth from the last in a listing of "the other 12 men." They were arranged in chronological order of prison arrivals, and Frank's simply stated, "Allen Frank Davis, imprisoned June 18, 1967 for murder in Garland County."

Rockefeller's goodwill gift allowed Frank to move into Tucker Prison's military-style barracks from his death row cell, where he'd spent 925 days. But now he had other issues to deal with, such as the general prisoners' frequent acts of theft, violence, rape, and intimidation.[4]

In the past, Tucker Prison had always been the home for white inmates but currently housed fewer than 300. Its racial counterpart, Cummins, only forty-eight miles south, held 1,219 black prisoners. Both prisons were modeled after antebellum plantations with the inmates performing various jobs, the unluckiest picking cotton, cucumbers, and rice.

Tucker used the "trusty" system, where they would designate inmates to guard the prison, enforce discipline, and be in charge of maintaining the daily operations. They were at the top of a hierarchy, while men like Frank were at the bottom of the prison's inmate society. The trusties, or bosses, supervised the inmates out in the fields, rode horses, and held guns or clubs and were called "long-line riders." Trusties considered themselves untouchable within the prison walls. They beat lower-ranking prisoners for small infractions, extorted inmates, and engaged in rape and murder.

Little of what happened at Tucker was known outside the prison until after Rockefeller took office in January 1967. Through the hiring of a new prison superintendent, the existing legal ban on the rawhide lash was enforced, and a crackdown on the worst abuses of the trusty system was attempted. So once again, Frank received a bonus of sorts, arriving after Governor Rockefeller had begun addressing the hideous conditions of Arkansas prison life.

Frank became a trusty in 1969, which gave him four hours of visitation rights each weekend. He had to complete an "inmate correspondence and visiting list" with the names of family and friends, whom the prison then rated as temporary, approved, mail only, or temporarily approved. He registered his mother, stepfather, a friend who owned a Hot Springs restaurant he'd frequented, his Lakeshore Drive buddy Troy Carter, and Wanda Castleberry, a woman from Hot Springs. A title such as "mother" or "friend" was noted next to each name, but Wanda had no such designation. That space was blank. However, Wanda was the person his friend Harold Tankersley thought Frank had married. They dated while he and Sharron were separated in the fall of 1966. In fact, Wanda was at Irene Davis's home the night Frank murdered Sharron, waiting for him to arrive so they could celebrate his mother's sixtieth birthday. At that time, Wanda was pregnant with Frank's fifth child, who would be born seven months later, in July 1967, six months after Frank murdered Sharron.

Prison records show Frank enjoyed his newfound freedom. His first assignment in the "Pen Store" led to a job at the "Cow Barn" on February 2, 1971. In the middle of July, he was sent to the Prison Board and then transferred to Cummins in August.

Two days after settling into his new prison home, Frank received a disciplinary action that resulted in 365 days of "good time" forfeited, but his "good time" reserve held only 161 days. With this infraction, his job assignment was changed to a restrictive area.

Oddly enough, six months later, on August 23, 1971, the Department of Corrections Division of Probation and Parole Services mailed a letter to Garland County Circuit Judge Britt, prosecuting attorney Walter Wright, and Sheriff "Bud" Canada. The Parole Board, "in accordance with Act 152-169, was requesting recommendations for Allen Frank Davis, who would be reviewed for Executive Clemency on August 28, 1971."

The Parole Board's executive clemency requests were like an employer delving into a prospective employee's work past by contacting previous employers to learn about job performance. In Frank's case, if the board received favorable answers, they would send the governor a recommendation based on those responses, and then it would be up to the governor's inclination to either shorten Frank's prison term, parole him, or do nothing.

Judge Britt replied immediately, saying, "There are not any extenuating or mitigating circumstances whatever to suggest any relief from the sentence that this individual is serving. He was convicted by a jury for a vicious, violent killing. There was another murder charge pending against him, and a charge of assault with intent to kill against him when he was sentenced to die for the homicide for which convicted in this case. It is this court's belief that this individual should be required to serve the life sentence now imposed and not be given any relief whatever. If he is granted relief, it is this court's opinion that law enforcement might as well cease and that the courts will be of no use to the public."

Hiram Ward was also contacted but not by the Department of Corrections. People who were afraid of Frank called Ward, asking that he intercede with the governor. "He [Frank] had threatened to kill the deputy coroner in Hot Springs for this particular case. He also threatened his insurance agent that he was going to kill him when he got out," Ward told me.

"It wasn't me! Could've been my partner, but I'm not certain of that," said Elza Young, the insurance agent Frank attempted to shoot only hours before he murdered Sharron.

Judge Britt's efforts, along with the other protesters, were successful. Frank didn't receive executive clemency. But despite his disappointment, he stayed out of trouble and restored his "good time" by the end of March 1972. Because of that, he was allowed to return to the dairy and work with the beef herd, which meant he could ride a horse.

When Frank wasn't working outside in the fields, he was in his cell block, singing and writing songs. He kept his playlist in a homemade briefcase made of black-tooled leather. Long strips of tan leather had been used for the handle, buckle latches, and a decorative oval on the front that had been embossed with his name in western font letters. The business-like portfolio held Frank's private papers, including the songs he wrote to help pass the time. Ledger pads were full of curvy handwritten lyrics of songs such as "Stronger Than Prison Walls," a prisoner's love story of the darling he dreams of night and day that eerily ends the same as his and Sharron's marriage:

> And you don't know how much it hurt,
> the day you said we're through.
> But I will just go on,
> although you don't care,
> we will meet in heaven,
> and that place we will share.

Another favorite, "Me + You Big as Dallas," sang of "the easy tender love he couldn't turn down with Fair Lady Brown, who said 'you and me big as Dallas or any big city around.' And that's why he knew she loved him—cause Dallas is a mighty big town."

Other songs on Frank's pad included "God Gave Me You" and "Sweetheart: With All My Love." Sheets of thin onion paper also contained verses to "Strange Rider" and "Murder First Degree," the latter becoming his masterpiece with the help of the music alphabet. The origins of this instructional paper are unknown. However, meticulous notes were written in capital letters, which said, "Remember these chords are all 6 string chords based strictly on the musical alphabet. The relative moves on the neck of the guitar will be the same in any of the 5 keys that you chose. And the movements will be relative to the respective key in which you are playing. What I'm saying is, is that if you will learn all the changes for the key of C. Then you will be able to play in any of the keys, C, ch, cd, D, dh, ed, E. It will only require moving up the neck alphabetically and obeying the law of relativity." A diagram with lines and arrows was drawn with more notes to accompany the "6 possible chord changes."

The finished tune made its way onto a piece of notebook paper where Frank drew musical lines and notes above the lyrics of "Murder First Degree":

> When shadows fall below these walls,
> another day has passed.
> We go inside
> and try to hide
> from the questions that they might ask.
> And I'm wishing now
> that I somehow
> could make them set me free.
> But I can't win.
> I'm in, my friend,
> for Murder First Degree.

Moderation was not a term or lifestyle Frank Davis embraced. His pursuits, whether collecting wives or cars, were conducted with reckless abandon—and now, behind bars, his sad songs had replaced women and automobiles.

• 28 •

The Fifth Marriage and the Escape

$\mathscr{I}$n January 1975, Frank received an approved prison furlough to marry his fifth wife, Wanda. Instead of holding their ceremony in Hot Springs, they went to Searcy, Arkansas, 136 miles north of the prison.[1] Frank and Wanda had begun dating in the fall of 1966 after Sharron's departure, and Wanda was at Irene Davis Hogan's birthday dinner the night he murdered Sharron on January 19, 1967. Seven months later, Wanda and Frank became the parents of a baby girl, Becky.

A year later, Frank was transferred to a minimum-security facility in Booneville, Arkansas, at the Department of Correction's livestock production center. His relocation was not only a perk for several years of good behavior but also based on his Texas A&M degree in agriculture and previous employment as a U.S. cattle inspector. Twenty years earlier, he had been skilled at inseminations, which was a plus at the prison's breeding center. He was driven to Booneville, where he would live and work with only twelve trusty inmates and three administrators, a world away from the chaos at Cummins.

A recommendation of Frank's eligibility for parole to Oregon was made a month after his arrival. The Arkansas State Pardon and Parole Board stated, "The recommendation is on the basis of his institutional record and performance of the tasks assigned to him during his incarceration at Cummins."

But once again, the parole board heard strong protests from Hot Springs. The *Sentinel-Record*, in a February 7, 1976, editorial, "Poor Decision by Parole Board," argued the following:

> What we have here is a failure to communicate.
> Let's put it another way to our esteemed Arkansas Parole Board.

On the night of January 19, 1967, less than ten years ago, a young woman with small children in tow, entered a local laundromat accompanied by her mother.

They didn't see the woman's husband, Frank Davis, lurking in the dark with a 30-30 rifle aimed at her head.

He fired. The bullet split her skull with a thud [*sic*]. He then trained the rifle on the woman's mother . . . blam . . . the second woman fell and lay in a pool of expanding blood.

Sharon [*sic*] Davis was killed instantly [*sic*]. Her mother was blinded.

But let's look even a bit further back to June 24, 1966, when 12-year-old [*sic*] Kathy Ward of Hot Springs had her head bashed in by a rock. Davis was indicted in that murder also, but never answered those charges because he had already been sentenced to death for the shooting.

The Parole Board unanimously and ignorantly recommended to Governor Pryor, on Jan. 23, that Davis' life sentence be commuted to parole eligibility and that Davis be paroled to the State of Oregon.

Frankly, we question whether Oregon really wants Davis.

We will be deeply disappointed if David Pryor signs the parole, after Davis has served only eight years of his original death sentence in prison.

Now, please don't misunderstand our position toward prisons. We believe in the rehabilitation of criminals when and if rehabilitation is possible. But we also believe in strong punishment for people who callously murder others.

In our opinion, Davis has served about one-fourth of his punishment term. After all, . . . eight years for cold-blooded murder?

To release him back on society would be a disgusting and deplorable act. But it appears the Arkansas Parole Board isn't the least bit concerned about how the citizens of Hot Springs and Garland County feel in this matter. They didn't bother to notify the circuit judge, the prosecuting attorney or the police chief of their plans to unleash Davis until after the decision was made—behind the comfort and security of closed doors.

What kind of Mickey Mousism are they trying to pull?

If, in their own minds, those board members can justify releasing a man like Davis back into society, then we hereby recommend each of them be equally committed to their warped interpretation of "rights and justice" by making a room available to him in each of their homes whenever he wants it.

And when it comes right down to the issue of "rights." We have to ask what about the rights of the late Sharon [*sic*] Davis and her mother? Their rights really haven't been considered in this, have they?

Does this ridiculous excuse for a board ever consider anyone else's "rights?"

We would urge the citizens of this community to write or telephone Governor Pryor immediately and voice disapproval of "our" Parole Board's decision. And we would also ask that any future boards be required to notify this community before they see fit to release a person like Davis upon Hot Springs and the nation.[2]

The newspaper performed due diligence on Frank's past crimes, although they reported a few details incorrectly, such as Cathie Ward's age at death, Sharron dying instantly, and Frank lurking in the dark. Sharron lived long enough to tell doctors her killer's name before dying in the emergency room, and Frank Davis was in full sight of his victims, although they were unaware he had a 30-30 rifle on the floorboard behind him ready to blast away when his bad temper exploded.

Frank didn't clip the local newspaper's initial commentary but did snip a more complimentary follow-up in the readers' response column, "What Our Readers Are Saying." Baker Kurrus, a Lakeside High School graduate[3] and political science/government major at the University of Arkansas,[4] submitted his take on Davis's treatment, which the newspaper titled, "Reader Blasts Davis Editorial." Kurrus wrote,

> Dear editor:
> I was taken back by your editorial which urged local residents to write Gov. David Pryor and request that the governor turn down the parole recommendation of Frank Davis.
> The introduction of unbridled emotion, animosity, and hatred should be avoided in all judicial and penal proceedings. Elements of vengeance should be cast aside, and reason should be interjected. Editorials such as yours which appeal to group sentiments and disregard the calculated, rational, and unanimous decision of the Arkansas Parole Board demonstrate the editorial irresponsibility common to this page.
> I have made no positive determination in the Frank Davis case. I realize that I do not have all the facts. Until one knows the record of Mr. Davis while in the penitentiary judgement should be reserved.
> To reiterate your editorial of February 7, 1976, urging specific actions by citizens was premature. I will be much impressed on the day that I see this newspaper introduce the voice of reason into any relevant issue.
> Baker Kurrus
> Hot Springs

(Kurrus did not address the *Sentinel-Record* editor's February 7 editorial recommendation, suggesting that parole board members in favor of releasing Frank Davis back into society should provide him hospitality in their own homes.)

State Senator Bud Canada was Garland County's sheriff when Frank committed the two murders. He had aligned with the anti-pardon faction with his letter to Governor Pryor. The *Arkansas Gazette* reported Canada's dismay in a February 11, 1976, story, "Probe Requested of Parole Board in Prison Releases." The statewide publication said Senator Canada alleged the board was releasing dangerous felons prematurely and unwisely. Canada stated, "In particular, Frank Davis, who'd been recommended for executive clemency at the board's February 4, 1976 meeting."

The newspaper quoted Senator Canada. "This man should not be released, not only for the safety of several other people, but for his own safety."

Not a week later, Frank received an envelope bearing the Arkansas state seal. It contained a letter from Alton L. Taylor, the governor's administrator, stating the governor had denied his request for executive clemency. Taylor advised Frank against discouragement, telling him that he could apply again in one year. Taylor said, "If you keep a good record, your case will look much better to the Governor at that time."

Nancy Britt, the eldest daughter of Judge Henry "Hank" Britt, who presided over Frank's 1968 trial, reported Governor Pryor's denial in the *Sentinel-Record*. She said Pryor's decision was based on "the seriousness of his crime, the short time he'd served, and the adverse public opinion."[5] She then added, "He believed it was against the best interests of the people to release a man of Davis' record and capacity for violence, according to published reports."

The governor noted Frank Davis was also charged with assault with intent to kill his mother-in-law, Pauline Knight, and explained that the statute of limitations on that charge ran out while he was on death row.

Britt dug up dirt on Frank that included "a rape charge dismissed in 1964 and a charge of cruelty to animals in connection with the alleged bludgeoning of a horse with a large stick."

Frank's last denial was ten months earlier. Now this third attempt would kick it out another year, and each time, there were people working to keep him locked up—forever. Two men, the insurance agent and the deputy coroner, were still frightened of Frank, and every time he went up for parole, they would call Hiram, the father of Frank's first murder victim, Cathie Ward, and ask him to please contact the governor.

Sharron Knight Davis's family was also fighting to keep Frank in prison. "Sharon [*sic*] was my cousin, and her mother, my aunt, lived after he shot her in the head," said Nancy Fager Anderson-Richard.[6] "I was only four at the time but can recall the feeling of sadness and anger as my mom comforted my aunt and helped with the two precious boys left behind. My aunt raised those boys to adulthood and passed a few years ago. Each time Frank came up for parole, my mom would fight to appeal. It was a great tragedy for our family but proved the strength of the women as they refused to allow the evilness of one man to destroy them."

Despite living with blurred vision after the shooting, Pauline Knight raised Sharron's two sons with the help of her daughters. One, who lived in Little Rock, would come over on weekends or during the week.

"She became the backbone for her mother, especially after my uncle Fred died on the job after Sharron's murder," Debby Fager Larsen told me. "The other two sisters probably helped too, especially the one who lived in Hot Springs."

Sixteen months after Sharron's murder, Fred Knight died while on the job at the Reynolds Aluminum plant in Jones Mill, Arkansas, about three miles past the Garland County line. His niece, Debby Fager, said it was by electrocution. The family never suspected foul play, and two years later, his death was called a heart attack.

Katie Weaver remembered having the oldest Davis boy in her class at East Side Elementary School, not far from the Knights' home. She knew the boys had attended Catholic school, where it was more structured and organized, and now they were in their first year at public school, which was "a little looser." She thought both the boys were "good kids" and said, "The grandmother took good care of them."

THE ESCAPE

Frank had spent nine months in Booneville's minimum-security prison when the prison board was in the process of moving him back to Cummins maximum-security prison in October 1976. The prison's regular transfer van was on its way to get Frank when it broke down, and by the time it reached Booneville, Frank had escaped.[7]

He was discovered missing from the bunk area around 1:30 a.m. Friday, October 15, 1976. When the prison's administrators found that a horse and saddle were also gone from the center's operations, they notified the Arkansas State Police. Roadblocks were placed in an eight-mile area west of Booneville where the state troopers concentrated their search.[8]

"Frank Davis is 5 feet 10 inches and 140 pounds, last seen wearing khaki-colored trousers and a green field jacket. He is not believed to be armed," the prison stated in a bulletin.

The Arkansas State Police, thinking Frank might call to ask for a ride, interviewed his mother and fifth wife, Wanda, and staked out their homes 100 miles away (on foot or horseback).

The *Sentinel-Record* notified Hot Springs residents of Frank's escape the next morning, Saturday, October 16, 1976. The disclosure of his getaway came from Garland County Sheriff Leon Barlow, who said, "Security measures are being taken to ensure his capture."

"It's entirely possible that at some time in the future, authorities may question why Davis was allowed to serve as a trusty at a minimum-security prison facility," Sheriff Barlow commented.

Not divulging his immediate plans of local law enforcement, the sheriff said, "Certain precautions are being taken should Davis try to hide out here."

The newspaper noted Frank's trusty status at the minimum-security facility at Booneville's Livestock Production Center but not that it was located 110 miles north of Murfreesboro in close proximity to the father of his first murder victim.

As Hiram remembers it, "He was on a work detail in Dierks one time, and he escaped. Stole a horse and escaped. They called me and told me, the police did, at that time. They thought I'd be afraid of him. I said, 'Just run him down this way and you don't even need to chase him,'" he laughed.

The next day, Sunday, October 17, Hot Springs residents were informed, "Search for Davis Continues."[9] The *Sentinel-Record* stated, "Additional law enforcement officers were brought in Saturday to help in the search." Tim Baltz, the prison spokesman, assured the general public that eight roadblocks were being maintained in the area and that bloodhounds were being used.

Hot Springs residents were relieved on Monday, October 18, 1976, to read the newspaper's headline, "Davis Recaptured Near Facility."[10] Frank had been apprehended Sunday about four and a half miles from the unit he escaped Friday night. State Trooper Tom Henson of Booneville spotted him in a wooded area around 5 a.m. and called for backup units. When they arrived, Trooper Henson went into the woods, found Frank, and took him into custody. Frank was unarmed and gave himself up after Trooper Henson confronted him.

The prison spokesman said Frank possibly went as far as ten miles from the facility but turned around and was heading back on foot in an attempt to evade officers. When he was caught, he told the trooper he'd tied up the horse because "it was give up."

"Disciplinary action will be taken against Davis because of the escape," the prison spokesman said, without elaborating. "The officers are looking into other charges, and Davis might be charged with taking the horse and some other things."

Frank was taken back to Cummins Prison and placed in the east building on investigative status pending action by the Unit Disciplinary Committee.

Talk of his prison break was swirling around Hot Springs. Four days later, the *Sentinel-Record* ran a story with the headline "Prison Officials Disagree: Weekend Escape of Davis Wasn't His First Absence." The reporter,

Nancy Britt, said, "Frank Davis had recently been in Hot Springs on at least one occasion when prison authorities say they didn't list him as being on furlough." She continued, "Reports indicate that at least three persons saw Davis at the Garland County Fair, held September 20–25, one of them a Garland County Sheriff's Deputy, even though Cummins Prison head Art Lockhart says through a spokesman that Davis was not on any formal furlough and the sheriff's office hadn't been notified of any escape."

Margie Hill, whose husband Teddy had helped Frank corral his cattle at Blacksnake Ranch, knew of Frank's prison disappearances. Margie told me, "Irene Davis made sure Frank had everything. When they put him in prison, he knew so much about the cattle and the horses and the animals, they put him in charge of the cattle on the prison farm. They gave him a horse to ride to tend to these cattle, and Teddy said that one time when he saw him at one of the [Garland County Fair] rodeos, he had ridden his horse all the way on the back side of the prison, tied the horse up, and had his wife meet him back there, and she brought him back to Hot Springs to the rodeo. Then, when he went back, he got back to the horse, rode back, and told them he'd been lost, for eighteen or twenty-four hours—he told them he'd been lost on the farm and couldn't find his way back."

"He didn't stay gone," claimed Harold Tankersley, Frank's bar-hopping buddy. Harold told me that Frank had been at the fairground's rodeo when he was supposed to be locked up at the penitentiary. "We used to see him all the time," Tankersley said. "I don't know who would bring him down, but he'd be there. So, I guess it was his wife or could've been his mother. She was crazy about that boy."

Irene Larsen, the court stenographer who endured Frank's menacing glares at his 1968 murder trial, was attending the Garland County Fair arts and crafts show when she felt uneasy, as if someone were watching her. She turned around and saw Frank Davis in the corner of the building. He was looking straight at her, and once their eyes met, he lifted his right hand to make a gesture as if he were shooting her. Frightened, she turned around and hoped he'd move on. That scene haunted her, and sometime after June 1979, she related the story to her son's new wife, Debby Fager Larsen—the cousin of Frank's last murder victim, Sharron Knight Davis.

Although Frank was now locked up in the maximum-security prison at Cummins, Sharron's mother, Pauline Knight, was still afraid of him. The back of her head had scabbed over, and after it was healed, she wouldn't venture out at night. She couldn't drive anymore because of brain damage from the shooting. She did, however, go out the back door of her kitchen onto three steps that led down to the backyard—and that's where she found Frank's cigarette butts. She knew he had left them, even though he was supposed to be in prison. Terrified that he was casing their home, she wouldn't answer the door at nights for fear it could be him.

"He said he was going to finish the job," Debby Fager told me. "Probably said it in court, that if he ever got out, he'd finish the job that he started, meaning he'd finish killing her [Pauline Knight] cause she knew too much from what Sharron probably told her."

An investigation into Frank's escape was begun by Arkansas Governor David Pryor. He had been given reports that at least three people had seen Frank Davis at the Garland County Fair a month earlier when he wasn't on official furlough.[11] Also, his aide, Don Harrell, had informed him that a staff member had heard Frank Davis was involved in a rape or attempted rape involving a sixteen-year-old girl before his escape. Prison officials were looking into possible other unauthorized absences by Davis as well as the fifty-year-old's reported incident with the girl.

Allen Kilby Jr. served on the jury of Frank's 1968 murder trial. Back then, the thirty-four year-old considered Frank Davis "a forty-year-old spoiled brat." Kilby felt Frank had killed others. He knew the jurors weren't allowed to talk in private about the case, but he told his wife "some of them mentioned the girl's death at the ranch, and there was hearsay of Davis renting a house where a woman's foot was found without a body."

Now almost a decade later, Kilby was living in "Little Chicago," the west Hobson Street neighborhood of Hot Springs full of Lithuanians who'd relocated from the Windy City. His two-level home was built on a slope with the master bedroom upstairs and a ground-floor bedroom for his son Marc. The teenager heard Frank Davis had been seen in town and knew his father had been a juror at Davis's trial and remembered the murderer's threats of revenge. Marc was so frightened Davis would come looking for his father that he wouldn't sleep in his bedroom for a month. Instead, he went upstairs each night and slept in a sleeping bag on the floor of his parents' bedroom.

Dr. Joe Little, who had employed Frank Davis's third wife, Carrie, recalled, "My father-in-law, David Whittington, was the prosecuting attorney in the early sixties, and for quite a few years, a lot of city officials were scared to death of Frank Davis. He had a lot of people worried about their safety. He was a psychopath. Frank Davis had made threats against city officials—before and after he killed his wife."

After Frank was apprehended, the prison spokesman said, "Authorities had some information that Davis might be having some family problems, and we were in the process of moving him back to Cummins when he escaped. Trusty inmates who are away from a location where they are regularly watched by guards and who have family problems provide the most frequent incidence of escapes. We may get information of such and pull one back under tighter control for a short while, until things settle down." He added, "Other possible charges in connection with the escape are still under investigation."[12]

Frank's family problems may have stemmed from his twenty-two-month-old marriage to Wanda. His fifth wife, a Garland County native, was rumored to live "somewhere in Hot Springs." Their child, Becky, was seven and a half years old at the time of their marriage.

During Frank's June 1968 murder trial, Irene Davis had become amnesic of her then one-year-old granddaughter's mother. Walter Wright, the prosecuting attorney, asked Irene who was present in her home when Frank returned on January 19, 1967 (after murdering Sharron).

Irene said, "There were three people."

Walter Wright asked, "And could you give us their names?"

Irene said, "I believe the boy's name was Hawthorn, and I think the girl's name was Castleberry and the other boy's name was Terry something." (Irene knew the girl's identity but wouldn't acknowledge Wanda, the mother of her fifth grandchild.)

Frank's reasoning for escaping in Booneville contrasted with the prison's viewpoint. The rambling note he wrote to justify his escape was found in his worn-out prison briefcase. It read,

> Hershell Neeley, Supervisor, Booneville Unit–ADC called and cancelled June 1st, 1976 for scheduled heart catheterization at St. Edwards, Ft. Smith. He called Dr. Roberts of Booneville Clinic. Mr. Harris, Security Officer. Mr. Harris was hired about June 10th and we then had full force of Security personnel. Mr. Neeley never Rescheduled me for Heart Catherization after he had adequate personnel. From June 10 to Oct 14, 1976 Mr. Lockhart and Mr. Henderson. Mr. Hawk asked me why I left assigned area. I told them in order to get to a V.A. Hosp. in Okla. and fight extradition until such time that I could get medical relief.

Frank's escape had stirred up the citizens of Hot Springs, who were frightened of Frank Davis. Just the mere mention of his name caused fear in children and adults. The *Sentinel-Record* editor was not immune to the town's recent panic and went after the governor of Arkansas in his October 26, 1976, "Local Comment," "Is Frank Davis Really in Prison?"[13]

> Gov. David Pryor and those who administer the state prison system owe Garland County an explanation. Area residents want and need to know why A. Frank Davis had apparently received preferential treatment while confined to state prisons.
>
> Davis recently escaped from the minimum security unit at Booneville. He was later captured but only after causing a weekend of fear for many in Hot Springs.

He was sentenced to death in Garland Circuit Court in 1968 after being convicted of first degree murder in the death of his estranged wife in 1967.

His sentence was later commuted [in 1970] by the late Gov. Winthrop Rockefeller. Before the commutation, though, in 1969, a year after his sentencing, he was made a trusty at Cummins. In 1975, Davis married again. His wife visited him regularly.

This past January he was transferred to Booneville. A month later, in Feb., Gov. Pryor denied a parole recommended for Davis by the State Board of Pardons and Paroles only after a loud outcry from Garland County.

Davis remained at Booneville after the parole was denied.

The Booneville operation apparently bears little resemblance to a corrections unit.

Although he was found guilty of first degree murder and was accused of various other crimes including murder, rape and cruelty to animals, Davis has managed to function apparently in a relatively normal manner, not much different from a freeworld existence.

Certainly rehabilitation is desirable, the eye for an eye code is long dead, but the exceptional treatment started for Davis long before any change could have occurred, and his recent actions indicate he is much the same as he was in 1967.

His entire history suggests a man who has little respect for life and who is determined to have his way in everything he does.

Gov. Pryor and his staff must explain to the residents of Garland County why Davis is so different from other convicted murderers that he deserves the treatment he's received. Law abiding citizens here should not be forced to experience even a few moments of fear over a man society put away.

Rumors continue to circulate in the county about Davis; rumors of continued misconduct and abuse of others; rumors of influence bought and sold.

Gov. Pryor and his staff owe the county an investigation into the Davis case and a complete explanation of why he has been treated as he has been.

On a warpath with the governor's office, the *Sentinel-Record* ran another editorial on December 2, 1976, titled "Frank Davis: Still No Answer":

The governor's office said earlier this week that it has concluded its investigation of the recent escape of Frank Davis from a minimum security unit at Booneville and of alleged "special treatment" he received during his prison stay.

In the investigation report a prison official indicated that Davis will not likely receive any unusual consideration in the future.

He is in maximum security and will remain there for at least a year the report said.

The prison officials are apparently "getting tough" with Davis because of the recent escape and because of local comment following his recapture which resulted in the governor's investigation.

The investigation and subsequent report and public revelations about its content are fine as far as they go. But there are no answers to the provocative questions raised about the treatment Davis received after he was sentenced to Cummins for the 1968 murder of his then estranged wife.

Davis became a trusty at Cummins in 1969 while still sentenced to death.

He repeatedly received what appears to be partial treatment. He recently remarried and was at the Booneville minimum security unit where his life was relatively unencumbered by supervision.

The spokesman for the governor who revealed information from the investigation said Gov. David Pryor might still look further into these circumstances.

That no determination was made concerning the treatment indicates a serious shortcoming in the investigation. The system apparently failed in dealing with Davis and only through understanding how it failed can the public be confident that it will not fail in the same way again.

While Davis was loose following his escape, a number of spa residents expressed fear that he might return here and harm them. There is no justifiable reason why persons in the outside world should have to experience these kinds of anxieties over a person who society has decided should be punished.

Certainly rehabilitation is a primary concern. The convict must have care and consideration, but so must those in the free world.

The saddest aspect of the current trend towards absolute "protection" for the criminal is that it allows too many misfits to escape punishment for a wrong they've committed only to return to society and perpetrate more tragedy.

Too often innocent people become victims of "justice".

To a certain extent, this is true in the Davis case. His apparent preferential care as a prisoner makes taxpayers who support the prison system, and those residents in the county who were wronged by him, and those who sought to implement justice, the victims.

Certainly Davis should be perceived as he now is. Perhaps he has changed. But his escape from Booneville only adds to the local theory that he is not ready to be returned to society, that he is not rehabilitated.

Gov. Pryor is aware of Davis now, but he has not satisfied the local need to know how a prisoner can receive preferential treatment. He has an obligation to do so.[14]

Frank was docked five years, two months, and twenty days of "good time" for his three-day escape. Now back at Cummins maximum-security prison, he remained unassigned for work duties until December 7, 1976, and then he was sent far away from cattle and horses to the garden squad—every inmate's worst nightmare.

· 29 ·

The Chest Pains and Newspaper Clippings

In the past, Frank spent time writing songs, but now his efforts were focused on freedom. He clipped newspaper articles and began working with the prisoners' attorney. An *Arkansas Gazette* story on "prisoners' rights to sue if their illnesses were ignored by officials" was his impetus to begin building a file. Over the years, he'd had plenty of stomach issues, but now he had a new ailment, coronary arteriosclerosis. Before he broke out of Booneville, a doctor in nearby Fort Smith had told him he needed a heart catheterization. Frank wrote his Hot Springs attorney, Bob Ridgeway, to inform him of his latest ailment but received a polite response saying he'd be out of the office. So, Frank took another route through the prison infirmary with a referral to the University of Arkansas Medical Center in Little Rock, where a physician agreed with the Fort Smith doctor's diagnosis.

While at the medical center on March 30, 1977, Frank explained his arduous prison work in detail. He said his chest pains became worse while carrying 100-pound sacks in ankle-deep mud and after complaining to prison authorities was told he was just hyperventilating.

The doctor ordered a stress test on April 4, 1977, which found the prison's previous claims of "hyperventilation" were incorrect. Instead, Frank was diagnosed with "ischemic chest pain." The doctor placed him on 10 milligrams of Inderal four times a day, limited his physical activity, and requested he return in one month for a follow-up exam.

Frank added the new diagnosis to his file and continued to explore other avenues. He asked officials for an opinion of his parole eligibility on September 30, 1977, and then began creating notes on a legal pad. Frank also gathered copies of his armed forces documents and past correspondence in addition to as many medical recollections as he could obtain. Feeling a kindred spirit, he clipped George Fisher's *Arkansas Gazette* editorial cartoon featuring a New Jersey policeman sitting outside a jail cell with a prisoner hunkered inside. The guard is raising his right fist and yelling, "Inhuman! Barbaric" as he reads a newspaper with the headline "USSR JAILS DISSI-DENTS." What brings this cartoon home to Arkansas is a sign above the jail cell that says, "UNCONSTITUTIONAL ARKANSAS DEPARTMENT CORRECTION." Below the jail cell door, a message had been scribbled: "ENTER A 'DARK EVIL' World!"

⌒

The restoration of Frank's meritorious good time was enacted on January 9, 1978. Twenty-two days later, James Mabry, director of the Arkansas Department of Corrections, received Opinion No. 78-6 by the Arkansas attorney general, which addressed Frank's parole eligibility. It contained information of applicable Arkansas statutes, court rulings, legal terminology, examination of the executive chief's (Governor Rockefeller's) commutation language and interpretations, and different time line correlations.

The five-page opinion addressed the issue of whether Frank Davis was eligible for parole consideration and, if not, what statute was applicable. "Parole, unlike pardon or reprieve, is not a matter of gubernatorial clemency, but is an administrative conditional release from imprisonment which may be controlled or prohibited by legislation that is not discriminatory," it stated at the beginning.

The time it took to research and write this opinion would probably be mind boggling, especially with the case examples, examinations of language, the history, and interpretations. However, the summary stated that the individual (Frank Davis) was ineligible for parole between June 17, 1968, and December 29, 1970, when his death sentence was commuted. After that, when he was given a life sentence, he was still ineligible through April 1, 1977, when a new law dictated that the controlling statute should be the one in effect at the time the felony was committed (Sharron's murder). The opinion covered all sides of the issue and concluded that the decision as to parole eligibility should be decided under Act 93 of 1977, which earlier stated it was the most recent embodiment of legislative intent on the subject of parole eligibility.

The document ended with the salutation, "The foregoing Opinion, of which I approve, was prepared by Assistant Attorney General Robert M. Lyford. Sincerely yours, Bill Clinton, Attorney General."

To some, the opinion might be considered "legalese" that could mean one thing or the other, but the value of it could be comparable to breaking into a bank vault. And Irene Davis Hogan had found the perfect lock picker,

Charles Sidney Gibson—a prominent southeast Arkansas attorney from a powerful political family with members serving in both the Arkansas Senate and the House of Representatives. Irene hoped Gibson's family name, connections, and know-how would provide a *legal* escape from prison for her dear "Sonny." Gibson wasted no time going to work for her in February 1978, filing a complaint for declaratory judgment.

While Irene was working on the outside, Frank was working inside. His daring attempt to gain freedom two years earlier cost him the exalted trusty position, riding a horse with the beef herd, and resulted in manual labor. He loathed the new assignment and began documenting each day's work on the back side of a legal pad. "Apr 3, 1978. Returned to field. 12 men loaded trailer truck potatoes sacks weighted over 100 lbs, 2 12 yd trucks of bricks fertilized, 20 acres of radishes, cabbage, onion, beets."

The next day, he wrote, "Apr 4th garden layed in due to shortage of Rider. However, we were required to mop and clean barracks and then mop and sweep about 150 yds of hall and dust bars and wash walls. Apr 5, Returned to Field chopped strawberries, loaded 2–12 yd trucks of bricks, fertilized about 20 acres of crops with 12–12–12 and then chopped about ¼ mile of shit ditch."

He continued, "Apr 6, one garden layed in, but we were required to clean Barracks and then go on up and lay 2 dump truck loads of Brick on a sidewalk out sally port door. Apr 7. Layed in for Dr Call to be reclassified due to call from Senator about university's order to not let me ever be placed in field, was advised that by Dr Adams. I'll let you never make any more requests on fresh air or sunshine again. On approximately March 17th Mr. Bradberry had discussed possibilities of my getting some fresh air or sunshine as I had been layed in for months by Dr. Douglas orders. Head cardiologist university of Ark. And to never return to field duty or they would be in trouble."

Frank used all the back side of his legal pad and then found a scrap of paper where he continued his notes. "On May 10th, finally after insisting that I see a cardiologist I was finally sent to the university to see Dr. [name illegible]. University ran an E.K.G. chest x rays and I was examined by Dr. [illegible]. He asked me what type of work I was doing & I told him that they had assigned me to the Kitchen and from there to the veg. House. He asked me my duties. I told him picking up 55 gallon barrels of slop, from 6:00 a.m. until thru usually and quite often 12 hrs per day. He ordered reclassification. Mr. Bradberry Hosp. Registered Nurse recommended to the classification officer on the 25th of May that I be changed to light outside yard work not to lift over 15 pounds, no long standing for no more than ½ day. I met classification on June 1st 1978 at approx. 8:30. Mr. Campbell said when he looked at Mr. Bradberry's typed request for reclassification that this just means we can work him outside but I want to leave him right where he is, thank you Frank that's all. I never even opened my mouth. I was [word illegible] out to return to work."

Frank clipped the *Gazette State News* article, "Husband Gets 5-Year Term in Gun Death,"[1] of a forty-nine-year-old Benton man who was charged with first-degree murder for the September 1977 shooting death of his estranged wife. The prosecutor asked for life, but the jury of eight women and four men gave him five years. His defense attorney, Ray Roberts, "contended his client was suffering from a mental disease at the time of the slaying and that he had no recollection of shooting his wife." The newspaper article noted the prosecuting attorney presented several shooting witnesses, including one who testified having heard the murderer tell his wife, "I told you I would kill you."

The article may have caught Frank's attention for two reasons: the murderer had threatened his wife with almost identical words, and the man received a five-year prison term instead of the death penalty. Frank wasted no time contacting Ray Roberts, the defense attorney.

Dan Runde, the inmate attorney, sent Frank a June 8, 1978, letter on Arkansas Department of Corrections letterhead in response to correspondence from Ray Roberts. Frank and his mother had contacted Roberts for the possible habeas corpus, which would compel those holding a prisoner to produce the prisoner and prove that they have legally incarcerated the individual.

The inmate attorney instructed Frank to send Roberts the case or memorandum brief that he intended to use in the habeas corpus. He suggested Frank also give Roberts his views to inform him of his wishes concerning his services and/or his acting as attorney for him.

With this new potential legal arrangement, Frank was two-timing his most recent attorney—Charles Gibson—who on June 10, 1978, filed a writ of habeas corpus ad testificandum with the U.S. District Court, Eastern District of the Arkansas Division. The main point of Gibson's contention in *Allen Frank Davis, Appellant, v. Jerry Campbell, Acting Warden, Appellee* was the reconstruction of Frank's incarceration time line to begin with his admittance to the Arkansas State Hospital for observation on January 30, 1967, instead of the June 17, 1968, sentencing date.

Gibson noted, "The Plaintiff has served in excess of fifteen years of which Plaintiff's credit for good time allowances does not exceed five years as contemplated by Ark. Stat 43-2807 (b) (2). (This is not a Stipulation that the cited Statute applies, only that if it does that Plaintiff has satisfied its requirements for parole eligibility.)"

The hearing was held five days later. A U.S. marshal escorted Frank to provide testimony for Federal District Court Judge (of the Eighth Circuit)

Elsijane Trimble Roy, who would determine if his imprisonment was unlawful. The hearing began at 9:30 a.m., and at the conclusion of testimony, the court requested briefs from Frank within thirty days. He was told the state would respond within thirty days, and a reply would be due ten days later. The court recessed at 2:36 p.m. after denying a motion for bail.

Supporting her son as he worked every legal avenue to gain his freedom, Irene wrote a letter on June 22, 1978, and added 3:00 p.m., the time she began writing. Irene said,

> Dear Sonny: Received your sweet letter written the 20th and post marked the 21st that is real fast mail service, [illegible] in this off the way place. Your letter to me had not been sealed, so anyone could read it if they had time to. I love hearing from you but don't want you to push yourself out so much unless you need to have me do things that can help you can cut mine short and tell Wanda the things you need to and save you some of the writing. You have so much to do with all the research you are doing. I wish you had a typewriter at your disposal, if you ever needed a secretary it is now. And you have had some good one like Jane and the shorthand.
>
> You should see Ray Roberts on a typewriter. I can do as well and see better. We were in his office when he was typing the summons up for the three witnesses. I didn't know at the time that we were having to pay him forty dollars an hour. I did ask him why he didn't let one of the secretarys [sic] do it for him and he said he only had 3 of the forms and he didn't want to take a chance on them messing one up. Maybe he is O.K. but slow.
>
> It is his fault that he has been so long in doing what he has and he owes you some consideration for doing all of the research for him. That is why Ray has charged so much as he knows how little Chas [attorney Gibson] has done and what he charged for nothing so far. Ray has done what Chas. should have done for what we have paid.
>
> Any way the cost would mean nothing if they only got you out, we could live on bread and water if it takes it the money doesn't mean anything compared to your freedom and being with us. I would never complain if only we could be on our own together. I wanted to go see Ray today but got a bug from something in [illegible] our water, it is going around the pharmacist said, and sent me some Infentol pink with opium & paregoric in it and I took two small doses of it and felt like an elephant was on my chest then I called my Dr's office and they said not to take any more of it.

Irene explained that she bought automobile tires for Wanda and mentioned how his daughter, now eleven years old, "had done a good job washing windows and raking the yard." Irene said, "I pay her so she has her own money. She is a lot like me when it comes to making money; you know I always was a workhorse when it came to making money."

In closing, she said,

I hate to think about how hard you are working. Wish you and Vic both could slow up. He is trying to get out from under so much expense on his ex's side. Mike Hindel is doing it for him but may have to pay to have his house repaired 750.00 before he gets it settled. Don't worry about my tummy ache. I will eat carefully. I love you dearly more than anything or body in the world. Love Mother

Irene's comments that "we could live on bread and water" and "I would never complain if only we could be on our own together" reveal a mother who couldn't let her little boy become a grown man. Her possessive love wouldn't allow him to be a responsible husband and father, or maybe she was covering up her parental mistakes that produced a multiple murderer.

"Vic," whom Irene mentioned at the end of her letter, was her fourth husband, Vic Lewis. He was employed at Brown Packing and resided with her at 163 Henderson Street, the house originally owned by her second husband, Athas Athanas.

Irene's third husband, Pat Hogan, was sixteen years her senior, and by 1978 when she was seventy-one years old, he would have been eighty-seven if he were still living. Two years before Frank began his 1966 murder spree, Irene and Pat Hogan were involved in a December 1964 four-car accident in Hot Springs.[2] A car driven by a twenty-four-year-old man sideswiped three cars on Third Street before hitting Irene and Pat's car head-on. Irene went to the hospital with "a possible broken jaw" and lacerations of the face, while her husband sustained a shoulder injury and facial lacerations. After murdering Sharron in 1967, Frank mentioned his mother and stepfather's debilitating accident and lengthy recuperation during sessions with the state hospital psychiatrist.

⌒⌒

Continuing to build his case, Frank returned to journaling on his legal pad. A page topped with the date, June 27, 1978, said, "On this day, we processed produce & loaded barrels as required approx. 29 or 30 barres. Called out at approx 0600 hrs and worked until 1200 hrs." The next entry, June 28, 1978, stated, "Made sick call was having jaw & neck pains & shortness of breath. Saw Mr. Bradberry at approx. 5:35 AM. He saw me again at infirmary at approx 9:00 AM. He asked me if I was taking Nitro and I replied like popcorn. He layed me in for the rest of day 3 hrs and the 29th day of June, stated he didn't want Old Frank dying on us."

Despite the efforts of Frank and his attorney, Governor David Pryor denied his latest application for executive clemency in a June 28, 1978, form letter that was identical to his previous denial. Once again, Frank was encouraged to reapply in one year.

After this bad news, he made a handwritten list of other possibilities for freedom:

1. What about a default Judgment on the Declaratory Judgment?
2. What about Medical Clemency? Length of Time, etc.?
3. What about Medical Suit?
4. What relief could be expected through Habeas Court?
5. What about Board relief in the event of a reversal & remand. Who Sets Bond?
6. What about change of Venue?
7. How Long before a hearing could be obtained on Medical Relief?
8. There is NO Diet available for Artery diseases at institution.

Disappointed at her son's latest rejection, Irene mailed Frank a July 1, 1979, *Sentinel-Record* newspaper clipping titled "Mentally-Ill First Offender Is Sent to Cummins."[3] The article explained that a twenty-one-year-old first-time offender with a five-year history of mental problems had received a six-month sentence at Cummins prison for stealing twenty-two cases of beer with friends. The young man's attorney, Bill Green of Hot Springs, reportedly furnished Judge Britt with letters documenting the man's illness, but Britt said in open court that he chose "to make an example" of him. "His sentence is apparently intended to 'set an example' for potential lawbreakers," the newspaper stated.

Irene scribbled a note on the second page of the article: "This is just what he did to you and said the same thing. I don't know why somebody doesn't say something about the way he does."

Encouraged by his mother, Frank wrote his name on the spine of an 8½- by 14-inch Scribbletex legal pad. He started a letter, dated July 21, 1978, to Mr. James Gardner, chairman of the Board of Pardons and Parole at a Post Office box in Blytheville, Arkansas. Across from the inside address, Frank placed his name, prisoner number, and status—"Sentenced to Life, 1st Degree Murder, Garland Co. Ar."

Frank asked Mr. Gardner for advice and consideration in his case and situation. He explained the steps of his incarceration (from the death sentence to Rockefeller's commutation), his many attempts for executive clemency, the various rulings, and the filing of his declaratory judgment. His narrative continued for two and a half pages, and then it fizzled out. The last paragraph began, "I have studied the attorney general's opinion and conducted research on the opinion and the laws governing my case on eligibility," dwindled into his feelings about "Act 93," and ended with an incomplete sentence.

Frank was desperate to flee the prison's backbreaking manual labor on his fifty-four-year-old body, so he decided to enlist help from his younger counterparts. He rounded up six prison mates who wrote affidavits of the grueling hard work he performed and their concerns for his health and welfare. He also accumulated doctors' notes and prescriptions on his visits to the prison infirmary. A June 15, 1978, doctor's permit stated, "May have Bottom Bunk" along with "No Duty thru 6-16-78."

Later that summer, Frank mailed his attorney, Charles Gibson, a drawing of the Pink Panther with a sly grin, a black cigarette holder in his right hand. A ball and chain that displayed a large "8" between the initials, "F" and "D," was attached to his left ankle. "August 28, 1978" was written atop the page, and Gibson's address was flush left, as if it were a memorandum. Under the Pink Panther, on the bottom of the page, Frank wrote, "What about the Declaratory Judgment? I expected to be on the August Board. What happened? Sincerely Frank Davis."

⌒

Staying busy, Frank inventoried his personal property. It included "one oxygen tank and mask; one portable TV; one AM Panasonic radio; one AM-FM radio; one pair new Sea Turtle Ben Miller boots; one pair Justin elephant skin boots; one pair Nocona nearly new brown calf boots; 2 western hats; 2 pair glasses; books, Black's Law, Webster Dictionary, other books; 2 upright lockers containing approx $25 commissary, picture albums, $50 cosmetics, under clothing, etc; one Alvarez guitar and case, value $350; 2 suits Free World Kaki's; pair of spurs; 2 Free World poncho, rain coats (New); other personal clothing, sweater, pajamas & etc.; one ½ carat white gold diamond ring 14 K gold; 4 dogs, 3 yellow curr, 1-1/2 curr & Border Collie; 2 Concho Rain Coats (New); Legal material, Records of case & etc.; one gold chain and one silver chain."

Then, on August 3, 1978, he reprinted this list on another piece of legal-size notepaper and placed "Affidavit, State of Arkansas, County of Lincoln" on top. Next, he enlisted a prison mate to swear "that while I was assigned to the Booneville Unit, Booneville Arkansas in the year of 1976, that Frank did have in his possession the following listed articles." The "affidavit" was notarized by Stephen G. Martin and showed the prisoner's name and signature along with his five-digit Arkansas Department of Corrections identification number.

⌒

Frank's lifelong health problems, coupled with acute health issues, provided him a way out with a new medical classification on August 31, 1978. The doctor prescribed no arduous duty, and he became an unassigned inmate.

While he was in the prison barracks, his attorney filed a writ of mandamus. This summons (*Allan Frank Davis v. James Mabry, Director, Arkansas Department of Corrections et al.*, Lincoln Circuit No. 78-27) had the same force as a court order. It demanded "a prisoner be taken before the court, and the custodian [usually a prison official] present proof of authority, allowing the Court to determine whether the custodian had lawful authority to detain the prisoner."[4]

The decision landed in the court of Judge H. A. Taylor, circuit judge of the Eleventh Judicial District, Second Division, where the prison was located. On November 14, 1978, Judge Taylor sent correspondence to Robert M. Lyford at the attorney general's office and to Frank's attorney, Charles Sidney Gibson, stating his "conclusions of law" to the writ of mandamus.

Judge Taylor wrote, "Inasmuch as Mr. Davis' new sentence occurred subsequent to the effective dates of Act 48 and 94 of 1969, he is not eligible for parole on serving a life sentence. Therefore, the plaintiff's petition for Writ of Mandamus is denied. Mr. Lyford will prepare a judgment consistent with the above, submit the same to Mr. Gibson for approval as to form and then to the Court for signature."

• *30* •

The String Pulling

$\mathcal{A}$ week before Christmas 1978, Frank sent a written request to Clifford Terry, the prison's treatment coordinator, requesting class 1 special visiting privileges "due to both mine and my mother's terminal incurable diseases." Frank said his mother had undergone three heart operations and was scheduled for a fourth at the Texas Heart Institute "as soon as she was fully recovered from the last."

Frank explained, "The gravity of our conditions makes every visit possible the utmost important." He assured Terry, "Visitations will be limited to my immediate family, my wife, daughter, stepfather and mother."

Frank then wrote Tom Cashion, an attorney in Eudora, Arkansas, an hour south of Cummins Prison. The February 16, 1979, letter explained how he'd waited for a visit from his attorney, Charles Gibson, but learned Gibson had been elk hunting for the past three weeks. "He has failed to get my motion filed for a probable cause and to give notice of appeal on Judge Roy's ruling on my Habeas. I will submit it Tues. and submit the brief," said Frank. "There is no doubt that this latest Att. Gen. opinion supersedes all other rulings pertaining to my parole eligibility under Act 50 and makes me eligible. You have been real helpful to my cause a long time. Also very comforting to my mother by answering her many questions. At present I feel like if I had someone to consult with Mr. Gardner and the other Board members and discuss the opinions that Mr. Gardner would place me on the February Board as a special due to my dire medical needs. If you could do this for me, I would be happy to retain you for your assistance and representation, also to reimburse any travel expense, telephone calls, etc. incurred."

Busy networking in and out of the prison, Frank accepted a business card from Dr. J. F. Cooley that said, "Whatever is right by God and better

189

for man, this I do." Dr. Cooley had taught eleven years in Forrest City, Arkansas' all-black Lincoln Junior-Senior High School until the John Birch Society gained control of their school board and fired him with no explanation in 1969.[1]

"His termination seemed to have stemmed from his activities in the civil rights movement, including the December 1968 formation of the Committee for Peaceful Coexistence," the *African American Heritage in Arkansas Guide* stated. "Cooley had also helped organize demonstrations and worked with black males to prevent juvenile delinquency. Cooley's firing fueled unrest among junior high students who vandalized Lincoln [school] in March and staged a student walkout in April," the guide explained.

Turning to a different platform, Cooley became a Little Rock constable in District 3 and also began advocating for prisoners and others who needed his helping hand. The card he had given Frank displayed his long list of legal affiliations: Legislative aide on prison reform; permanent captain, North Little Rock Police Department; prosecuting attorney's office; sheriff's department; notary public, prison and parolee counselor; deputy registrar; permanent lieutenant colonel, law enforcement; circuit court clerk's office; and editor, *Arkansas Weekly Sentinel*.

Frank kept a May 3, 1979, edition of Cooley's publication, which showed a photograph of the middle-aged black man dressed in a white shirt, black tie, and dark jacket with a law enforcement patch on the left sleeve and wearing a trooper-style uniform hat with gold braids and a crescent-type emblem. Across the page from his picture was "Editorial Observations," where Cooley stated, "Many inmates are becoming mentally ill or sick otherwise in our Correctional Institutions."[2] He listed different diseases and gave his belief that "even though some of these inmates are serving long sentences for vicious crimes, their continued confinement is not serving any purpose whatsoever." He felt they should be released to organizations or relatives for care, claiming it would save money for Arkansas and reduce crowded cells that housed more than 3,000 inmates. He noted the state also had almost 3,000 parolees, who, coupled with the inmates, made a "large family of criminals."

"It is time something be done to either reduce this number or place them in a better location," Cooley said. "Two evils of the same nature never solved anything. And, whereas I deplore any type of crime, and pray that all criminals will be fully punished; I feel it is morally, psychologically, socially, educationally and spiritually wrong for a person to be punished, if they are unable to be fully punished."

Cooley claimed there were a few inmates serving time that he thought would "relieve the state of much obligation and trouble if they were released." He noted they learned that crime didn't pay and had fully or partially paid for their crimes. He said, "If they were to be paroled now or given Executive Clemency, they may be of some use to others before the 'curtain falls.'"

Frank Davis led a list of eleven inmates whose conditions he felt were worsening during several years of his counseling. Adding a disclaimer, Cooley stated, "There are many more. I do not agree with their crimes in any way. But, under their present condition and frame of mind, plus the good changes that have come into their hearts, I see no need for confining them any longer. Why place an additional burden on the State, when these people are ready to live constructive lives outside or be cared for at the family's or their own insurance's expense."

To compensate Cooley's efforts, Irene Davis began her own form of advocacy, especially after Frank's early 1979 executive clemency denial. In March 1979, she contacted a family friend from Lake Forest, Illinois, to write a letter in Frank's support. It stated,

> To Whom It May Concern, I have had the privilege of knowing Frank Davis's family since I was a little girl. Frank Davis, as a Son, as a soldier, as a businessman, as a pilot, as a horseman has always demonstrated great skill, ability and genuine concern for what he was doing or involved in. And, in response, has received great love and respect. Irene Davis, Frank's mother, is a fine, intelligent and loving woman who has remained steadfast in her love for her son. She has maintained a warm and stable home for her son and family, in spite of tremendous adversity, heartbreak and serious illness. She is a woman of a strong and loving disposition. I love her as one would a mother or dearest Aunt.

The woman mentioned Irene's fourth husband, Vic Lewis, and Frank's fifth wife and child. She said his wife had been with him for over twelve years, "and never had there been the least doubt of her love or devotion to him." The family friend claimed, "They all made up an extraordinary home that would be precisely the environment for a man to come back to after his 'rehabilitation.' I urge Frank Davis's immediate release and return to his family."

Letters were flying everywhere, and Frank zipped one off to Charles Gibson on April 2, 1979. "I hate to keep writing but I feel this noteworthy," he said, before informing his attorney of a recent *Arkansas-Gazette* article of the correction board's acceptance of Prison Director Mabry's resignation and their plans to replace him.

Frank explained the article mentioned a "Liberalized Furlough, SCR6," which he felt could be his ticket out of prison. He wrote, "With the U.A.M.C. Doctors, V.A. Doctors, and my medical records along with our political support. This may be the fastest possible relief. What is your opinion?"

Frank's reasoning contained two good possibilities. The first included his suit against the prison administrator, arguing he was parole eligible "due to having served in excess of fifteen years," and the second was "the political support" he mentioned in his letter to Gibson.

Another Arkansas governor could be providing Frank's pathway to freedom. And this time, it was the Hot Springs hometown boy, thirty-two-year-old Bill Clinton, who, at his January 1979 inauguration, became the youngest governor in the nation.[3]

When only a child, Bill moved from Hope to Hot Springs with his mother, Virginia. His new stepfather, Roger Clinton Sr., was rejoining his brother, Raymond, at Clinton Buick, the family business. Roger had been working in their Hope dealership when he met Bill's mother, Virginia Cassidy Blythe. After the relocation to the popular resort town, Bill attended Hot Springs public schools and graduated in 1964. Three years later, Roger Sr. died.

In 1969, Virginia married Jeff Dwire, who, like her, was born in Bodcaw,[4] only fifteen miles from Hope.[5] Her third husband, a hairstylist, owned Jeff's Hair Fashions, which in the early 1970s was the same salon space where Sharron Knight Davis worked at the time of her 1967 murder. Dwire and Irene Davis were professionally associated until his death in 1974, but that didn't stop Irene's personal connection to Virginia—especially in 1979 when it could come in handy knowing the governor's mother.

Irene never hesitated asking favors from others. Her bankers had written letters to the parole board and the four governors who had been elected during Frank's incarceration. Now, in 1979, she started a petition campaign for his parole. She gathered signatures from her contacts around Hot Springs, such as Dorys Covington, Vera M. Cook, Frederick Dale, Martin J. Lax, Dorothy G. Finch, Margaret Holiman, Mrs. Harry Harrelson, and Howard Caldwell. The long list included names of a dentist, a well-known savings-and-loan officer, an antiques dealer, Lakeshore Drive and Henderson Street neighbors, beauty shop clients, business owners, wives of business owners, and even a man named Will Rogers, who was actually the manager of the Garland County Farmers Association where she'd purchased many bales of hay for Frank's livestock.

Her efforts, along with expensive lawyers and Dr. J. F. Cooley's advocacy, came to fruition on September 11, 1979, when a notification from the Department of Corrections Probation and Parole Services in Pine Bluff was delivered to persons connected to Frank Davis's imprisonment. The letter stated, "Subject is eligible for parole under Act 50 pursuant to recent Supreme Court Action," then asked for "input on the request for his parole."

Wasting no time in responding, Garland County Circuit Judge Britt wrote, "This court strongly and without reservation recommends and requests that parole and other relief from sentence be denied this inmate because this was a brutal and violent murder of his wife and the attempted murder of his mother-in-law. Further, this court has good reason to believe that if this inmate is released on parole or otherwise, he or others may very well die or be killed as a consequence. There are no mitigating circumstances."

A week later, on September 18, 1979, the *Sentinel-Record* ran the headline "Davis Eligible for Parole."[6] The article announced the Arkansas State Supreme Court ruled the previous day that Frank was now eligible for "consideration for parole." Their ruling overturned the decision made by Lincoln County Circuit Court Judge Taylor, who less than a year earlier said Frank wasn't eligible to be considered for parole by the state parole board.

Judge Britt, who'd sentenced Frank to death in the electric chair, was asked his opinion of this recent action. "I didn't know he went to the Supreme Court. However, I do oppose parole in that case," he said. "The facts and circumstances are too horrible to release that man on parole."

The newspaper explained the Arkansas Supreme Court declared in its ruling that it wasn't saying Davis was entitled to parole, only that he was entitled to be considered for parole by the state parole board. "The legal question in this case was whether his eligibility for consideration for parole should be determined by the law that was in effect at the time of his original sentence or the different law that was in effect at the time of the commutation," it stated.

A further explanation included Lincoln County Circuit Court Judge Taylor's previous ruling of "the law that applied was the one that was in effect at the time of the commutation." Taylor said that the commutation was a new sentence and that eligibility for parole consideration would have to be determined by the law that existed at the time, which was less in Davis's favor than the law that was in effect at the time of his sentence.

Associate Justice John A. Fogleman maintained the opinion of the Arkansas Supreme Court was that the law existing in 1968 was the one on which Davis's eligibility for parole consideration had to be based. The 1968 law provided "the consideration for parole of a lifer after he had served fifteen years, with up to five years of that time being time credited to the inmate for good behavior." Under that formula, the Supreme Court said, "Davis is eligible for consideration."

People throughout Hot Springs were surprised and frightened when they read the startling news. Many remembered Frank Davis's threats.

Debby Fager said, "He didn't like anybody that was in the courtroom, the stenographer and the judge, the attorneys, and my family members that might've been there. I'm pretty sure a lot of them felt like they were being threatened and feared for their life because he probably would've killed them. If I remember right, I think he did say he was going to kill anybody and everybody that had anything to do with the trial. He was crazy."

Hot Springs residents couldn't understand how a man who had murdered his young wife and a teenage girl could qualify for parole. Over the years, they had watched Frank's prison status change from death by execution to life in prison as well as the dismissal of Cathie Ward's first-degree murder charges.

Some may have second-guessed the Garland County Circuit Court. Maybe if they hadn't dropped the charges for Cathie Ward's murder, he would've faced a second sentence and would've received another death sentence or at least a second term of life in prison. But who in their right mind, back in January 1970 when Cathie's murder charge was dropped, would have imagined in only twelve months Frank would be plucked from death row and then undergo a bizarre chain of events that would allow him the possibility of parole in 1979?

The Keep Forever Letters

*F*rank Davis received two letters on September 28, 1979. The first one was dated two days earlier, on September 26, and just as his mother Irene had written on previous correspondence, she included the time, "6: P. M.":

Dear Sonny,

Received your letter written on the 24th today, sorry to hear that you did not get our letters that we mailed Sunday at 6: P.M. I know how disappointing it can be. Hope by now you have had my letter written both Monday and Tuesday also hope you received my message today from the Chaplins office as I know how much you needed to hear from us also to know what is going on.

I have talked to Charles once on Monday and wrote to you that he wanted me to be there Friday so I received my permission today from Mr. Gardner. And Wanda & I will be there with you and so will Charles and Dr. Cooley but Charles wants to present both the medical and the other so I told him that was fine, also told Dr. Cooley that and there would not be enough time for everyone to talk and be interviewed.

The board members are familiar with your case and will not have so much to review except all new medical records and the supreme courts findings regarding your case so you already know. I hope by now that Charles has let you hear from him some way. He said he needed to talk to you so maybe he won't be late Friday. My letter said to be there at 8:30 so we will get started by 5:30 that way we won't have to leave Becky with someone and Lynn can see that she gets off to school o.k. So don't worry about us and just try to be calm so you won't be so upset over everything.

We have got to make it this time as our time is sure short. So far I am doing fine and trying to be prepared for whatever we have to do. Just take it one day at a time and today is almost over and tomorrow will just be one more day to wait and then we will try to be calm and pray that God will see us through the suspense.

He always has been our consolation. Until I see you Friday this will be the last letter you will get so put your trust in the Lord and know that he loves you and that I love you so very much.

All my love,
Mother.

The second letter Frank received was on the same writing paper but had endearing love notes in both upper corners of each page. His wife Wanda had drawn hearts for every "O" in "I Love You! So Much!" Then she wrote the date and time, "Sept. 26, 1979, 4:00 PM":

Sweetheart,

I received your sweet letter of the 24th today. I sure was ready for it also. I am so sorry you didn't have our letter Monday. We both got our letter in the post office before 6:30 PM. You should have had it Monday. I know how I feel when I don't have a letter from you. They really are the highlight of my day. Becky and I are going to the wash as soon as Vickie comes by to pick up her pants. She gets off work at 4:30.

Your mother and I will be down for the Board Friday. We will be there by 8:30 AM. I have my fingers crossed. We will make it and don't you even think any different.

Sweetheart don't ever forget for one minute how very much I love and need you. Our love is so very special and wonderful to me. I know I may repeat myself on that but I just never want you to forget. There is no way I could ever think of a future without you in ("it"). You are stuck with me so put that in your pipe and smoke it. I don't ever intend to be without you. Ever! You are the most wonderful husband in the world.

From what you said, things are really going to change down there. You won't be there to see them all take place. We are going to be together and away from it all very, very soon.

Right now our next visit seems like a year away. Soon we won't have to wait for visits and letters but be together all of the time. It will be so fantastic. Friday will be our day.

I'll close for now and be looking forward to our next visit and your sweet letters. All of my love till I can see you. Lots of Love Forever, Wanda. P.S. I love my sweet and wonderful husband more than anything in the world. Don't you ever forget that either. Not a chance because I won't let you. I love you!

Irene and Wanda arrived on time for the Friday, September 28, parole board hearing, and that evening, after returning to Hot Springs, Irene pulled out her notepad to begin another letter. Across the top, she wrote, "To Day is Friday" followed by "Sept. 28th, 1979," as if it were a newspaper headline:

Dear Sonny,

This is the day we have waited for. It has been a long hard fight we have had for so many precious years, but we finally received Justice the hard way. Thank God for his compassion, and I hope We can soon get this all behind us and have a few days of peace of mind and body together again. I thank God for watching over you through all of the danger around you and keeping you from the destructing that comes from being surrounded by the environment that goes with prison life. You have to be strong to overcome the temptations that can destroy so many high standards of living. It has never destroyed your will power like one party thought. You are still a man of honor and dependability. A man of your word and that is what America was built on when a man's word is not good he has lost everything. You can stand up and be counted on any time anywhere.

I was so sorry that you did not get to see Wanda today she wanted to see you so much but then we thought we would get the special visit Sunday until we got home and read your letter. Charles had already told us we could go on down as he was sure to get one. I wish you could have seen us when the man told us we were going to Oregon. I was speechless and Charles grabbed me around the neck. He to[o] was shocked he was so happy about it. Then Wanda came over and I told her to hug both Dr. Cooley & Charles. I have never seen anyone any happier than Dr. Cooley was. I had to hug him for his kindness and prayers. He said this was the one thing he wanted to see, was your freedom and he wanted to be there when we got the word. I hope you knew it as soon as we did.

The girl in the tower hollered down to me and said someone must have some good news and I told her we did. So maybe you know that it came then and the vote was 100% only 4 members and they all voted for your release to Oregon. Mr. Wells was not present or he would have voted for you. I talked to Charles and he is going to rush your release as soon as possible. It will be Monday before they can do anything and Charles said as soon as they make the contact with the Oregon board. We can go by car and take our time traveling.

I called Travis & Bobbie [Frank's uncle and aunt in Oregon]. They are so happy for us. Travis was so glad he was excited more than I have ever known him to be. I talked to Bernice & Lester and they too are happy.

Dr. Cooley said he would get them to call Oregon to rush things up Monday if Charles doesn't. I know you know by now what happened, hope you got a call for tonight. We can also get a special visit to you on business Dr. Cooley said so maybe we could see you Sunday awhile if Dr. Cooley called and request that we need to talk about some plans as soon as possible.

I hope you don't have any bad effects over this excitement. It can have a reaction on any one with a heart condition. We are hoping for a call from you tonight, so be sure to rest all you can and try to relax and I will too. We will start planning things next week and let our minds rest a day or two by meditating and praising and thanking God for his goodness to us now—

Your four leaf of clover sure came thru today. It will always be our symbol. I want a solid gold one for my neck as a Memorial. Wanda said she would have these laminated on a bracelet that would be sweet to carry on a card in your purse or billfold as a good luck token. Take it easy and be careful. I love you so much.

All my love, Mother.

P.S. Vic is not home yet so he doesn't know the good news we had. We had Susie with us today she enjoyed the ride.

Wanda followed her mother-in-law's lead, dashing off a long letter to Frank. And once again, she adorned the top of every page with the message "I Love you! So Much!" and swapped each "O" for a heart:

Hi Sweetheart,

I had your sweet letter of the 26th today. I sure was ready for it also. Today was our day and wasn't it fantastic. Well it all came true for us today. The day of our being together forever is really on its way now. I sure did want to see you today. It was so hard to be so close and yet so far away. But our visits and letters are over forever. That is a very wonderful feeling. I sure do hope you get a call tonight. Your Mother and I left about 6 AM this morning. We left Becky in bed and Betty called her at 6:45 to wake her up. I left her a note telling her to wash her face and brush her teeth. She wrote on the bottom of the note "Okie Doki."

Sweetheart don't ever forget for one minute just how very much I love and need you. Our love is really so wonderful and special to me. There is no way I could ever think of a future without you in it. EVER! You are the most wonderful husband in the whole world. We are going to be together soon. I just hope you don't get tired of my being around all of the time. You will just have to get used to it. I can hardly wait till I can see you. This Sat. & Sun. is a fifth Sat and Sunday. The next weekend seems like a year away. I can hardly wait for it to get here. I would give anything if I could be with you right now. We will be soon though. Right! Right!

I'll close for now and be looking forward to our visit and the time we can be together all of the time. It will be very soon now. All of my love till I can see you.

Lots of Love Forever, Wanda

P.S. I love my sweet and wonderful husband more than anything on earth. Don't you ever forget that. OK!

Frank put the two sets of letters into his mother's September 28, 1979, postmarked envelope bearing a fifteen-cent Oliver Wendell Holmes stamp. Then in the space above his name in the recipient's address, he wrote "Keep Forever" and underlined his words. He placed it in his prison briefcase.

෧

Days after the loving words from his mother and wife, a piece of mail arrived from Berry Creek, California, that he'd also stash away for safekeeping. Written on the envelope where most people would place their return address was the exclamation "Oran! Bingo!" Inside, was a sheet of three-holed notebook paper that had been folded three times. A musical score had been drawn on the back side of the paper with notes and lyrics that sang, "It's Been a Long Long Time." The writer placed the date, "29 Sept 79," on the upper-right side of the one-page letter:

> Sonny, !!!
> I just peed in my pants! and I'm a big boy now, but when Maggie called out here to my workshop and said I had a call from Irene, I broke all speed records getting to the house—My god, what a beautiful day it is! I talked with our elegant Irene for at least 10 minutes, but could hardly do so, because I was crying so hard. I must have sounded like I was gargling. We were laughing and crying together and I even had a real good talk with Vic. Frank, I can't say what's really in my heart, that's Mission Impossible, but YOU know! Now, get your paroled ass out here, you hear? Oh God, Son, how happy I am—I never asked "Old George" up yonder, for too much but the few I did on your behalf, must have been heard. I'm so damned happy, that I just think I'll take Ole Spook down the canyon, where there's a bitch dog in heat, and let him try it, ONE MORE TIME! Sonny, welcome home, kid brother!!! In my book, you can do no harm, and if you do, I'll break both your arms! Oh how happy! Oran

The connection between Frank and Oran is unknown despite several attempts to gain that information.

• 32 •

Oregon or Bust

The residents of Hot Springs didn't learn of Frank's actual parole until October 5, 1979, when the *Sentinel-Record* announced, "If Accepted by Oregon, Parole Board Okays Release of Davis."[1] The newspaper reported the Arkansas Supreme Court had ruled him eligible to be considered for parole two weeks earlier. "However, this didn't mean he was entitled to parole," they stated. "They [the parole board] based their decision on the law in effect at the time of his sentence, which made him eligible for consideration after serving fifteen years with up to five being credited for good behavior."

With that consideration, Frank was now eligible for parole, per the court, but with a caveat. Corrections board spokesman Tim Baltz said, "Davis will be required to go to Oregon or be held in violation of his parole and subject to parole revocation." He added, "The board did not indicate what reasons were given in paroling Davis to Oregon."

The newspaper repeated Judge Britt's distress of Frank's parole situation and his belief that the circumstances were too horrible to release him.

Garland County Sheriff Elza Young told the newspaper reporter he "planned to write to the parole board and question what the value of the local community's input to the board if letters and other opinions were not to be considered."

Tim Baltz addressed the community's concern, saying, "If he is released from our custody, it will be to the state of Oregon. Davis is not coming back to Hot Springs. And, if he did, he would be in violation of his parole. We are still working on the paperwork to see if Oregon will allow him to come there, and until that is completed and we get an answer, Davis will remain in our custody."

Robert Ridgeway, Frank Davis's trial co-attorney, speculated that Frank would be going to Oregon to be near relatives and said, "I personally can see no reason for anyone to be upset about Frank's parole."

With the parole to Oregon being contested, Irene Davis began canvassing the objectors. She approached Garland County Sheriff Elza Young, not knowing back in 1967, only hours before her son murdered Sharron, he attempted to murder Elza. She was also unaware Frank had continued to make death threats against him from behind prison walls.

"His mother came to me while I was sheriff and asked me to go along with having him transferred to Oregon to serve out his time," Elza told me. "I checked with prison officials, and that was their plan, to swap prisoners. I had no objection. I just wanted to get him out of this part of the country. I didn't want him to eventually get out and be here."

The news of Frank's new status not only roused the citizens of Hot Springs but also peeved Mike Masterson, editor of the *Sentinel-Record*. He'd written passionate editorials against the special treatment of Davis by the Arkansas governor and the parole board. Now he moved his editorial from the usual "Local Comment" section on page 2 to the front page, taking up the entire bottom half on October 6, 1979. The editorial, "Parole Opportunity for Davis a Crime against Society," began with an incorrect date for the Redbird crime and Sharron's fatal injury but continued with a passionate delivery of the basic facts:

> In a reckless and appalling move last week, the Arkansas Board of Pardon and Paroles voted to parole convicted murderer Frank Davis of Hot Springs to the state of Oregon . . . if they will accept him.
>
> We believe the state of Oregon (which has publicly announced its distaste for additional population) should be aware of the quality of citizen they might be welcoming into their populace.
>
> It was June 17, 1968, when a wild-eyed Davis carried a high-powered rifle into a local laundromat and blew part of his wife's head off. He also had earlier used the same gun to critically wound his mother-in-law in the presence of his children, ages three and eight months.
>
> This man, now eligible for parole, was also the prime suspect in the brutal murder of another young girl and the questionable death of a black man in a farm pond near Hot Springs.
>
> Circuit Judge Henry M. Britt, who is one of several Davis has threatened to kill, sentenced the man to die in the electric chair. However, former governor Winthrop Rockefeller saw fit to commute Davis' sentence, along with the death sentence of others [inmates] at Cummins before he left office in 1970.

By his action, Rockefeller opened the door for Davis to be considered for parole in subsequent years. Sure enough, less than nine years later, a handful of political-appointee cronies have now voted to turn this murderer back on society. Their action to pardon Davis came despite protests from Judge Britt, Prosecutor Walter Wright and Sheriff Elza Young, not to mention a number of concerned citizens. But apparently, these good ole boy appointees do not consider the feelings of society in releasing the likes of Frank Davis back into their midst. Perhaps these political hacks do not have children or families of their own. Obviously, they are unaware of their actions.

We consider this vote not only a shameless breach of public confidence but a serious crime in itself against law-abiding citizens who do not deserve to suffer the anxiety that will inevitably grow should Davis be released.

After all, we are talking about a man who has threatened "other lives in Hot Springs" and whose only "rehabilitation" has come in a pathetic and shameful institution like Cummins prison, where a prison guard can take a human life and not even be held accountable for it. You can bet he has received plenty of psychological uplifting down on that farm during the past 12 years.

It is also asinine to assume that just because such a murderer is paroled to Oregon, he can't physically return to Arkansas to carry out these death threats.

To compound our aghast at this situation, when attorney Robert Ridgeway who represented Davis during his trial, was asked Thursday for his opinion about the possible parole, his reply caused many to double-read for accuracy. "I personally can see no reason for anyone to be upset about Frank's parole," he said.

Well, we could probably list several hundred from this community right now who would be more than merely upset at releasing this murderer. We cannot believe anyone could possibly suggest otherwise.[2]

The significance of the front-page editorial was more proof that Frank Davis was more feared by Hot Springs lawmakers and citizens at large than the Chicago gangsters who once frequented the city. Even though they were involved in gangland murders, Al Capone, Lucky Luciano, Frank Costello, and Bugs Moran never evoked a scathing front-page editorial during their visits (and/or hideouts) in Hot Springs.

Frank was sitting in prison, as the slow wheels of justice were processing his parole, when a piece of mail dated "10-18-79" arrived from Dr. J. F. Cooley. Frank opened the letter and began to read:

Dear Mr. Davis,

Received your letter today and was very happy to hear from you. I have been ill for the past several weeks, but feel a little better today. I must say without reservation that your letter was one of the finest and decent ones I have ever received from an inmate, and I have helped to free over 3,000 during the past 21 years. I am going to frame it and hang it on the wall for anyone to see. It really touched me. I believe you meant what you said.

Truly, you cannot pay for things like this because there is much time involved. But, a thankful letter like yours is worth thousands of dollars. I do hope you will get away soon so that you may get the treatment that you and your mother need. It should not take too long to get the papers in order. But, try to keep yourself in good condition so that you will be ready for the long trip to Portland.

Oh yes, I called your Mother today after I got your letter. I just had to tell her about such a very nice letter. She is very nice and sweet. We just had to try and keep her controlled because she deeply loved you and wanted your freedom so bad. But she never did get out of hand (smile). I deeply agreed with her actions but could not let her know it because of the protests from the other side. But, all in all, we got the job done, and I do feel very great. I am thankful to God that was helpful in getting a person down from the electric chair of death, to life, and finally to freedom. I do pray and hope you will value this freedom highly. Please keep in touch with me. May God guide you in all things.

Sincerely,

Dr. J. F. Cooley

The prisoner advocate had stood by Frank and his family to the parole board's favorable end, prompting Frank to stash the kind letter in his brief-case for posterity. Dr. Cooley's mention of Irene's "actions" is unknown.

◌2◌

A week later on October 25, 1979, cries of sorrow at Irene Davis's home were smothered by loud shouts of joy across Hot Springs as residents read the front-page headline, "Oregon Refuses Davis." Carol Hickingbotham reported that the deputy administrator of Oregon's Interstate Compact Program said Frank Davis's petition for parole failed to meet the national program's minimum requirements of residency and employment.

The article included a recap of Sharron Davis's murder, Frank's arrest, his time spent in prison, and the Arkansas Supreme Court's decision. It said the reason Oregon yanked its welcome mat was due to the Interstate Compact System not being set up to transfer unwanted parolees to another state for supervision because "it was designed to allow a prisoner already holding residency in one state, or firm employment, in some cases, the opportunity to leave the state in which he is incarcerated."[3]

Oregon's deputy administrator explained in Davis's case that "he had only an uncle's Oregon residence listed as substantiation for parole to the northwestern state." In questioning the petition's validity, the administrator said, "Normally a full investigation is made; however, in Davis's case things never progressed that far since minimum requirements were not met."

Sharron Knight Davis's family was pleased to hear Frank wouldn't be released to Oregon, the newspaper reported, "but expressed fear of what the future might hold since he has been paroled and now is without destination."

The botched Oregon parole hit Frank hard, and more than a week later, the *Sentinel-Record* ran a front-page headline, "Two Strikes against Him, Frank Davis Wants to Start a New Life." The Associated Press story noted, "*The Oregon Statesman* in Salem learned of Davis' case from a Hot Springs banker who started a letter-writing campaign to Arkansas and Oregon officials protesting Davis' release."[4]

The banker, who conducted the campaign against Frank Davis, was not noted in the article, but it more than likely was Sharron Knight Davis's uncle, Charles Fager, a well-respected trust officer and vice president of Arkansas Bank Trust.

The article stated, "Sentiment is running high against his release in Hot Springs, Ark., where Davis, authorities said, shot and killed his 22-year-old estranged wife and wounded his mother-in-law. Also, Oregon Corrections Division officials have refused to approve his parole until Davis is assured of employment in this state."

Highlighting Frank's crime bio along with his death row commutation and Supreme Court decision, the Oregon newspaper said, "He'd rather stay a prisoner than be a free man in Arkansas where notoriety is attached to his name and many persons still consider him dangerous."

Then they repeated the *Sentinel-Record*'s recent editorial proclamation that several hundred Hot Springs residents would be more than merely upset if "this murderer" was released.

Frank's parole rejection by the Oregon Corrections Division was based on a technicality. The deputy administrator for the Interstate Compact for the Support of Parolees and Probation screened applicants for parole from one state to another and rejected Frank Davis's request because Frank didn't state his job plans, nor had he ever lived in Oregon. However, Frank's uncle, Travis Martin, a retired U.S. Immigration and Naturalization Service officer, lived in Portland and managed an apartment complex in northeast Portland, where Frank planned to work and live with his mother, wife, and daughter.

The uncle said, "The Davis family has $100,000 in savings and extensive property holdings in Arkansas, and Frank Davis receives a $1,000-per-month disability pension for an ulcer condition dating from his military service during World War II."

Travis said his nephew was a skilled horse trainer with a degree in animal husbandry from the University of Texas at Arlington. "He's not a habitual criminal. I don't think he's more violent than anyone else. Nobody was more surprised than me, or my wife, when he killed his wife. It was a spur-of-the-moment thing," the uncle said.[5]

Travis continued, "The Davises were a wealthy family in Hot Springs. He's served his time."

Travis and his wife believed the ill feelings against Frank were prompted by jealousy. She said, "He'd like to have another chance at life before his days are over, and he wants to be with his mother (in her 70s) before she passes away."

The Arkansas Parole and Pardons Board approved Davis's parole on the condition he be accepted by Oregon. David Gunthrop of the parole board, said, "Davis probably will resubmit his application."

Each morning, Hot Springs residents such as Mary Sue and Frances, stalwart members of the legions of "locals who'd be upset if Frank Davis were released," rushed to scan the newspaper for information of his status. Days turned into weeks with nothing about Frank Davis in the local newspapers. Thanksgiving and Christmas came and went, and by the time New Year's Day 1980 arrived, not a mention of Frank's parole had been seen or heard by anyone in Hot Springs. It seemed as if they were getting their wish. Or were they?

· 33 ·

The Logjam Loosened

$\mathscr{T}$hose who believed Frank Davis would never leave prison were stunned when they opened the February 13, 1980, newspaper and read the front-page headline, "Frank Davis Is Paroled to Oregon."[1] "Quietly, with none of the public attention, the case received 12 years ago, Davis was remanded to the jurisdiction of the Oregon Pardon and Paroles Board," Carol Hickingbotham reported.

She explained how Frank "played a three-month waiting game in prison after Arkansas agreed to let him go to Oregon, but the northwest state would not accept his application." Hickingbotham said the deputy administrator of the Interstate Compact System made it clear that "Oregon was not a dumping ground for the unwanted prisoners of other states. Then on February 5, 1980, the paperwork logjam was overcome when Oregon agreed to let Davis come under its supervision."

"Local sources knowledgeable in the Davis' case," she noted, "speculated perhaps the fact Davis, who is reportedly of independent means, with property in Arkansas and a $1,000 a month disability pension from an ulcer condition dating from World War II military service, had a bearing on Oregon's ultimate decision."

Those "sources" could have been anyone who was staying informed of Frank Davis's ongoing story in the newspaper and merely repeated what his Uncle Martin had divulged to the press.

Frank's wife, Wanda, who had stayed by his side since the night he murdered Sharron, given him his fifth child in 1967, married him in January 1976, and written him love letters, especially at the end of his incarceration, was not mentioned in his future plans.

207

Hickingbotham stated, "He will be living, it has been reported, with his mother and stepfather at an apartment complex his uncle manages in northwest Portland."

(Sources confirm, however, that Wanda and Frank's fifth child did live with him in Oregon.)

The reporter called Frank's uncle in Portland for a quote, but his wife answered and said, "I don't think I have anything to say to you," and abruptly hung up.

But Judge Britt, whom Hickingbotham reported presided over the highly publicized trial a decade earlier that ended in his only death sentence, said he considered Davis's Oregon parole "a mistake." Britt told the reporter the Arkansas Parole Board had not contacted him about Davis's parole and stated, "They did not comply with the law."

When asked if Frank Davis could return to Arkansas, Judge Britt said, "There is a constitutional provision which prohibits banishment."

Hickingbotham then noted the "violent death of Sharon [*sic*] Davis, the rancher's fifth wife in the presence of their two children . . . and the shooting of Mrs. Davis's mother, had prompted a substantial public outcry when the subject of parole first became known." She added, "Relatives of the deceased woman were unwilling to comment publicly on Davis's parole." (Sharron Davis was Frank's fourth wife.)

Sharron's family talked to the press when they saw a glimmer of hope that he would not be paroled. Now they were being close-lipped. The thought of him securing freedom probably consumed them as it had other Hot Springs citizens, who hoped Frank's parole would be a bust. I'm sure Mary Sue and Frances were just as disgusted as the Knight family.

Conversations about Frank Davis's parole began moving across Hot Springs like an out-of-control wildfire. Margie Hill, whose husband Teddy had helped Frank in the past, recalled the hubbub during a conversation with her uncle, Harold Tankersley.

"We were told when he got out of prison and went to Oregon, the only way he could get paroled was to leave Arkansas."

Harold said, "After Frank got out of the pen—after they paroled him out—he was supposed to stay away from here, but he would slip back to the parades and the fairs. He wouldn't ride in the parades. He'd come and sit in the [rodeo] audience and walk all around the fairgrounds."

"And nobody seemed to be surprised he was there," Margie interrupted him. "They kind of whispered, 'You know Frank Davis is here.'"

"It wasn't any secret," Harold said.

And Margie added, "Everybody knew Frank had always been a free being and did just what Frank wanted to do."

⌒

Frank signed his February 5, 1980, "Order of Parole" paperwork with a signature that included a backward "F" for "Frank." The document stated his employer as "disabled" and noted he would be residing by "self" on N.E. 102nd Avenue. His release was based on immediately reporting to a State of Oregon parole officer in Portland. It included thirteen stipulations, such as avoiding excessive use of alcoholic beverages and "not owning, purchasing or having under your control any deadly weapons or firearms or imitations thereof, or be in the company of any persons possessing the same." Along with his ticket to freedom, he was given $75 cash.

He missed his mother's seventy-fourth birthday on January 19, 1980, the thirteenth anniversary of Sharron's murder. But when he walked out of prison seventeen days later, his freedom was Irene's belated birthday gift.

A woman who knew Irene Davis told me, "I think his mother would use whatever resources she had to help him. She was a very gracious lady and real nice. I think if there were any strings pulled, I would say it would have to come from her or some association that she had, and I do believe that she had enough money."

Once again, Frank and his mother would be together in a family setting, where she could baby him and make up for what they had missed during the past thirteen years. They celebrated his fifty-sixth birthday on June 24, 1980. Then, six months later, on December 29, Irene Davis passed away.

· 34 ·

The Final Headline

$\mathcal{F}$rank Davis had befriended Tiny Browne and her daughter Cathy Browne-Robbins a year before he murdered Cathie Ward. During that year, he chauffeured little Cathy to his ranch and gave her discounts to ride his horses in reciprocity for her mother's kindness in allowing him to distribute his pamphlets at her business, the Best Tourist Court on Ouachita Avenue. He earned their trust and the nickname "Mr. Frank."

However, they, just like everyone else in Hot Springs, began avoiding Frank Davis after Cathie Ward's suspicious death at Blacksnake Ranch in June 1966. Then seven months later, when he murdered Sharron, Tiny and her daughter were shocked and frightened, especially little Cathy, who had considered him "a nice man."

She told me about her days at Blacksnake and how excited she'd been when Frank and Sharron would invite her into their home and allow her to hold the baby and play with their toddler. Little Cathy and her mother never knew Frank and Sharron's marriage had imploded less than two months after Cathie Ward's death and that he was stalking his then-estranged wife.

Tiny kept up with Frank's murder trial and would see his name in the newspaper throughout the years. But once he was gone from Arkansas, his headlines stopped—until Tuesday morning, June 5, 1984.

Tiny's now thirty-two-year-old daughter, little Cathy, who had married and moved out of state for her husband's job, was home for a visit with her toddler. She and Tiny were drinking coffee when Tiny picked up the newspaper. She began reading the front page and gasped.

"Here look, Mr. Frank died," she said, her hand shaking as she handed the paper to Cathy.

Glancing down where her mother had pointed at the article, Cathy saw what had shaken her mother. Frank's news, which had always garnered bold front-page headlines in the past, was now relegated to "The *Sentinel-Record* Digest," news flashes running down the left column of the front page. Frank wasn't even the lead story. That was reserved for the June 12 election runoff information. Next was a bomb threat at Hall Printers. Then Frank's death came third. The headline announced, "Convicted Murderer Dies of Apparent Heart Attack."[1] His story from Portland, Oregon, stated, "Convicted murderer Frank Davis, formerly of Hot Springs, died Friday in Washington state of an apparent heart attack."

After finishing the four-sentence story, Cathy handed the paper back to her mother, who grabbed some scissors and clipped the surprising news of Frank's passing. It served as his only death notice in Hot Springs. His obituary never graced the pages of the *Sentinel-Record*, where the continuous appearance of his name in the 1960s and 1970s created pure, unadulterated hatred and fear throughout the town.

Remembering "Mr. Frank," Cathy told me, "Mother didn't ever say anything, but I could feel that she really didn't like him. She felt like he was shady. Kind of what she would say about somebody, that 'they were a little shady.'"

Frank's death on June 1, 1984, was ten days shy of his sixtieth birthday, the same occasion his mother was celebrating the night he murdered Sharron in 1967. Irene spent the rest of her life—and probably the majority of her money—seeking freedom for her son, and after succeeding, she savored only ten months and twenty-four days with him.

Although his post-penitentiary time with Irene was brief, Frank spent his last three years, three months, and twenty-seven days with his daughter, Becky, and fifth wife, Wanda. She sent his body to Big Springs, Texas, where he was buried in a family plot beside his parents, Ray B. Davis and Irene C. Davis.

∽

Sharron Knight Davis's cousin Debby Fager Larsen received a phone call from Inez Cline, a local historian. Cline had read of Frank Davis's death and wanted to write a follow-up story about the man who was known for murder in Hot Springs. "She asked me how I felt about him passing away and if she could get some stuff from me to write about it," Debby told me. "But I declined."

∽

An Order of Discharge, which was a fill-in-the-blanks form used by the State of Arkansas Board of Pardons and Paroles, completed Frank's prison file. The June 1, 1984, document announced, "This is to certify that *Davis, Allen Frank Number 61749* is hereby discharged from the Board of Pardons and Parole by reason of *Death*." In tiny print under the date of issuance were the instructions, "You may discontinue making monthly reports." Someone had typed "OREGON" at the bottom left of the page.

Fourteen days later, on June 15, a letter was mailed from Lewis L. Flint, the adult parole/probation officer of the Portland Branch North, to Bob Wallace with the Corrections Interstate Compact in Salem, Oregon. A copy of the correspondence was forwarded to the Arkansas Department of Corrections. Below the date and inside address was the reference line, "RE: Allen Frank Davis, ADC #61749."

The letter stated, "This officer has been supervising Allen Frank Davis since June of 1980. On June 1, 1984 his body was found in his parked pickup just off of State Road #140, Milepost 10, near Washougal, Washington. He was actually on the property of a friend, Mr. Bill T. Walker, with whom he dealt with from time to time in buying and selling horses. An autopsy was subsequently performed on Mr. Davis' remains, and it was determined that he died of natural causes."

~~

Several years later, a group of girls went on a camping trip that included Madelyn, who had invited Cathie Ward to go horseback riding the day she was murdered. One of the girls, who had been there at the time, told me, "We were sitting around the campfire, talking about rape, and Madelyn said when she was young, she had a friend who was raped. It was Cathie Ward, and Frank Davis made Madelyn go with him to find her. And she's the one who found her. He set it up so it would look like he didn't know what really happened."

• 35 •

The Cathie Road Trips

$\mathscr{I}$ find it quite fitting that forty-nine years after Leslie, Mitsy, and I viewed Cathie Ward from the backseat of a moving vehicle on the day she died, we would once again be in the same setting to reunite with her. During those decades, we hadn't known Cathie's burial site, nor had we searched the local cemeteries. But that was before the forty-eighth anniversary of her death in 2014 and the eerie event that brought her to the forefront of our attention.

In 2015, we were on our way to Murfreesboro to find Cathie. Our hour-long trip began with memories of her. It's remarkable how vividly we could picture Cathie walking down the street in 1966. I marveled at the fact that over all those years, we still had the image of her walking home and me leaning out of the back window of Mrs. Letha's Rambler sedan to wave and holler, "Hi, Cathie!" Why that scene remained with us is unexplainable, especially after research showed Cathie was already deceased at the time. But somehow we saw her that day, and the mental picture has been stored in our minds like an online digital photo file.

Her death made an indelible mark on us and others, then rippled outward, depending on the closeness of the contact. We were all swept away with grief and fright and were pulled out of our once-comfortable childhood existence as if caught in a high tide. However personally it touched our junior high school classmates, it also reached kids throughout town, our parents, and the community at large. Cathie's death had become a personal experience on many different levels. Most everyone in town had been touched with the sadness, fright, and disbelief of something so tragic happening in our happy-go-lucky town, built on the premise of luck, chance, or skill.

On the drive west, we didn't discuss the one similarity we shared with Cathie, how she had an older brother who was just as smart and nerdy as ours. They all had their quirks. Leslie's collected Beatles albums, never drank Cokes, and became a doctor; ours talked to ham radio enthusiasts around the world, won science fairs, and later was on a 3-D camera design team; and Cathie's was a percussionist in the band and a Boy States delegate who became an engineer. Our three brothers weren't as quick with a smile as us and definitely never went to a Y-Teen dance.

Other than our brothers, our home life was so different from Cathie's. We never knew what it was like to not have a father at home and a young mother who was trying to forge a happy existence away from her home and children. We hadn't known what it was like to be uprooted from a core family and dropped into a neighborhood and school with kids who were second- and third-generation residents. We couldn't have understood her pain, trying to fit in with school friends while hiding a dysfunctional home life. But she did a great job and had surpassed all her obstacles and come out victorious by June 24, 1966.

Now forty-nine years later, Leslie, Mitsy, and I arrived in the middle of Murfreesboro, which had the feel of a stop on Route 66. Stores selling crystals, assorted Cracker Barrel–type goods, ice cream, and hardware lent a small-town charm to the rustic, outdated rural community. I skirted past them and found a remote entrance to the cemetery by the Murfreesboro Fire and Rescue Department on South School Street. Pulling through a gravel parking lot, I parked behind their building, which stood sentinel to the eastern plots, where we spotted the huge Ward monument. Jumping out of the car and heading that direction on foot, we found Cathie's small headstone two rows away.

I had always noticed the sweet baby section at my parents' cemetery in Hot Springs, and for some reason, I had envisioned the same for Cathie. But no, that wasn't the case. She was in a regular plot near her grandmother Ruth Lilly Ward, who at her death in 1992 at the age of ninety-one had outlived her granddaughter by a quarter of a century. Then I was surprised to see Cathie's headstone. I had pictured it with an angel near her name or something sweet like a rose or little bird. But that also was fictional on my part. It bore three somber lines: her name, Catherine Ward, along with her birth and death dates.

In fact, the entire cemetery, void of trees, rolling hills, or lush lawns, was a bit disappointing. It was simply a field with an old wrought-iron Murfreesboro Cemetery sign above an overgrown entryway on the northern side. I felt sorry for Cathie in her flowerless grave, but at least she was with family. I remembered the sad story she wrote in grade school, saying how she missed her father and didn't like being in Hot Springs, and I thought, *Sadly, she got what she wished for*. My first encounter with Cathie's eternal residence didn't reach the hype I had conjured in my mind, but I was happy to have started my new relationship with her and vowed to research and develop her murder story, wherever it took me.

Two years passed before I could make it back to Murfreesboro on June 24, 2017. The three of us returned again, but this time, Leslie brought Cathie's skateboard. We walked up to her grave, and Leslie stood for a photograph, holding the skateboard in her hands. I snapped her photo, then handed my cell phone to her so she could take one of me. We took turns, taking our pictures with the skateboard. We spent seventeen minutes at her grave, and when I got into the car, I opened up my photo file to check the pictures and was shocked. Leslie's first photo with the skateboard had an odd distortion, like the pixels had been scrambled from the ground up. A blur arose from the right side of Cathie's headstone and shimmied upward to where it reached a black box that covered half of the photo. It didn't obscure Leslie but stood beside her, like another person. I showed it to her, and I could tell she was thinking the same thing as me, the energy of afterlife. That issue has never happened before or since that experience.

We put that oddity behind us and went over to one of the downtown stores to shop. Mitsy wanted to keep shopping, but Leslie and I had seen enough. "We're going outside, and we'll catch you at another store," we told her. We walked out onto the sidewalk and no sooner had we gotten outside than a truck passed us with a sign on its door announcing "Ward Shavings." It turned the corner onto Main Street at the exact moment we walked out of the store. We didn't feel that was a coincidence, nor that the photo was at the cemetery. We felt Cathie was trying to get our attention the same as she'd done four years earlier on the anniversary of her death.

A bit of dread hovered over us as we drove to Murfreesboro in 2019. We were leery of what might happen, but as it turned out, the visit was unremarkable. We placed the flowers and some small statuary at her grave and took pictures. Leslie's thirteen-year-old granddaughter, Sydney, had accompanied us, and Leslie realized the enormity of that fact. She turned to her and said, "You're the exact same age now as Cathie was then, when she died, murdered by a horrible man." She went on to lecture her granddaughter about the good and evil of people.

Leslie and I didn't let the 2020 coronavirus restrictions keep us from going to Cathie's on June 24. By now, it had become an annual event similar to Thanksgiving or Christmas. We knew where we'd be on that date—at Cathie's grave. I bought some beautiful fresh flowers and a tiny skateboard to leave at her headstone. We took our annual photograph, but this time, I also spoke to Cathie. I told her everything that had happened after her murder, giving her a brief synopsis of the killer's life story and that *he had been charged with her murder.* When I finished, Leslie bent down, put two fingers to her lips, and then placed them on the headstone and said, "We'll see you next year, Cathie." As we started to walk away, I turned and said, "I hope wherever your soul might be, it's in another life filled with happiness and joy."

After we left Murfreesboro and were headed home, I said, "Nothing happened this year."

"I think it's because Cathie's at peace. She knows the book is finished, and her story will be told. She's gotten her life back, now," Leslie replied.

Cathie will forever be the tall, pretty, and perky thirteen-year-old remembered more for how she affected us in death than in life. I found a *1966 Hallmark Date Book* in my junior high school scrapbook and thumbed through it while conducting research. I know Cathie had to be at Leslie's birthday party on February 2, 1966, but I don't remember. She was also most certainly at the Y-Teen dance more than a week later when fifteen-year-old Jon Provost, who played Timmy on the popular TV show *Lassie*, made an appearance. Yet I can't say for certain. I'm sure she was at the school dance on March 11 when the Ascots played. Can't pinpoint that either. She more than likely gave me one of her seventh-grade school photos. Nevertheless. it's missing. All of the pieces of Cathie's existence are gone from my memory except the day she died.

One last glance at the 1966 date book caused me to cringe when I saw a September 13 notation that said, "County Fair Parade." Despite Frank Davis being double-crossed by the rodeo club on Sharron's departure a month earlier, I can't help believing he was once again riding with the rodeo club on the one day the general public could admire him. The daredevil on a horse most assuredly enjoyed the adulation from throngs of kids lining Central Avenue—who unknowingly waved to Cathie's killer. However, along the parade route, a scribbled note was hidden away in a bank lockbox that would snare the cocky cowboy seven months later. His estranged wife Sharron gained her revenge from the grave. She made sure her information on Cathie's killing was safe until it was needed—and Frank Davis wouldn't get away with murder.

What Happened to Them?

FRANK DAVIS

Frank Davis was the father of five children, two from his third wife, Carrie; two from his fourth wife, Sharron; and one from his fifth wife, Wanda. At the time of his death in 1984, his children ranged in age from sixteen to twenty-two, with the youngest being the only one to spend a memorable amount of time with their father.

Frank neither admitted nor denied murdering anyone. He never mentioned Cathie Ward's name in discussions with the State Hospital doctor, but he did admit reading a newspaper article that said he'd shot his wife. The words "killed" or "murdered" never passed Frank's lips. He showed more compassion for the death of his faithful ol' gray mare in the early 1960s than the two lives he took in 1966 and 1967.

SHARRON KNIGHT DAVIS

Sharron Knight Davis, Frank's fourth wife, was buried at Greenwood Cemetery in the heart of Hot Springs, Arkansas. Oddly, less than a week later, Lieutenant Commander William Ray Davis Jr. was interred a few plots away, followed by his wife a month later. The Davises, who owned a real estate company and a bookstore near the Garland County courthouse, were not related to Frank Davis.

ALLAN RAY DAVIS

Allan Ray, Sharron's oldest son, was born July 30, 1964, and died of cancer at the age of forty-four on November 15, 2008. He was buried in Hot Springs, not near his mother but on the east side of Hot Springs, close to the neighborhood where his grandmother Knight had raised him.[1]

FREDRICK ALLAN DAVIS

Fredrick, Sharron's youngest son and the baby who was in the front seat when she was murdered, will not address Frank Davis as "father" or "dad." In the fall of 2018, Fredrick drove to Big Springs, Texas, and spit on Frank's grave. He also took photos of Frank's headstone beside his parents, Ray B. Davis and Irene C. Davis—the grandmother he never knew.

Fredrick said Pauline Knight wouldn't allow Irene Davis to see him or his brother. He remembered Pauline saying, "It's all Knights, or nothing!"

Fredrick , a psychiatric nurse, read the State Hospital's psychiatric evaluations he found in Frank's briefcase and was convinced the man he wouldn't call "father" was not mentally ill but sane. He said, "You go find me someone's who's bipolar, true bipolar, and believe me, I have dealt with a number of them, they won't confess they're bipolar. It would be a cold day in hell. A true bipolar [person] will deny it to the bitter end!"

Fredrick recalled his half sister Becky's tales about their grandmother Irene Davis, who forbade the name "grandmother." Becky told him that her mother was treated by her grandmother like she was the maid.

Because he'd never met his grandmother, Fredrick was surprised when Becky told him, "All Irene could ever talk about were her grandsons from Sharron." He felt Becky knew more about his history than him.

Fredrick remembered another sibling conversation, this time with older brother, Allan Ray, who was sitting in the backseat grinning at their father only minutes before he murdered their mother. "He told me he didn't remember Frank," said Fredrick. "But he did remember either our grandmother Knight or our aunt Cheryl, telling him 'about the little girl's murder at the ranch' and how Frank had tied the little girl up to the horse and let it run around the field for a while." He paused and then added, "After he probably killed her!"

The status and whereabouts of Frank's first and third wives are unknown. Carrie, the third wife, wanted to keep it that way. His second wife, Shirley, left Hot Springs after fleeing Frank and enjoyed a successful second marriage and career. Although her location is known, it wasn't divulged out of respect for her privacy. His second and third wives were members of the same Hot Springs High School 1950s graduating class and would be eighty-five years old in 2022.[2] After Frank's death in 1984, his fifth wife, Wanda, returned to Hot Springs with their sixteen-year-old daughter. Ten years later, forty-nine-year-old Wanda died at a local hospital and was buried in a small community cemetery outside the city limits of Hot Springs.[3]

FRED KNIGHT

Fred Knight, Sharron's father, was fifty-seven years old when he died of a heart attack at work on May 30, 1969. He was buried next to his daughter.

PAULINE KNIGHT

Pauline Knight, Sharron's mother, got the last laugh on Frank Davis—outliving him by thirty-two years. Although he was seven years younger, he died only days shy of his sixtieth birthday in 1984. Pauline lived to the ripe old age of eighty-nine and then passed away on April 12, 2006. She was buried beside her husband and shared a tandem husband-and-wife headstone.

DEBBY FAGER LARSEN

Debby Fager Larsen, the thirteen-year-old who called Sharron Knight Davis "her favorite cousin," was another example of the many coincidences weaving through this true story. Debby married the son of the deputy court clerk at Frank's murder trial. She was a lifelong Hot Springs resident but died in July 2020 at Altamonte Springs, Florida.[4]

WALTER WRIGHT

Walter Wright, the Garland County prosecuting attorney who won Frank's murder trial, was elected circuit judge for the Eighteenth Judicial District (East) in 1987,[5] three years after Frank's death. During a 2016 phone interview, Judge Wright said, "What I said in court speaks for itself. I think I could try the case again. That was the first murder case I tried." Judge Wright passed away on January 21, 2017.[6]

SARAH WARD

Sarah Ward, Cathie's mother, moved her two children to Little Rock, Arkansas, after her son's high school graduation in 1968, two years after Cathie's death. Sarah went back to college, earned a degree as a social worker, and began working at the University of Arkansas Medical Sciences.[7] She joined the Unitarian Universalist Church and didn't seem eager to pursue her interests in the arts as she had in Hot Springs. Although she was a very attractive woman, Sarah never remarried after her divorce from Dr. Ward in 1963. She died on May 10, 2013, at the age of eighty-four and is buried in a mausoleum outside of Little Rock.

HIRAM WARD

Hiram Ward, Cathie's father, who was just two years younger than his daughter's murderer in 1966, passed away on July 29, 2021. Ward had always considered his daughter a typical teenager but with a different personality than his other two children. When asked "if Cathie's death had affected her siblings," he said, "Well I'm sure it did. They never talked about it, nor discussed it as a family. We were never together as a family since we separated [in 1960 when Cathie was seven years old]."

Ward devoted his life to medicine. The Arkansas Hospital Association noted on November 19, 2007, that he single-handedly saved the Pike County Memorial Hospital by coming out of retirement (at eighty-one years old) to provide around-the-clock medical coverage for the hospital—twenty-four hours a day, seven days a week. Because of that and his forty-five years of dedication to rural medicine, Ward was named recipient of the "2007 Country Doctor of the Year Award."[8] A reception at the Murfreesboro High School cafetorium was held by Staff Care of Irving, Texas, to honor Ward. "Letters of praise were read by representatives of former president Bill Clinton, Arkansas Gov. Mike Beebe, U.S. Sens. Blanche Lincoln and Mark Pryor and U.S. Rep. Mike Ross," Jan Williamson stated in the *Texarkana News* on December 10, 2007.[9]

After his second wife, Pat, passed away, he married her friend Janice, a nurse. This information is startling due to its coincidence—Janice was the cousin of Bettye Jo Tucker's father. She called him to break the news of Cathie's death because she knew Bettye Jo and Cathie were close friends. That evening in June 1966 when she passed along the tragic news, she never suspected that someday she'd become Ward's third wife.

DICK WARD

Dick Ward, Cathie's older brother, had just completed tenth grade when she died in 1966. After graduating college with an engineering degree, he moved to California, where he still resides.

Cathie's younger sister was aware of this story being written about her sister and Frank Davis but didn't wish to participate. However, her father shared information about his daughter and gave permission for its use. Hiram said, "She's a computer programmer. That's not what she's doing right now." He went on to tell of her earlier employment with a highly regarded governmental agency known worldwide for its incredible achievements.

BETTYE JO TUCKER WILSON

Bettye Jo Tucker Wilson was Cathie's friend who couldn't go with the group of girls that fateful day at Blacksnake Ranch because her father knew Frank Davis and wouldn't give her permission. Remembering her past, Bettye Jo said, "It was a shock. I kind of blocked—the whole time—the time period is like stunted. It was so bad that I don't even remember, this is the honest truth, I don't remember what happened to Madelyn after that. She'd invited us, and I don't remember if we ever saw each other again . . . if she moved out of town. To me, it was almost like she dropped out of sight. Something happened at that point. It was so devastating. Because I wasn't there, I was left to deal with it on my own. So, it's been a big thing in my life that no one knew was a big thing. I was devastated, just devastated."

"My now ex–father-in-law served as a juror on Frank Davis' trial," Bettye Jo said. "I remember asking him about what he knew, and he would just say, 'Nuh, uh,' and shake his head. And that's all I know. Evidently it came up in the trial about Cathie because he did know stuff about it, but he wouldn't ever say anything."

Bettye Jo is married and living in a southeastern state where she was a dance and theater choreographer.

MIKE LANGLEY

Mike Langley, the thirteen-year-old quarterback who was dating Cathie at the time of her murder, said, "I never knew the details of her death, but I remember the suspicion of foul play and have always kept her in my prayers. I kind of put it behind me like everybody did, but I always wondered what it would have been like if she hadn't been killed because I was very infatuated with her and that was the ages and the times when you're creating new relationships that lasted a long time. So, I always wondered what was lost there between us and what was lost in her life, obviously everything. Would my life have been different if she had lived?"

Mike attended the U.S. Naval Academy, was a navy pilot on surveillance and intelligence missions worldwide, earned an MS degree in information systems, and became a successful chief executive officer and globally recognized economic development strategist.

JOHN JAMES

John James, who considered Cathie his first girlfriend, said, "I was in shock the day I heard about her death. Then when I found out more, I was angry. I'm still angry about it! I always thought, 'What a waste, and what a waste of humanity he was—and got away with it!'"

LORNA GARNER ELLIS

Lorna Garner Ellis, who played with Cathie at the Jones School bell house and later suffered the disturbing encounter with the man she suspected was Frank Davis, said, "I've thought about Cathie from time to time. How many kids that age have been murdered? Here is this sweet kid, fun and funny, who was a friend. Don't know how he chose her to murder. I've always felt like her spirit is still here. I drive down Prospect two or three times a week. I feel like she is still talking, laughing. I can still feel her having a good time with us kids. Which is good for me. She wasn't a close friend but a friend who was a nice person, who was going to have this life, date, get married, have kids. I've always felt like she's still around. She's there."

FRANCES "BIG GABY" GABRIEL FORSBERG

Frances "Big Gaby" Gabriel Forsberg was a prominent actor in the Hot Springs Fine Arts Center's theatrical productions during Sarah Ward's mid-1960s involvement. Frances's roots were deep in Hot Springs because of her Greek heritage. Her father's restaurant was located next door to Arkansas' tallest structure from 1930 to 1960, the sixteen-story Medical Arts Building. Her father was good friends with another Greek restaurateur, Tom Athanas, who became Irene Davis's second husband. Frances Gabriel Forsberg passed away on March 14, 2017.

MARY SUE TRACY

Mary Sue Tracy, Leslie's mother, died in 2002 with Cathie's heart-wrenching grade school paper still tucked away in her bedroom drawer.

LESLIE TRACY SWINFORD

Leslie Tracy Swinford found Cathie's paper many years before her mother's death. She read it as an adult, explaining, "It was superb. It was like, you could never think a child in grade school could write such stuff. Cathie just had a different outlook at that age that the rest of us knew nothing about. I don't know what happened to it, I guess when both my parents were gone and I sold the house, it was still in the furniture. But I really wish I had it because it could really give an insight into who she was—an old soul in a young body."

Leslie also described Cathie as "kind of a loner child."

"She seemed a little timid," said Leslie. "But I remember the kindness in her, the innocence of her. I can see now, probably looking back, how she got into that situation because she probably did trust an adult she shouldn't have. Especially back then in the sixties when we were thirteen and taught that we could trust adults. We were taught we could go to policemen. We were taught to go to teachers. We were taught that these are the people you can trust, people in authority. You know, here's this man who owns this horse farm. He owns a business. There was no reason not to trust somebody, especially in Arkansas. Back then I probably would have trusted Frank Davis. He probably came on real nice. Now knowing that he had that capability in him to harm people in that way makes it even more affirmative to me that he murdered her. He was probably obsessed with her. She was a beautiful girl.

She was young, and he obviously had some issues. Any man that can go to a gas station and shoot his wife in the head and shoot his mother-in-law clearly had some issues. Hopefully it wasn't hard for Cathie . . . very long."

Leslie married and had two very bright children, who have made her a proud grandmother of six accomplished grandchildren. While Leslie raised her family, she kept Cathie Ward in her heart by quietly preserving her skateboard, the medium of their childhood friendship.

Leslie always maintained Cathie "died and was forgotten," but she couldn't let it stay that way. If not for her genuine love for a friend, the truth of Cathie's murder and the story that followed would have never been investigated.

I believe Leslie's enduring concern and connection to her long-ago-murdered friend may very well have been her sole mission in life. I also feel there was a reason for Leslie, Mitsy, and I to have carried our lifelong vision of Cathie Ward on her death day. The complete true story has been revealed, allowing her and Sharron Knight Davis to live eternally through *Snake Eyes: Murder in a Southern Town*.

Acknowledgments

$\mathscr{I}$ spent six years researching and writing *Snake Eyes*, which made it into people's hands only because of the enthusiasm and steadfastness of my literary agent Linda Konner, Globe Pequot Press acquisitions editor Jake Bonar, writing mentor Bonnie Hearn Hill, and production editor Nicole Carty.

I'm forever indebted to Leslie Tracy Swinford and her story of Cathie Ward's skateboard that appeared on the forty-eighth anniversary of her murder. What happened to Cathie on June 24, 1966, affected people in different ways and created memories of the event through their connections to her—and the terror that took over Hot Springs. However, there are those of us who were touched by her shortened life like a high-water mark after a flood. We've been tethered to her all these years, but now, with *Snake Eyes*, we can cut that cord.

Immense thanks for aiding me in research goes to Renee Lambert Lucy, Donnie Kilgore (deceased October 21, 2017), Nat Martin (deceased January 5, 2021), Linda Hogaboom, Paulann Turner, Orval Albritton, Clyde Covington, Melanie Pearce, Gail Ashbrook, and Liz Robbins and Donnavae Hughes (technical help) at the Garland County Historical Society; St. Luke's Episcopal Church Reverend Sarah Milford; Brian Irby and Tatyana Oyinloye with the Arkansas State Archives on the Arkansas Capitol Grounds; Barbara Erdman, Anita Millard, Margie Hill, and Charleen Nobles with the Melting Pot Genealogical Society in Hot Springs, Arkansas; Charleen Nobles, while at home, performing online newspaper searches; Boyd Heath (deceased January 26, 2018); Greg Williams, supervisor, Garland County Library, along with the great Garland County Library staff who gave me many, many reels of microfilm; the *Sentinel-Record*'s September 15, 2016, "Letters to the Editor" editor; and Jeanne Lou Counts Dean for loaning me several 1960s

Hot Springs City Directories before I located a stash for sale at the Garland County Historical Society.

I'm very grateful for the memories and, in some cases, personal mementos from Bettye Jo Tucker Wilson, Leslie Tracy Swinford, Frances Gabriel Forsberg (deceased March 14, 2017), Cathy (Browne) Robbins, "Anonymous," Clyde Covington, Gary Jackson (deceased October 15, 2019), Gail Ashbrook, Sue McGuire, Bill "Bunny" Dever, Glen Peake, Debby Fager Larsen (deceased July 14, 2020), Margie Hill, Harold Tankersley, Patsy Searcy (deceased January 5, 2017), Judge Walter G. Wright (deceased January 21, 2017), Lorna Garner, Pam Johnson Rains, Mitsy Martin Findley, Dr. Donald Harper, John James, Dr. Hiram Ward, Richard "Dick" Ward, Janice Ward, Gail Rader Ross, Paula Seay Wise, Dr. Joe Little, Frank Davis's second wife's sister-in-law, Phyllis Davis Spahn, Mary Nan Carter, Mary Claire Atkinson McGarry, Margie Hawthorn Golden, Debby Franks Shackleford, Suzanne Franks, Jan Harrison Wood, Laura Melton Garrett, James "Jim" and Janie Smith, Jan Johnson, Linda Livingston Harris, Katie Weaver, Kathy McConkie, Elza Young (deceased January 16, 2019), Janette Woodcock, John Dean, Mike Langley, Mary Lou and Allen Kilby, and Delia Cook McBride. Several of these personal interviews were possible thanks to arrangements made by Patsy Burtness, Elizabeth Jefferson Smith, Nancy Fager Anderson-Richard, Leslie Tracy Swinford, Rebecca "Becky" Beasley Dennison, Margie Hill, Lisa Harper Duranleau, Patty Carlson Roddenberry, Pam Hill, Mary Whittington Little, Margie Hawthorn Golden, and Sherry Young Bracy.

I was extremely fortunate when Bill Dever didn't hesitate to share his many copyrighted Red Bird crime scene photographs.

Jim Smith, a classmate since grade school who now owns the property that once was Blacksnake Ranch, was so generous to share invaluable documents attached to his property deed.

A major coup for the book came from out of nowhere when Renee Lambert Lucy connected me to Frank Davis's fourth child, Fredrick Davis, who was a baby when his father murdered his mother. Although he detests the father he never knew, he obtained Frank Davis's personal prison files from a sibling who wanted nothing more to do with them. He brought the files to his interview and allowed me to inventory the many items that had once been in the same hands of Hot Spring's notorious 1960s killer—and, I can't thank him enough!

I was lucky to receive information, advice, or assistance from Gail Sheehy, Jill Marr, Vicki Threadgill Rima, Judge Homer Wright, J. D. Gingerich (then director of the Arkansas Administrative Office of the Courts), Mike Nawojczyk, Roy Smith, Doug Harp, Stuart Smedley (Hot Springs coroner), Doug Lackey, Mike Ellis, John Reed (Arkansas Senate information officer), John Westfall, Beverly Burch Jackson, Susan Whittington Batterton, and Wayne Threadgill.

Recognition for locating and supplying me with decades-old documents is attributed to Kristie Womble, chief deputy, Garland County Circuit Court; Jim Smith and his assistant, Carla Miles; Gina Moore, deputy clerk and office manager, Garland County Circuit Clerk's Office; and Shelli Maroney, ADC classification administrator, Arkansas Department of Corrections.

I want to thank my fellow Hot Springs Writer's Group members Nancy Smith Gibson, Sherri Ungerer, Charles "Chap" Harper, Jane Dews Benkart, Carole Katchen, Bill Schuler, and Jennifer Schroeder for keeping me on track when my writing would go off the rails.

I valued the input from beta readers Margaret Campbell, Lily Kersh, Kathy Graham Rucki, Dinah Dugan Marrall, and Jennifer Schroeder.

A huge credit goes to Leslie Tracy Swinford and Mitsy Martin Findley for reading parts of the manuscript to check the validity of historical events as we remembered them. And finally, I truly appreciated the consistent support from my creative cheerleaders Haley Findley, Mitsy Martin Findley, Leslie Tracy Swinford, Gail Martin Montouri, and Tansill Stough Anthony.

Source Interviews

"Anonymous" Madelyn friend personal interview, Hot Springs, Arkansas, February 24, 2016.

Atkinson McGarry, Mary Claire, e-mail (see "Source Documents").

Beasley Dennison, Becky, personal interview, Hot Springs, Arkansas, September 25, 2015.

Bowman Maves, Mary, phone interview, Hot Springs, Arkansas, January 17. 2018.

Browne Robbins, Cathy, personal interview, Hot Springs, Arkansas, June 30, 2015.

Burnette, Melinda Koen, personal interview, Hot Springs, Arkansas, October 10, 2017.

Burtness, Patsy, text, July 29, 2020.

Carter, Mary Nan, phone interview, August 28, 2017.

Cook, Delia, phone interview, November 11, 2020.

Covington, Clyde, personal interview, Hot Springs, Arkansas, August 28, 2014.

Davis, Fredrick Allan, personal interview, Hot Springs, Arkansas, February 28, 2019.

Dean, John, personal interview, Hot Springs, Arkansas, November 16, 2018.

Dever, Bill, personal interview, Hot Springs, Arkansas, December 1, 2014; July 19, 2016; and multiple e-mails.

Fager Larsen, Debby, personal interview, Hot Springs, Arkansas, December 15, 2014; phone interview November 6, 2017; and multiple e-mails.

Findley, Mitsy Martin, personal interview, Hot Springs, Arkansas, June 24, 2015; December 5, 2015.

Forsberg, Frances Gabriel, personal interview, Hot Springs, Arkansas, August 27, 2014; November 20, 2014.

Franks Shackleford, Debby, and Suzanne Franks, phone interview, November 1, 2017.

Fullbright Gates, Margaret, phone interview, July 4, 2018.

Garner Ellis, Lorna, personal interview, Hot Springs, Arkansas, January 27, 2015.

Garrett, Laura Melton, personal interview, Hot Springs, Arkansas, April 4, 2018.

Gibson, Janette Woodcock, phone interview, July 1, 2019.

Harper, Don, phone interview, July 21, 2016.

Harris, Linda Livingston, personal interview, Hot Springs, Arkansas, August 19, 2018.

Harrison Wood, Jan, by Facebook Messenger correspondence, January 8, 2018.

Hawthorn Golden, Margie, personal interview, Hot Springs, Arkansas, November 1, 2017; July 29, 2020.

Heath, Boyd, phone interview, July 28, 2016.

Hill, Margie, personal interview, Hot Springs, Arkansas, February 10, 2015.

Jackson, Gary, personal interview, Hot Springs, Arkansas, August 28, 2014.

James, John, personal interview, Hot Springs, Arkansas, August 12, 2016.

Johnson, Jan, personal interview, Hot Springs, Arkansas, April 5, 2018.

Johnson, Pam, personal interview, Hot Springs, Arkansas, February 22, 2016.

Kilby, Mary Lou, and Allen Kilby Jr., phone interview, December 31, 2020.

Langley, Michael, phone interview, December 12, 2019.

Little, Joe, phone interview, September 7, 2017.

Martin, Bitty, comments, November 16, 2018.

McConkie, Kathy, personal interview, Hot Springs, Arkansas, October 9, 2018.

Milford, Sarah, St. Luke's Episcopal Church, phone interview, December 14, 2016.

Peake, Glenn, personal interview, Hot Springs, Arkansas, December 1, 2014.

Perkins, Margie, personal interview, Hot Springs, Arkansas, August 9, 2018.

Ross, Gail Rader, phone interview, August 18, 2016.

Searcy, Patsy, personal interview, Hot Springs, Arkansas, July 15, 2015.

Sister-in-law of Frank Davis's second wife, phone interview, February 12, 2015.

Smith, Janie, personal interview, Hot Springs, Arkansas, August 1, 2018.

Smith, Jim, personal interview, Hot Springs, Arkansas, August 1, 2018.

Spahn, Phyllis, phone interview, October 16, 2017.

Swinford, Leslie Tracy, personal interview, Hot Springs, Arkansas, August 14, 2014; August 19, 2014; August 26, 2014; August 27, 2014; February 17, 2016; August 16, 2016; November 16, 2018.

Tankersley, Harold, personal interview, Hot Springs, Arkansas, February 10, 2015.

Wade, Ann, personal interview, Hot Springs, Arkansas, August 9, 2018.

Ward, Hiram, personal interview, Murfreesboro, Arkansas, August 25, 2014.

Ward, Janice, personal interview, Murfreesboro, Arkansas, August 25, 2014.

Ward, Richard "Dick," personal interview, California, February 19, 2017.

Weaver, Katie, personal interview, Hot Springs, Arkansas, September 16, 2018.

Wilson, Bettye Jo Tucker, phone interview, October 30, 2014, and multiple e-mails.

Wise, Paula Seay, phone interview, August 22, 2017.

Wright, Walter, phone interview, December 13, 2014.

Young, Elza, personal interview, Hot Springs, Arkansas, September 28, 2018; phone interview, April 5, 2018.

Source Documents

"Agreement, Exhibit A; Exhibit B; Summons by Equitable to Frank Davis x2 and Minor Children x1; Application for Appointment of Guardians-Ad-Litem; Order Appointing Guardians Ad Litem; Separate Answers of Sam L. Anderson, (minors); Separate Answer of Robert Ridgeway, Guardian Ad Litem for A. Frank Davis; Decree; Commissioners Sale Notice; *Sentinel-Record* advertisement contract; Commissioner's Report of Sale," Garland County Circuit Clerk's Office, Hot Springs, Arkansas (July 31, 2018).

Allen Frank Davis prison file, e-mail attached documents from Shelli Maroney, ADC Classification Administrator, Arkansas Department of Corrections (July 27, 2016).

"Bench Warrant #12,846, Allen Frank Davis, Murder in the First Degree," April 13, 1967, by Garland County Circuit Clerk (November 17, 2017).

"Complaint for Foreclosure of Land Contract, James A. Culberson and Charlotte S. Culberson vs. A. Frank Davis, Arkansas State Hospital, Little Rock, Arkansas (and two minors), in the Chancery Court of Garland County," June 20, 1967, Garland County Circuit Clerk's Office, Hot Springs, Arkansas (July 31, 2018).

"Complaint in Equity, Sharon Davis vs. Frank Davis and Irene Davis, No. 37,232, in the Chancery Court of Garland County," October 19, 1966, Garland County Circuit Clerk's Office, Hot Springs, Arkansas (July 31, 2018).

Frank Davis Court Case ID 26CR-12827: online and Arkansas State Hospital, Psychiatric Hospital and Mental Status, Psychologists' Report, Diagnostic Staff Conference Report, February 1967, Garland County Circuit Clerk's Office Staff and Kristie Womble, Chief Deputy, Garland County Circuit Court, Hot Springs, Arkansas (August 27, 2015).

Frank Davis's personal prison files, which also included Arkansas State Hospital, Psychiatric Hospital and Mental Status, Psychologists' Report, Diagnostic Staff Conference Report, February 1967, shared by Fredrick Davis (February 28, 2019).

Hallmark Date Book 1966, from Steigler's Greeting Card Headquarters, 520 Central Avenue and 419 Albert Pike, Hot Springs, Arkansas, property of Bitty Martin.

Indictment #4128 Circuit, #12846, Audit #272977693, Kristie Womble, Chief Deputy Garland County Circuit Court, Hot Springs, Arkansas (November 17, 2017).

Indictment #4128, Allen Frank Davis, Garland Circuit Court, Murder in the First Degree, June 24, 1966, Walter Wright, Prosecuting Attorney, Garland Circuit Court, Kristie Womble, Chief Deputy Garland County Circuit Court (November 17, 2017).

"Mary Claire Atkinson McGarry's Recollection of Events Surrounding the Death of Cathie Ward.docx," Mary Claire Atkinson McGarry e-mail (June 20, 2017).

"Notice to Frank Davis, in the Chancery Court of Garland County," December 2, 1966; Garland County Circuit Clerk's Office, Hot Springs, Arkansas (July 31, 2018).

Photos from Bettye Jo Tucker, Facebook Messenger (June 1, 2017).

"Separate Answer by Frank Davis to Plaintiff's Complaint in Equity, in the Chancery Court of Garland County," December 15, 1966, Garland County Circuit Clerk's Office, Hot Springs, Arkansas (July 31, 2018).

"Separate Answer of Irene Davis, in the Chancery Court of Garland County," December 15, 1966, Garland County Circuit Clerk's Office, Hot Springs, Arkansas (July 31, 2018).

"Summons Action by Equitable Proceedings, State of Arkansas, to the Sheriff of Garland County, Case No. 37,232," October 19, 1966, Joann Newkirk, Deputy Circuit Clerk, Garland County Circuit Clerk's Office, Hot Springs, Arkansas (July 31, 2018).

Notes

CHAPTER 1: THE TEENAGE GIRL
AND THE RANCH OWNER

1. Orval E. Albritton, "Al Capone," *Dangerous Visitors: The Lawless Era* (Hot Springs, AR: Garland County Historical Society, 2008), 342.

2. Nancy Hendricks, "Charles 'Lucky' Luciano (1897–1962), A.K.A., Salvatore Lucania," updated July 27, 2006, https://www.enclyclopediaofarkansas.net/entries /charles-lucky-luciano-3690/ (retrieved August 26, 2019).

3. "Hot Springs Art Center," *Sentinel-Record*, February 13, 2000, 7H.

4. "Girl Killed in Horseback Riding Accident," *Hot Springs New Era*, Hot Springs, Arkansas, June 25, 1966, 1.

5. "Girl Killed in Horseback Riding Accident," 1.

6. "Black Snake Angus Ranch, Inc." *Polk's Hot Springs National Park (Garland County, Ark.) City Directory 1966* (Dallas, TX: R. L. Polk & Co. Publishers, 1966), 42.

7. James Collett, "McCamey, Texas," https://www.tshaonline.org/handbook/entries /mccamey=tx (retrieved September 15, 2018).

8. "Ray B. Davis," https://www.ancestry.com/radybdavis (retrieved July 23, 2017).

9. "Girl Killed in Horseback Riding Accident," 1.

CHAPTER 3: THE FUNERAL AND THE SKATEBOARD

1. "Girl Killed in Horseback Riding Accident," *Hot Springs New Era*, Hot Springs, Arkansas, June 25, 1966, 1.

2. "St. Luke's Hot Springs Story," https://www.stluke.shs.org/about-us (retrieved August 8, 2018).

CHAPTER 4: THE KILLER

1. "Flight Officer," https://military.wikia.org/wiki/Flight-Officer (retrieved August 6, 2020).

CHAPTER 5: THE DROWNING, THE WOMEN, AND THE MOTHER

1. *Old Gold Book 1954*, Hot Springs High School, Hot Springs National Park, Arkansas, page omitted for privacy.

2. "Definition of Undulant Fever," www.medicinenet.com (retrieved March 20, 2017).

3. *Old Gold Book 1962*, Hot Springs High School, Hot Springs National Park, Arkansas, 137.

4. *Polk's Hot Springs National Park City Directory 1966* (Dallas, TX: R. L. Polk & Co. Publishers, 1966), 282.

5. "Ray Davis," *Polk's Hot Springs (Garland County, Ark.) City Directory 1951* (Dallas, TX: R. L. Polk & Co. Publishers, 1951), 64.

6. "Ray Davis," 1930 U.S. Census, www.ancestry.com/raybdavis (retrieved July 23, 2017).

7. "Irene Davis," *Polk's Hot Springs (Garland County, Ark.) City Directory 1951* (Dallas, TX: R. L. Polk & Co. Publishers, 1951), 63.

8. "Obituaries, Ray B. Davis," *Sentinel-Record*, December 19, 1954, 10.

9. *Polk's Hot Springs (Garland County, Ark.) City Directory 1951* (Dallas, TX: R. L. Polk & Co. Publishers, 1951), 63.

10. *Polk's Hot Springs National Park City Directory 1955* (Dallas, TX: R. L. Polk & Co. Publishers, 1955), 69.

11. "Winston M. Athanas Family," www.flickr.com/photos/36357437@NO2 /4354117784; Charlene Nobles e-mail attachment, May 4, 2017.

12. "Athanas, Athas," U.S. Census, www.ancestry.com/AthasAthanas/1920 (retrieved August 24, 2017).

13. "Athas Athanas," 1920 U.S. Census, www.ancestry.com (retrieved August 24, 2017); and "Athas Athanas Veterans File," Garland County Historical Society (retrieved January 15, 2019).

14. "Athas Athanas, Arkansas Marriage Licenses 1920–1949," www.ancestry.com (retrieved September 1, 2017).

15. "Athas Athanas," 1930 U.S. Census, www.ancestry.com (retrieved September 1, 2017).

16. "Davis-Athanas," *Arkansas Democrat*, May 23, 1957, 9; Charlene Nobles e-mail attachment, May 1, 2017.

17. "Athanas Service," Obituaries, *Sentinel-Record*, July 8, 1963, 9; Charlene Nobles e-mail attachment, May 1, 2017.

18. *Polk's Hot Springs National Park City Directory 1963* (Dallas, TX: R. L. Polk & Co. Publishers, 1963), 311.

19. "Girl's Death Resulted from Riding Accident," *Sentinel-Record*, July 14, 1966, 3.

CHAPTER 6: MENTAL HEALTH AND THE GETAWAY

1. "Runoff Primary Today, Campaign Workers in Circuit Judge's Race Clash Contacted over Circulars," *Sentinel-Record*, August 9, 1966, 1.

2. "Hebert Defeats Ridgeway in Circuit Judge's Race," *Sentinel-Record*, August 10, 1966, 1.

3. Bond for Marriage License, Affidavit and Marriage of License, Frank Davis and Shirley, State of Arkansas, County of Garland, November 8, 1958.

4. *Old Gold Book 1954*, Hot Springs High School, Hot Springs National Park, Arkansas, page omitted for privacy.

CHAPTER 7: THE RUMORS

1. *Spartan Spirit*, vol. 12, no. 1, Central Junior High School, Hot Springs, Arkansas, October 1966, 1.

2. *Strike Up the Band*: *Spartan Spirit*, vol. 12, no. 1, Central Junior High School, Hot Springs, Arkansas, October 1966, 3.

CHAPTER 8: THE SPREES

1. "Meprobamate," Wikipedia, https://en.wikipedia.org/wiki/Meprobamate, October 24, 2017.

2. "Hawthorn G E Meat Co," *Polk's Hot Springs National Park (Garland County, Ark.) City Directory 1966* (Dallas, TX: R. L. Polk & Co. Publishers, 1966), 215.

CHAPTER 9: THE STALKER

1. "Complaint in Equity, Sharron Davis vs. Frank Davis and Irene Davis, No. 37,232, in the Chancery Court of Garland County," October 19, 1966, Garland County Circuit Clerk's Office, Hot Springs, Arkansas (retrieved July 31, 2018).

2. "Summons Action by Equitable Proceedings, State of Arkansas, to the Sheriff of Garland County, Case No. 37,232," October 19, 1966, Joann Newkirk, Deputy

Circuit Clerk, Garland County Circuit Clerk's Office, Hot Springs, Arkansas (retrieved July 31, 2018).

3. "Separate Answer of Irene Davis, in the Chancery Court of Garland County," December 15, 1966, Garland County Circuit Clerk's Office, Hot Springs, Arkansas (retrieved July 31, 2018).

4. "Separate Answer by Frank Davis to Plaintiff's Complaint in Equity, in the Chancery Court of Garland County," December 15, 1966, Garland County Circuit Clerk's Office, Hot Springs, Arkansas (retrieved July 31, 2018).

CHAPTER 10: THE REDBIRD

1. "Did It as Favor to Davis, Witness Says He 'Watched' Wife of Man Accused of Her Murder," *Sentinel-Record*, June 13, 1968, 2.

2. Gary Rowland comment in *Remember in Hot Springs* public Facebook group: "Some of you older people might remember that awful, awful murder that took place at the Red Bird Laundromat" (George Linnington post, September 4, 2014) (retrieved October 16, 2017).

3. Lois Aicholz comment in *Remember in Hot Springs* public Facebook group: "Some of you older people might remember that awful, awful murder that took place at the Red Bird Laundromat" (George Linnington post, September 4, 2014) (retrieved October 16, 2017).

CHAPTER 12: EVIL PERSONIFIED

1. "Woman Fatally Shot, Mother Wounded at Laundromat Here," *Sentinel-Record*, January 20, 1967, 1, 4.

CHAPTER 13: THE PICTURE IN THE CASKET

1. Mrs. Thelma Sharron Davis obituary, *Sentinel-Record*, January 23, 1967, 4.

CHAPTER 14: THE POST-MURDER MELTDOWN

1. "Woman Fatally Shot, Mother Wounded at Laundromat Here," *Sentinel-Record*, January 20, 1967, 4.

2. "Woman Fatally Shot, Mother Wounded at Laundromat Here," 1.

3. "Woman Fatally Shot, Mother Wounded at Laundromat Here," 4.

4. "Davis Bound to Grand Jury in Murder Case," *Sentinel-Record*, January 25, 1967, 4.

5. "Jack Holt Sr.," *Encyclopedia of Arkansas History & Culture*, www.encyclopedia ofarkansas.net/entries/jack-wilson-holt-sr-7549 (retrieved November 16, 2017).

6. "Davis Bound to Grand Jury in Murder Case," 4. Subsequent quotes in this chapter are from this source.

CHAPTER 15: THE STATE HOSPITAL

1. April Goff, "Arkansas State Hospital," https://encyclopediaofarkansas.net/entries arkansas-state-hospital-2238/ (retrieved October 15, 2017).

2. "Butisol," Wikipedia, https://en.wikipedia.org/wiki/Butabarbital (retrieved October 16, 2018).

CHAPTER 17: THE POSTHUMOUS BIRTHDAY GIFT

1. "Man Indicted in Death of Resort Girl," *Sentinel-Record*, April 14, 1967, 8.

2. *1966 Hot Springs National Park City Directory* (Dallas, TX: R. L. Polk & Co. Publishers, 1966), 553.

3. "Man Indicted in Death of Resort Girl," 8.

CHAPTER 18: THE FORECLOSURE

1. "Complaint for Foreclosure of Land Contract, James A. Culberson and Charlotte S. Culberson vs. A. Frank Davis, Arkansas State Hospital, Little Rock, Arkansas (and two minors) in the Chancery Court of Garland County," June 20, 1967, Garland County Circuit Clerk's Office, Hot Springs, Arkansas (retrieved July 31, 2018).

CHAPTER 19: THE TRIAL *STAY* TO *FIRST DAY*

1. "Frank Davis Trial Gets Stay," *Sentinel-Record*, July 27, 1967, 2.

2. "Murder Trial Begins, Jury Selected in Davis Case; State May Ask Death Penalty," *Sentinel-Record*, June 12, 1968, 1–2.

3. "Henry Middleton Britt III," https://military.wikia.org/wiki/Henry_M._Britt (retrieved January 17, 2018).

4. "Murder Trial Begins, Jury Selected in Davis Case; State May Ask Death Penalty," *Sentinel-Record*, June 12, 1968, 1.

5. Jurors' occupations from *Polk's Hot Springs National Park (Garland County, Ark.) City Directory 1966* (Dallas, TX: R. L. Polk & Co. Publishers, 1966), and Allen Kilby Jr. from *Polk's Hot Springs National Park (Garland County, Ark.) City Directory 1963* (Dallas, TX: R. L. Polk & Co. Publishers, 1963).

6. "Murder Trial Begins, Jury Selected in Davis Case; State May Ask Death Penalty," 2.

CHAPTER 20: THE ADMISSION

1. "Jack Holt Sr.," *Encyclopedia of Arkansas History and Culture*, www.encyclopedia ofarkansas.net/entries/jack-wilson-holt-sr-7549 (retrieved November 16, 2017).

2. "Did It as 'Favor' to Husband, Witness Says He 'Watched' Wife of Man Accused of Her Murder," *Sentinel-Record*, June 13, 1968, 1.

3. "Admits Wife's Slaying, Death Penalty Asked at Frank Davis Trial as Testimony Begins," *Hot Springs New Era*, June 12, 1968, 1.

CHAPTER 21: FAKING BAD

1. "Murder Trial Continues, Psychiatrists Testify Davis Suffering from Mental Illness," *Sentinel-Record*, June 14, 1968, 2.

2. "Murder Trial Continues, Psychiatrists Testify Davis Suffering from Mental Illness," 1.

CHAPTER 22: THE PSYCHIATRISTS' SAY

1. "Murder Trial Continues, Psychiatrists Testify Davis Suffering from Mental Illness," *Sentinel-Record*, June 14, 1968, 1.

CHAPTER 23: THE JURY DELIBERATES

1. "To Be Sentenced Monday, Jury Finds Davis Guilty; Death Penalty Automatic," *Hot Springs New Era*, June 15, 1968, 2.

2. "Case Goes to Jury Today, Four Psychiatrists Split Evenly on Issue of Frank Davis Sanity," *Hot Springs New Era*, June 14, 1968, 1.

CHAPTER 24: THE VERDICT

1. "James Waybern Hall," https://murderpedia.org/male.H/h/hall-james-waybern
.htm (retrieved October 23, 2018).
2. "Arkansan's 'Hitchhike Killer' Recounts Slayings of James 'Red' Hall," in Janie
Nesbitt Jones, *The Arkansas Hitchhike Killer: James Waybern "Red" Hall* (Cheltenham:
History Press, 2021).
3. "James Waybern Hall."
4. "To Be Sentenced Monday, Jury Finds Davis Guilty; Death Penalty Automatic," *Hot Springs New Era*, June 15, 1968, 1.

CHAPTER 25: THE SENTENCE

1. "Davis Standing Stoically, Receives Death Sentence; Execution Set in 60 Days,"
Hot Springs New Era, June 17, 1968, 1.
2. "Davis Standing Stoically, Receives Death Sentence; Execution Set in 60 Days,"
2.
3. "Davis Receives Death Penalty" (Hot Springs AP), *Arkansas Gazette*, June 18,
1968.

CHAPTER 26: THE DEATH ROW INMATE

1. "WR Commutes 15 Sentences, Arkansas Death Row Is Emptied," *Sentinel-
Record*, December 30, 1970, 1.
2. Rex Nelson, "The Peck Legacy," *Arkansas Democrat-Gazette*, March 28, 2018,
7B.
3. "Winthrop Rockefeller (1912–1973)," https://encyclopediaofarkansas.net
/entries/winthrop-rockefeller-122/ (retrieved December 26, 2017).
4. "Tucker Telephone," Wikipedia, https://en.wikipedia.org/wiki/Tucker_Tele
phone (retrieved December 26, 2017).
5. Colin Edward Woodward, Lee Family Digital Archive, Stratford Hall,
"Tucker Unit, AKA: Tucker Prison Farm," https://encyclopediaofarkansas.net
/entries/tucker-unit-7608/ (retrieved December 14, 2017).
6. Andrea Ringer, "Rockefeller and Death Row, Governor Commuted Death
Sentences in 1970," *Arkansas Times*, February 27, 2014, https://arktimes.com/news
/arkansas-reporter/2014/02/27/rockefeller-and-death-row (retrieved October 24,
2018).
7. Justice Byrd, "Davis v. State," https://law.justia.com/cases/arkansas/supreme
-court/1969/5378-0.html (retrieved August 21, 2014).

CHAPTER 27: ROCKEFELLER'S GOODWILL
AND PEACE TO PRISONERS

1. "WR Commutes 15 Sentences, Arkansas Death Row Is Emptied," *Sentinel-Record*, December 30, 1970, 1.

2. "Winthrop Rockefeller," Wikipedia, https://en.wikipedia.org/wiki/Winthrop_Rockefeller (retrieved October 25, 2018).

3. "Mrs. Winthrop Rockefeller Will Divorce Former Governor," *New York Times*, February 20, 1971, https://www.nytimes.com/1971/02/20/archives/mrs-winthrop-rockefeller-will-divorce-former-governor.html (retrieved October 25, 2018).

4. Colin Edward Woodward, Lee Family Digital Archive, Stratford Hall, "Tucker Unit, AKA: Tucker Prison Farm," https://encyclopediaofarkansas.net/entries/tucker-unit-7608/ (retrieved December 14, 2017).

CHAPTER 28: THE FIFTH MARRIAGE AND THE ESCAPE

1. Nancy Britt, "Prison Officials Disagree: Weekend Escape of Davis Wasn't His First Absence," *Sentinel-Record*, October 22, 1976, 1.

2. "Poor Decision by Parole Board," *Sentinel-Record*, February 7, 1976, 4.

3. "Baker Kurrus," *Arkansas Democrat-Gazette*, February 18, 2015, https://www.arkansasonline.com/news/2015/feb/18/kurrus-will-head-panel-on-lr-schools-fi-1/?latest (retrieved January 28, 2021).

4. "Baker Kurrus," RocketReach, https://rocketreach.co/baker-kurrus-email_39033452 (retrieved January 28, 2021).

5. Nancy Britt, "Prison Officials Disagree: Weekend Escape of Davis Wasn't His First Absence," *Sentinel-Record*, October 22, 1976, 19.

6. Nancy Fager Anderson-Richard, comment in *Remember in Hot Springs* public Facebook group: "Some of you older people might remember that awful, awful murder that took place at the Red Bird Laundromat" (George Linnington post, September 4, 2014) (retrieved October 16, 2017).

7. Britt, "Prison Officials Disagree."

8. "Frank Davis Escapes from Prison Facility," *Sentinel-Record*, October 16, 1976.

9. "Search for Davis Continues," *Sentinel-Record*, October 17, 1976, 6.

10. "Davis Recaptured Near Facility," *Sentinel-Record*, October 18, 1976, 1.

11. Nancy Britt, "Governor's Office Probes Davis Case—No Record of a 'Leave' Found," *Sentinel-Record*, November 6, 1976, 1.

12. Britt, "Prison Officials Disagree," 19.

13. "Is Frank Davis Really in Prison?" *Sentinel-Record*, October 26, 1976, 2.

14. "Frank Davis: Still No Answer," *Sentinel-Record*, December 2, 1976, 2.

CHAPTER 29: THE CHEST PAINS AND NEWSPAPER CLIPPINGS

1. "Husband Gets 5-Year Term in Gun Death," *Gazette State News*. (Frank Davis personal prison file contained clipped newspaper article without publication date. Acquired from Fredrick Davis, March 4, 2019.)

2. "Three Persons Injured in 4-Car Accident," *Sentinel-Record*, December 13, 1964, 8.

3. "Mentally Ill First Offender Is Sent to Cummins," *Sentinel-Record*, July 1, 1979.

4. http://www.casetext.com/case/davis-y-cambell-2#.UuOMyhv1Fl. "This is not a Stipulation that the cited Statute applies, only that if it does that Plaintiff has satisfied its requirements for parole eligibility" (*Allan Frank Davis v. James Mabry, Director, Arkansas Department of Corrections et al.*, http://www.opinions.aoc.arkansas.gov/weblinks8/0/doc/186197/page3.aspx [retrieved August 25, 2014]).

CHAPTER 30: THE STRING PULLING

1. "John Birch on the School Board, Dr. J. F. Cooley," *African American Heritage in Arkansas Guide*, http://creativefolk.com/travel/pdf/civil_rights_guide.pdf (retrieved June 26, 2019).

2. J. F. Cooley, "Editorial Observations," *Arkansas Weekly Sentinel*, May 3, 1979, 2.

3. "Bill Clinton," Wikipedia, https://en.wikipedia.org/wiki/Bill_Clinton (retrieved June 28, 2019).

4. "Jeff Dwire," Wikipedia, https://en.wikipedia.org/wiki/Jeff_Dwire (retrieved June 28, 2019).

5. "Virginia Clinton Kelly," Wikipedia, https://en.wikipedia.org/wiki/Virginia_Clinton_Kelley (retrieved June 28, 2019).

6. "Davis Eligible for Parole," *Sentinel-Record*, September 18, 1979, 1.

CHAPTER 32: OREGON OR BUST

1. Carol Hickingbotham, "If Accepted by Oregon, Parole Board Okays Release of Davis," *Sentinel-Record*, October 5, 1979, 1.

2. "An Editorial: Parole Opportunity for Davis a Crime against Society," *Sentinel-Record*, October 6, 1979, 1.

3. Carol Hickingbotham, "Oregon Refuses Davis," *Sentinel-Record*, October 25, 1979, 1.

4. Associated Press, "Two Strikes against Him, Frank Davis Wants to Start a New Life," *Sentinel-Record*, November 3, 1979, 1.

5. Associated Press, "Two Strikes against Him, Frank Davis Wants to Start a New Life," 15.

CHAPTER 33: THE LOGJAM LOOSENED

1. Carol Hickingbotham, "Britt: 'A Mistake,' Frank Davis Is Paroled to Oregon," *Sentinel-Record*, February 13, 1980, 1.

CHAPTER 34: THE FINAL HEADLINE

1. "Digest: Convicted Murderer Dies of Apparent Heart Attack," *Sentinel-Record*, June 5, 1984, 1.

APPENDIX: WHAT HAPPENED TO THEM?

1. "Crestview Memorial Park Cemetery," Find a Grave, November 15, 2008, www.findagrave/crestviewmemorialparkcemetery (retrieved June 1, 2018).

2. *Old Gold Book 1954*, Hot Springs High School, Hot Springs National Park, Arkansas, Melting Pot Genealogical Society, Hot Springs, Arkansas.

3. Wanda's obituary, *Sentinel-Record*, December 24, 1994, p. 2A.

4. Deborah L. Larsen obituary, *Sentinel-Record*, September 23, 2020, p. 8A.

5. Gross Funeral Home obituary, January 23, 2017.

6. Gross Funeral Home obituary, January 23, 2017.

7. "Sarah Catherine Ward" (obituary), *Arkansas Democrat-Gazette*, May 12, 2013, https://www.arkansasonline.com/obituaries/2013/may/12/sarah-ward-2013-05-12 (retrieved August 22, 2014).

8. "Physician Saves Arkansas Hospital, Receives Award," *The Notebook, a Weekly Publication of the Arkansas Hospital Association* 14, no. 44 (November 19, 2007): 1.

9. Jim Williamson, "Rural Doctor Receives National Award," *Texarkana Gazette*, December 10, 2007, https://www.texarkanagazette.com/news/texarkana/story/2007/dec/11/rural-doctor-receives-national-award/40476 (retrieved August 21, 2014).